curry
cuisine

curry
cuisine

Fragrant dishes from India, Thailand, Vietnam, and Indonesia

LONDON NEW YORK MUNICH
MELBOURNE DELHI

Commissioning Editor
Jeni Wright

Art Director
Peter Luff

Project Manager and Editor
Norma Macmillan

Creative Publisher
Mary-Clare Jerram

Senior Art Editor
Susan Downing

Operations Publishing Manager
Gillian Roberts

Senior Editor
Dawn Henderson

Publisher
Corinne Roberts

Project Art Editor
Caroline de Souza

DTP Designers
Adam Walker, Traci Salter

Designers
Sue Storey, Simon Daley

Production Controller
Stuart Masheter

Editorial Assistant
Zoe Moore

Photographer
Hugh Johnson

Americanization Editor
Christine Heilman

U.S. Recipe Consultant
Wes Martin

Published in the United States by
DK Publishing, 375 Hudson Street,
New York, NY 10014

First paperback edition published in 2010 by DK Publishing

10 11 12   10 9 8 7 6 5 4 3 2 1

A Cataloging-in-Publication record for this book is available from the Library of Congress.
ISBN: 978-0-7566-6207-3

DK books are available at special discounts for bulk purchases for sales promotions,
premiums, fund-raising, or educational use. For details, contact: DK Publishing Special Markets,
375 Hudson Street, New York, NY 10014 or SpecialSales@dk.com

Color reproduction by GRB, Italy
Printed and bound in Singapore by Star Standard

Discover more at
www.dk.com

CONTENTS

PAKISTAN MAHMOOD AKBAR 120

Ingredients • Spinach and lamb curry • Lamb and tomato curry • Ground lamb and kidney curry • Sliced beef curry • Special chicken curry • Quail in yogurt curry • Shrimp curry • Vegetable biryani • Chickpea pilau • Black-eye bean curry • Mixed vegetable curry • Potato curry • Leavened roti • Fried roti • Plum chutney • Pickled garlic • Apple chutney • Mango pickle • Cilantro chutney • Mint raita • Onion raita • Cucumber raita • Cumin raita

MYANMAR & MARITIME SE ASIA SRI OWEN 154

Ingredients • Compressed rice • Spiced tamarind relish • Dried shrimp relish • Peanut sauce

MYANMAR 172
Burmese chicken noodle soup • Pork curry with mango • Chicken curry with lime and tomatoes

MALAYSIA 177
Beef rendang • Red curry of beef • Laksa with shrimp and tofu

SINGAPORE 182
Chili crab • Fish-head curry • Sour fish curry

INDONESIA 187
Rich curry of duck • Duck breasts in Balinese spices • West Sumatran mutton curry • Hot and sour shrimp curry • Javanese lamb curry

PHILIPPINES 195
Chicken adobo • Squid adobo • Braised oxtail with peanut sauce

THAILAND DAVID THOMPSON 200

Ingredients • Coconut milk and cream • Cooking Thai curries • Green curry paste • Steamed jasmine rice • Coconut and turmeric curry of red snapper • Sour orange curry of brill and Asian greens • Southern curry of chopped beef • Crab stir-fried with curry powder • Northeastern curry of pork ribs and mustard greens • Fermented fish sauce • Jungle curry of chicken with vegetables and peppercorns • Red curry of oyster mushrooms and tofu • Red curry of beef with peanuts • Pineapple curry of mussels • Grilled halibut curry • Steamed scallop curry • Green curry of heart of coconut • Green curry of shrimp with eggplant and basil • Aromatic curry of pumpkin • Cucumber relish • Aromatic curry of chicken and potatoes • Chiang Mai pork curry • Muslim curry of duck with potatoes and onions

Curry Cuisine explores the culinary phenomenon known broadly as "curry" across an international spectrum. Very much in keeping with the evolution of expanding tastes in food over the past 20 years, recipes range from the more common spiced stews, to steamed traditional custards, to inventive stir-fries. Culture, history, health and well-being, and numerous other aspects of distinctly spiced dishes are explored in over 100 recipes that include the evolutionary beginnings of basic dishes, national and regional variations, and newly developed pan-Asian hybrid and fusion cuisine examples.

Curries, it seems, share a structurally similar spice and herb concoction, seemingly rooted in South Asian home cooking, that was spread outward by war, commerce, religious practice, and migration. While curries with common roots now span the globe, variations too numerous to mention can also be described—this is attributable to regional interpretation, ingredient availability, and individual cook.

Dating back centuries, and named by the globe-conquering, adaptive, and culinary cross-pollinating British (the English word "curry" is an interpretation of the Tamil word *kari*), curry now has morphed into a major part of world cuisine. Whether broth or paste, dried powder or ground fresh ingredients, packaged or just harvested from the garden, hot-pepper-laden or dominated by pungent herbs, stew or soup, plated, served in a bowl, or served as a sandwich, it is somehow curry just the same.

This book comprises the work of nine celebrated experts who cover North and South India, Pakistan, Myanmar and Maritime Southeast Asia (Malaysia, Singapore, Indonesia, the Philippines), Thailand, Mainland Southeast Asia (Cambodia, Laos, and Vietnam), as well as some of the many other parts of the world that curry has reached in the final chapter, Outposts (Africa, the Caribbean, Britain, and Japan). Each writer expands upon the basics, sometimes joyfully contradicting them.

The book explores the spicy dishes apt to be called *salan* in Pakistan, *geng* in Thailand, and *gulai* in Malaysia. The North Indian–rooted tandoori variation evolved through the use of a specific oven (*tandoor*), and the Filipino adobo has its ancestry in the Spanish *adobado*, possibly casting the Spanish as another global cross-pollinator in matters of the kitchen.

Thai curries delight in expanding the number of ingredients in service of subtly layered flavors and often includes rich coconut milks and creams, while Pakistani versions value a minimalist approach, disavowing coconut ingredients altogether and emphasizing each individual item's intensity.

The Japanese got curry not from their Asian neighbors but from the British in the mid-19th century, and inheriting it twice removed from its Indian roots, rejected traditional South Asian rice grains, favoring their own "sushi" short-grain rice and otherwise "Japan-ified" versions. To this day, curries in Japan are referred to as *Yo-shoku*, meaning (with an unconscious historical irony) "Western food."

A link to the historic past, a window onto and virtual map of the host country and its cultural values, trend-setting now and likely a stepping stone to our joyfully globalized culinary future, curry is here to be discovered, tasted, and, in the end, savored.

Corinne Trang

CONTRIBUTORS

Vivek Singh

As a boy, Vivek spurned family expectations by announcing his intention to become a chef. After catering college, he joined the Oberoi Hotel group as a specialist in Indian cuisine, first working at their busy flight kitchens in Mumbai. He then moved to the Grand Hotel in Kolkata, before being fast-tracked to Indian chef of the Oberoi's flagship Rajvilas in Jaipur—at the age of just 26. From early on, Vivek read Escoffier and devoured books by Marco Pierre White and Charlie Trotter. When Iqbal Wahhab, the founder of The Cinnamon Club in London, approached him with ideas of marrying Indian flavors with Western culinary styles, Vivek saw his opportunity. Since opening in 2001, The Cinnamon Club has redefined expectations of Indian cooking, by liberating it from the straitjacket of tradition and crafting a brilliant and exotic marriage of Indian and Western cuisines.

Das Sreedharan

Das is the founder chef of Rasa restaurants in London. Since starting up in 1994, he has created a new awareness of regional Indian cuisine. With a humble upbringing, Das learned traditional cooking skills and vegetable gardening from his mother. Now, through his restaurants, he passionately champions the simple, subtle flavors of Keralan food, offering his customers a fresh alternative to typical curry-house dishes. Das has published three cookbooks about his native cuisine, and organizes annual festivals promoting Indian food and culture. He conducts weekly classes in London and has recently launched a cooking school in India, teaching traditional techniques. Through the school, he aims to encourage healthy home cooking and ethical living. Das lives in London, taking regular trips to Kerala to seek new flavors and seasonings for his customers' delight.

Mahmood Akbar

From an early age, Mahmood was exposed to the pleasures of food and cooking by both his father, a great food lover, and his mother, an excellent cook. He obtained his degree in hotel management in the US, then joined Hilton International, where he spent five years as a food and beverage manager, including time in Hong Kong and East Asia. In 1982, Mahmood decided to start up his own restaurants, including the now famous Salt 'n Pepper Village restaurants in Lahore and Karachi. In his business he is assisted by his wife and, recently, by his daughter, who also graduated in the US with a hotel management degree. Mahmood's passion for food is undiminished. The lesson he learned as a child from his father about using only the freshest ingredients has become his guiding principle in running his own restaurants: all food is purchased fresh every morning and consumed the same day.

Sri Owen

Sri was born in West Sumatra, and it was there, as a child in her grandmother's kitchen, that she acquired a love of good food. After graduating from university in Yogyakarta, Central Java, she became an English literature professor, and she met and married Roger, an English colleague. Together they came to London, where she made a successful career with the BBC Overseas Service, at the same time writing her first cookbook. This was published in 1976, and has been followed by ten more books as well as much other writing on Indonesian and other Southeast Asian food. In 1994 her best seller, *The Rice Book,* won the André Simon Award for food and cookery book of the year; it was also nominated for a James Beard Award in New York. She and her husband live in London. They travel widely and are currently working on *The Oxford Companion to Southeast Asian Food.*

David Thompson

In the 1980s, David traveled to Thailand from his native Australia and became enamored of the country, its people and culture. There he met Khun Sombat Janphetchara, whose mother was attached to one of the palaces of Bangkok. From her, David learned the fundamentals of Thai cuisine. In 1993, he and his partner, Peter Bowyer, opened Darley Street Thai in Sydney, followed in 1995 by Sailors Thai. In 2000, David was approached to start Nahm restaurant in London, which opened in the Halkin Hotel in 2001 and was awarded a Michelin star in 2002. The same year, David published *Thai Food*, which won numerous awards, including the Guild of Food Writers' book of the year. At the Tio Pepe ITV Awards, David was honored as London Chef of the Year. He returns to Thailand regularly to continue his research, unearthing long-forgotten recipes that he can draw on for his restaurants.

Corinne Trang

Corinne is the New York–based award-winning author of *Authentic Vietnamese Cooking*, *Essentials of Asian Cuisine*, and *The Asian Grill*. Dubbed "the Julia Child of Asian Cuisine" by the media, she is well known for her writing, teaching, and radio broadcasts, as well as appearances on television programs such as *Martha Stewart Living* and *The TV Food Network*. Corinne has traveled extensively in Asia and teaches and lectures worldwide on the subject of Asian cooking. She is on the faculty at several universities, including New York University, where she is adjunct professor in the Department of Nutrition, Food Studies, and Public Health. Corinne is also a food consultant, a published food stylist, and an accomplished food and travel photographer. She is a member of the International Association of Culinary Professionals, New York Women's Culinary Alliance, and Les Dames d'Escoffier.

Roopa Gulati

Born and raised in Cumbria, Roopa's taste for culinary adventure took her to India, which for 18 years was her home. A Cordon Bleu chef, she blended Western and Asian styles of cooking while working as a consultant chef with the Taj group of hotels, and cooking on a daily live show on the Star TV channel. Roopa returned to Britain in 2001 and now lives in London, where she is Deputy Channel Editor with UKTV Food. She enjoys exploring the tastes of multicultural Britain and has been a judge for BBC Radio 4's Food and Farming Awards, as well as a regular radio broadcaster and a restaurant critic for *Time Out* magazine. Her recipe-led features have been published in many magazines, including *Good Food*, *Olive*, and New York–based *Gourmet*. She's particularly interested in how cooking styles travel—from market stand, to Maharajah's palace, to fine restaurant dining.

Judy Bastyra

Judy was born in London and has written about food for more years than she can remember. She prefers eating fruit bat that has feasted on mangoes, but feels that piranha will taste sweet and musty whatever it eats. Many years ago, Judy realized that if you love food and travel, what better job could you have than to be a food and travel writer? She is occasionally torn away from her first love to other meaningful subjects like sex or homelessness, writing books about them, too, but then the hunger takes over and she is off again in search of new culinary experiences. Her latest travels have taken her walking in the High Atlas Mountains in Morocco, climbing the "stairway to heaven" at Angkor Wat in Cambodia and eating bay scallops in Martha's Vineyard. But her heart remains in the Caribbean, where she frequently returns to continue her love affair with Caribbean cuisine.

Yasuko Fukuoka

As a musician and composer, Yasuko traveled all over Japan in the course of many concert tours. Coupled with her love of good food, this enabled her to gain a deep understanding of Japan's regional specialties and traditional culinary culture. Her curiosity led her to create her own recipes based on Japanese home cooking. Since moving to England, Yasuko has continued to work as a musician while developing her career as a journalist and food writer. Her first cookbook, co-authored with Emi Kazuko, won the Best Asian Cookery Book Award in 2001 at the Gourmand Cookbook Awards. As well as publishing several more Japanese cookbooks in English and contributing to Japanese publications, she develops recipes that combine traditional and contemporary Japanese cooking and British products. She lives with her photographer husband and their daughter in London.

NORTH INDIA

< **Dried red chilies,
Mapusa Market, Goa**

The cooking of northern India has its roots in Persia, where the *tandoor* originated. The *tandoor* was brought to India by the Mughals, Muslim invaders who ruled most of India for almost 200 years, until the early 1700s. With the arrival of the *tandoor* began the great phenomenon of "tandoori" cooking, which has spread all over the world and, with the curry, come to broadly represent Indian cuisine.

Under some Mughal rulers, great levels of culinary sophistication were achieved. There were periods during which cooking flourished and its practitioners were nurtured like artists, enjoying a status similar to celebrity chefs today. Vast sums of money were spent on kitchens run by skilled master chefs, or *rakabdar*, as they were called. Each ruler aspired to outdo the other, in hospitality and in the dishes his chefs devised.

From this, it might seem as if all of North Indian cooking was influenced by Mughal rulers alone, but this could not be further from the truth. Like every cuisine, the cooking of a country or region is shaped by what grows there, the seasons, the climate, and the availability of ingredients, as well as religious and socioeconomic factors.

Rulers in some parts of northern India made great efforts to preserve their own culture and identity. They included the Rajput rulers from Rajasthan, who were avid hunters of deer, wild boar, partridges, and sand grouse, which is why this region has a fine tradition of game curries. In this arid desert climate, little grows, and cooking is earthy and rustic. Dried vegetables, roots, berries, and fruits are more common than fresh ones. Sangri beans, which need little water to grow, are much eaten. Rather than cattle and buffalo, goat and lamb are reared for both milk and meat. Yogurt is used for cooking and as a drink, as it has a cooling effect on the body. Chickpeas, corn, and millet are the staples here, unlike the rest of the country. In such a dry climate this makes sense, because consumption of chickpea flour and cornmeal helps the body retain water.

Punjab, Delhi, and the rest of the north are relatively much better off in terms of fertile land, kinder climate, and better irrigation, as a result of the five rivers that feed the region. This is a land of plenty, and plenty of milk, cream, butter, and other milk products are used; fresh vegetables, such as spinach, mustard greens, and fenugreek, are abundant; wheat is grown; and lamb and chicken are reared. Just about the best of everything is available and is used in the cooking in this region.

The *tandoor* has had a major impact on the way of life here—even today most households have a tandoori oven tucked away in their courtyard. If not, the village has a communal *tandoor*, where women will gather at midday or early evening to make their bread or simply exchange news and gossip. The mighty *tandoor* is so much more than just a means of cooking food—it is an essential part of the fabric of life in this region.

Bengal and the eastern states have very fertile land in the plains, as the Ganges River brings with it the rich soil from the north. The climate is mild, and monsoons mean that two crops can be harvested each year. One of them is rice. Local vegetables are plentiful; mustard grows in abundance, so mustard seeds and oil are used in cooking. With the proximity to the sea, fish is frequently used in Bengali curries.

When the British arrived in India, they made Kolkata—or Calcutta, as it was formerly known—their headquarters. As a result, British influences can be seen in some Bengali dishes (and vice versa). Kedgeree and Bengali vegetable "chops" are just two examples of the crossover of cultures.

Today in northern India, 65 percent of the population is vegetarian, which explains why there is such a wide variety of vegetarian curries in the Indian culinary repertoire. The majority of North Indians are Hindus and Muslims, followed by Sikhs and those of other religions. Because cows are sacred to Hindus and pork is banned in the Muslim faith, beef and pork are rarely eaten.

While history, geography, and religion have all played an important role in shaping North Indian cuisine, there is one other important aspect—without which no cuisine can develop and survive—and that is creativity. And it is creativity that has enabled North Indian curries to travel all around the world, finding new homes wherever Indian migrants have settled. In adapting recipes to what is available locally, new curries have been created, but they are still identifiable as North Indian in their essence.

Vivek Singh

Frying whole spices >
Add them to hot oil so they
crackle and toast

The Taste of North India

1. cilantro leaves
2. saffron threads
3. gold leaf
4. split green lentils
5. split red lentils
6. split black lentils
7. whole black lentils
8. split gram lentils
9. split yellow lentils
10. carom (ajowan) seeds
11. black onion seeds
12. mustard paste
13. ground garam masala
14. coriander seeds
15. cumin seeds
16. dried fenugreek leaves
17. chili powder
18. crushed dried chilies
19. dried red chilies
20. fresh green chilies
21. fresh root ginger
22. garlic
23. mustard oil
24. mustard seeds

The raw materials

One of the things that makes North Indian cuisine so special is the spectacular variety of ingredients available to the cook. Each of the four regions has its own distinctly different cooking style, based on the climate and crops grown, religious influences, and the cooking mediums preferred. Everywhere the cooking is enhanced with fresh aromatics, herbs, spices, and other flavoring ingredients.

Chilies

Many different chilies, both fresh and dried, are used in North Indian cookery, varying in their fieriness and pungency. Kashmiri chilies, which are large and deep red, have a good flavor and color but are not too hot, and can be used in larger quantities than the smaller, much hotter green chilies. Whole dried chilies can be stored for up to a year in a cool, dark place (exposure to light will fade their vibrant color), whereas crushed or ground dried chilies will lose their power and spiciness after a few months.

Ginger and garlic

After salt, these are probably the most-used ingredients in the cooking of Delhi and Punjab. They are added to marinades for meats, fish, and vegetables when preparing them for the *tandoor*, as well as being a flavoring in many curries. Ginger and garlic are normally made into a paste, which can be done separately or in combination: take about 4 oz (100 g) peeled fresh ginger and 3 oz (75 g) peeled garlic and blend with 3/4 cup water, using a food processor. The paste can be kept in an airtight jar in the refrigerator for up to 5 days.

Cilantro/coriander

In its leaf form, called cilantro, this herb is used to finish curries and as a garnish. The seeds, known as coriander, are used as a spice, whole or ground. Thought to have been cultivated for over 3,000 years, the plant is said to have a cooling effect on the body and an infusion is a cure for fever.

Fenugreek

The fresh leaves of this aromatic plant are eaten as a vegetable; when dried (*kasoori methi*), they are used to flavor all sorts of Indian savories and curries (the best quality *kasoori methi* comes from Qasoor in Pakistan). The seeds of the plant are used as a spice. Ancient herbalists prescribed fenugreek to aid digestion, a remedy that continues to be used today.

Cinnamon leaves

Although commonly referred to as "bay leaf" in Indian recipes, what is meant is actually the dried leaf of the cassia tree. I like to call it cinnamon leaf. Used in most dishes all over northern India, cinnamon leaves have a mild, sweet flavor. They are not edible, so should be removed before serving. Should you find it difficult to obtain them, you can use bay leaves instead.

Turmeric

One of the most widely used spices in Indian cooking, turmeric flavors most Indian curries, be they meat, vegetable, or lentil, and also gives them a rich yellow-orange color. The roots (or rhizomes) are sold both fresh and dried, or ground to a fine powder. Turmeric has good preservative properties, too, so it is used in the making of many Indian pickles.

Asafetida

This essential Indian flavoring, which is a dried resinous gum, has a very unpleasant smell and bitter taste, so it is never used alone, but when cooked in a dish it enhances the other flavors. It is sold as powder, granules, or lumps, and will keep well for up to a year. In addition to its

Dried Kashmiri chilies >

culinary uses, it is supposed to be a cure for flatulence and to help respiratory problems like asthma.

Garam masala

Garam masala, which literally means "hot spices," is a mixture of roasted spices that is used whole or ground to a fine powder. Each region of India has its standard version of garam masala, using the spices available and popular and the cooking of the area, and the recipes change according to individual taste. (See recipe p28.)

Saffron

The costliest of all spices, saffron is the dried stigmas of a variety of crocus. Just a few saffron threads (stigmas) will give intense golden color and a unique, slightly bitter, perfumed taste to savory and sweet dishes. Store this precious spice in an airtight jar in a dark place, to retain its color and fragrance.

Royal cumin seeds

Also called black cumin, these spice seeds are very dark brown, long and very thin, and smaller than regular cumin. Their aroma is earthy and strong during cooking; the taste is nutty and warm. Royal cumin is used extensively in Kashmiri cuisine, and in Mughal cuisine as a tempering for meats.

Fennel seeds

A very commonly used spice in India, whole or ground fennel seeds add a warm and sweet flavor to all kinds of curries. Fennel seeds are also used in pickles and chutneys and in desserts. Fennel is thought to have digestive properties, so roasted seeds are often served after a rich Indian meal.

Nigella seeds

Although more commonly known as black onion seeds, this spice has nothing to do with onions and is actually the fruit of an herb related to the garden plant "love-in-a-mist." The small black seeds have an unusual, slightly bitter taste. Much used in Bengali cooking, nigella (*kalonji*) also garnishes many Indian breads.

Carom seeds

Closely related to cumin, which it resembles in appearance and fragrance, carom seeds (*ajowan*) have a hot and bitter taste. However, when they are cooked with other ingredients, the flavor mellows. Carom seeds are particularly good in seafood dishes and with root vegetables.

Pickling spices

This combination of equal quantities of fennel, carom, onion, fenugreek, mustard, and cumin, either as whole seeds or ground, is used in pickles as well as to flavor sauces and marinades for meat. You can buy ready-made pickling spices in India; elsewhere you will need to mix the spices together yourself.

Coconut

The hard, brown, hairy fruits of the coconut tree contain "water," which makes a refreshing drink enjoyed straight from the fruit. The crunchy, sweet white flesh is used to make rich coconut milk (p213), which is an important part of many Indian curries. Freshly grated coconut flesh is used in Bengali cuisine, while desiccated coconut features in Muslim cooking.

Kachri

A sour, tomato-like compound fruit native to Rajasthan, this has a hard skin and seeds inside. Available fresh and dried, it is used to tenderize meat and in the making of certain chutneys.

Black lentils

Also known as black *gram* (or *ma* in the Punjab), these are primarily used whole in North India, most famously in a festive Punjabi dish with red kidney beans. Whole black lentils (*urad*) have a stronger aroma and richer, earthier taste than split black lentils (*urad dal*). Whole black lentils can be kept in an airtight container for up to 4 months.

Split lentils

The most common variety of split lentils in India are *toor dal*, also called split yellow peas. They are used all over India to make the dishes known as *dals*. *Chana dal* are split *gram* lentils, a type of chickpea, from which the husk has been removed. A very versatile ingredient, *chana dal* are used in many ways in different parts of the country, and are also ground into a flour (see opposite). *Masoor* or red lentils are the easiest to cook and digest, and are commonly used to make lentil soups and *dals*, as well as kedgeree, which is essentially food for invalids and children. When whole, *moong dal* (mung

< Cinnamon leaves

beans) have a green skin; it is these whole beans that are sprouted to use in salads and other cold dishes. Split, they are used in northern India for a variety of things, such as in the making of popadums, batters, and fritters, but *moong dal* are rarely cooked on their own.

Ghee
This is clarified butter, the pure butterfat, clear and golden in color. Traditionally in India, ghee is made from buffalo milk, which is higher in fat than cow's milk, and the process involves souring milk to make yogurt and then churning this to yield butter. Unsalted butter made from cow's milk can also be used for ghee.

Paneer cheese
An Indian version of set cottage or pot cheese, paneer is made by separating the whey from milk by adding lemon juice to curdle it. The solids are collected in muslin, tied, and pressed under a weight for a few hours to set—to soft curds or firm for slicing. On its own, paneer tastes quite bland. It is widely used as an alternative to meat in vegetarian dishes.

Chickpea flour
Also known as *besan* and *gram* flour, this is obtained from husking and then grinding split *gram* lentils (*chana dal*) into a powder. It is a very versatile flour, commonly used to make dumplings (p37), in batters for fritters, and in bread doughs. Chickpea flour can be kept in an airtight jar for up to 6 months. Another form in which chickpea flour is available is *daria dal*, for which the split *gram* lentils are roasted before grinding. Roasting takes away the raw flavor and increases the flour's ability to absorb water. Roasted chickpea flour is often used as a thickener at the end of cooking.

Chapatti flour
This finely ground whole-wheat flour is used to make unleavened breads (see recipe p40).

Rice
Rice is grown all along the plains of the Ganges, from the foothills of the Himalayas right down to Bengal in the east. Although basmati is the best known, there are hundreds of other varieties of rice available, patna being another notable one. In Indian homes, rice is most often cooked by the boiling method; pilau rice and rice cooked by the absorption method are reserved for special occasions as they require more skill.

Kasundi mustard
This ready-made mustard paste is commonly used in Bengali cooking. It is made by soaking mustard seeds in vinegar, then grinding them to a paste with mustard oil and the addition of dried mango. Kasundi mustard adds its characteristic flavor to numerous dishes from the region. If not available, it can be replaced with Dijon or any other prepared grain mustard.

Mustard oil
As the name suggests, this oil is extracted from mustard seeds. It is pungent in taste and smell and deep gold in color. Mustard oil is greatly favored in Bengal and eastern India, and certain Rajasthani dishes get their flavor from it. When used, the oil is normally heated almost to smoking point, then cooled down and reheated again, which tones down its aroma.

Rose water and screwpine essence
Essences have been a part of Indian cookery since antiquity. During the time of the Mughal emperors, rare flowers were grown in the royal greenhouses to make attars, or fragrant essential oils, and some of these turned up in the kitchen. Floral essences such as rose water and screwpine essence (*kewra*) are the most popular today, used to flavor biryanis, pulaos, kebabs, desserts, and treats.

Gold leaf
This is the ultimate in exotic, luxury cooking. While edible silver leaf is quite commonly used to adorn dishes and decorate sweets in India, gold leaf is not as easy to find. Used as a decoration, it lifts up a dish in every sense.

Ghee Clarified butter

The process of "clarifying" butter to produce ghee, or pure butter fat, makes it an excellent cooking medium able to withstand high temperatures and constant reheating. It also prevents it from going rancid, an important consideration in a hot country such as India. Ghee has a unique rich, nutty taste.

INGREDIENTS
2 sticks (1 cup) unsalted butter

METHOD
Step 1
Place the butter in a heavy saucepan to heat. As the butter melts, let it come to a gentle boil.

Step 2
Simmer the melted butter for 20–30 minutes to evaporate all the water. Skim off the froth that appears on the surface and discard.

Step 3
The butter will separate into cooked milk solids, which will settle to the bottom of the pan, and clear, golden ghee at the top. Carefully pour off the ghee into a bowl.

Step 4
Allow the liquid ghee to cool. It will solidify, but will have a creamy consistency, somewhat like soft tub margarine; if refrigerated, it will become hard. Ghee can be stored for several years if kept in a tin or glass container in a cool, dark place, free from any obvious moisture or contact with water.

Yields about ¾ cup

Step 1

Step 2

Step 3 >

Garam masala Hot spice mix

This aromatic blend of spices may be used whole or ground to a fine powder, depending on the dish. Whole garam masala is often added at the beginning or early in the cooking, whereas ground mixes are used to finish a dish. The basic mixture usually includes coriander seeds, cumin seeds, cardamom, cinnamon, cloves, mace, peppercorns, and cinnamon leaf, in varying proportions and with other spices added according to the individual cook's preferences and the dish being prepared.

INGREDIENTS
3 tbsp coriander seeds
3 tbsp cumin seeds
20 green cardamom pods
10 cinnamon sticks, 1 in (2.5 cm) long
2 tbsp cloves
10 blades mace
10 black cardamom pods
$1/2$ nutmeg
1 tbsp black peppercorns
4 cinnamon leaves or bay leaves
1 tbsp dried rose petals
1 tbsp fennel seeds

METHOD
Heat a dry frying pan and add all the spices. Stir them and shake the pan as they start to crackle. When they smell roasted and aromatic, remove the pan from the heat and pour the spices onto a plate. Allow to cool.

To grind the spices, use a mortar and pestle or a spice mill (or a clean coffee grinder).

**Makes about
5 oz (150 g)**

Laal maas Fiery lamb curry

As the name suggests, this is a very hot dish, not for people with a weak constitution. It is by far the hottest dish in this chapter, and is one of the few Indian dishes that contains heat in every sense—both "chili hot" and "spice hot." You can decide the amount of heat you'd like in your finished dish—discard most of the seeds from the chilies if you want to reduce the heat, or keep them in if you want it really hot. I think this is perfect for cold winter evenings or even a Friday night gathering. You can use either lamb or goat—they are interchangeable.

INGREDIENTS

25–35 dried red chilies, stems removed
$1^{1}/_{2}$ tsp cloves
$5^{1}/_{2}$ oz (150 g) ghee or vegetable oil
9 oz (250 g) plain yogurt, whisked until smooth
2 tsp cumin seeds, roasted
$1^{1}/_{2}$ tbsp ground coriander
1 tsp red chili powder
2 tsp salt
3 cinnamon leaves or bay leaves

6 green cardamom pods
5 black cardamom pods
$2^{1}/_{2}$ oz (75 g) garlic cloves, finely chopped
9 oz (250 g) onions, finely chopped
$2^{1}/_{4}$ lb (1 kg) leg of lamb or goat with bone, chopped into 1-in (2.5-cm) cubes
3 cups lamb stock or water
2 tbsp finely chopped cilantro leaves

METHOD

Set aside 3 or 4 of the dried chilies to use later; put the remainder to soak in $^{1}/_{2}$ cup water. Also put aside 4–6 of the cloves and 1 tbsp of the ghee.

Mix the yogurt with the cumin seeds, ground coriander, chili powder, and salt in a bowl. Set aside.

Heat the rest of the ghee in a heavy-based pan. Add the remaining cloves, the cinnamon leaves, and the green and black cardamoms. When they begin to crackle and change color, add the garlic. Sauté for 2 minutes or until the garlic begins to turn golden. Add the onions and cook for 10 minutes or until golden brown, stirring constantly.

Stir in the meat and cook for 2–3 minutes. Drain the soaked red chilies and add to the pan. Continue cooking for 10–12 minutes or until the liquid has evaporated and the meat starts to brown slightly. Now add the spiced yogurt and cook for another 10–12 minutes or until the liquid from the yogurt has evaporated.

Add the stock or water and bring to a boil, then cover the pan, reduce the heat, and simmer until the meat is tender. Adjust the seasoning. Remove from the heat and keep warm.

To prepare the *tadka*, or tempering, which boosts the flavors, heat up the reserved ghee or oil in a large ladle over a flame (or in a small pan) and add the reserved cloves and dried red chilies. Cook for 1–2 minutes or until the ghee changes color and the spice flavors are released. Pour the contents of the ladle over the lamb curry, sprinkle with the chopped cilantro, and serve.

Serves 4

chili hot

Makai ka soweta Lamb and sweet corn curry

This is a true example of regional Indian cooking using local ingredients to make a dish that is not only unique but also appropriate for the region. The climate in most of Rajasthan and the Thar Desert is arid, and, while not a lot is produced here, corn is grown and consumed in abundance. Sweet corn helps water retention in the body, and yogurt is also cooling in a hot climate. I've made this recipe with lamb, but it would work just as well with goat or mutton, if you can get some.

INGREDIENTS

2¼ lb (1 kg) boned shoulder of lamb, cut into 1-in (2.5-cm) cubes
½ cup ghee or corn oil
1½ tsp cumin seeds
5 green cardamom pods
4 black cardamom pods
10 cloves
2 cinnamon leaves or bay leaves
3 cups lamb stock or water
1 lb (450 g) canned sweet corn, drained and coarsely chopped
juice of ½ lemon
2 tbsp chopped cilantro leaves

Marinade

10 oz (300 g) plain yogurt
2 tsp ground coriander
1 tsp ground turmeric
2 tsp salt

Onion paste

7 oz (200 g) onions, finely chopped
3 oz (75 g) garlic cloves, finely chopped
12 green chilies

METHOD

Mix together the ingredients for the marinade. Add the cubes of lamb and turn to coat, then cover and set aside for about 15 minutes.

Meanwhile, make the onion paste by blending together the ingredients in a blender until smooth.

Heat the ghee in a heavy-based pan over moderate heat, then add all the spices and the cinnamon or bay leaves. As the spices crackle, add the marinated cubes of lamb, with the marinade, and turn up the heat to high. Cook for 12–15 minutes or until all the moisture has evaporated, stirring constantly.

Next, add the onion paste and cook for a further 10 minutes, still stirring to ensure that the paste does not stick to the pan and burn. Add the lamb stock and reduce the heat. Simmer for 30 minutes or until the meat is about 85 percent cooked.

Add the sweet corn and cook for another 10 minutes, stirring constantly. The dish is ready when the consistency is glossy. Remove from the heat, adjust the seasoning, and transfer to a heated serving dish. Finish with the lemon juice and fresh cilantro. Serve with steamed rice or bread.

Serves 4–6

warmly spiced

Pounding grain with a pestle, Rajasthan >

Achari khargosh Rabbit leg cooked in pickling spices

This is the type of dish that would have been cooked on a *shikaar*, or hunting expedition, when the Rajput princes went out hunting with their entourage. It would originally have been made with hare but works just as well with rabbit.

INGREDIENTS

4–6 rabbit legs, about 2 lb (900 g) in total
1 tsp salt
1 tsp ground turmeric

Sauce
$3^1/_2$ tbsp mustard oil
$^1/_3$ cup ghee
4 dried red chilies
1 tbsp mixed pickling spices (p24)
8 garlic cloves, finely chopped
2 onions, about 6 oz (150 g) in total, finely chopped

1 tsp salt
$^1/_2$ tsp ground turmeric
1-in (2.5-cm) piece fresh ginger root, cut into julienne strips
2 tbsp palm sugar or molasses
10 oz (300 g) plain full-fat yogurt
2 tsp chickpea flour
juice of 1 lemon
1 tbsp finely chopped cilantro leaves

METHOD

Place the rabbit legs in a pan and add the salt and turmeric. Pour in $1^1/_2$ quarts (liters) water and bring to a boil over moderate heat. Reduce the heat to low, cover with a lid, and simmer for 45 minutes or until tender. Remove the rabbit legs from the liquid and drain; reserve the cooking liquid.

In another heavy-based pan, heat the mustard oil to smoking point over moderate heat. Add the ghee and, as it melts, add the whole red chilies and allow them to crackle for a few seconds. Next, add the pickling spices and, as they begin to crackle and change color, add the garlic. Sauté the garlic for a minute or so until golden brown, then add the onions. Sauté for 10 minutes or until the onions are soft and translucent but not brown.

Stir in the salt and turmeric and add the cooked rabbit legs. Add the ginger and palm sugar and stir for a few minutes, until the legs start to acquire a light brown color. Now stir in the reserved cooking liquid and let it simmer for 5 minutes.

Serves 4

spicy, tangy, and sour

In a bowl, whisk the yogurt with the chickpea flour until well combined. Increase the heat and bring the liquid in the pan back to a boil. Slowly add the yogurt mixture, stirring constantly to prevent it from separating. When all the yogurt has been incorporated, continue simmering for 2–3 minutes. If the oil starts to separate out at the sides of the pan, that's fine.

Adjust the seasoning and, just before serving, stir in the lemon juice and cilantro. Serve with either rice or bread.

Pitod ka saag Chickpea flour dumplings in yogurt sauce

This is a very unusual vegetarian dish using yogurt and chickpea flour as the primary ingredients. The texture of the dumplings and the complex mix of spices make a very interesting dish. This is good in the summer, served with steamed rice.

INGREDIENTS

1 lb 10 oz (750 g) plain Greek-style yogurt
$3^1/_2$ oz (100 g) chickpea flour
1 tsp salt
$^1/_2$ tsp ground turmeric
$^1/_2$ tsp sugar
$^1/_2$ tsp ground garam masala
1-in (2.5-cm) piece fresh ginger root, finely chopped
2 tbsp ghee
1 tsp fennel seeds
pinch of asafetida
vegetable oil for frying

Yogurt sauce

2 tbsp corn oil
pinch of asafetida
$^1/_2$ tbsp cumin seeds
4 cloves
1 onion, finely chopped
7 oz (200 g) plain Greek-style yogurt
2 tbsp ground coriander
$^1/_2$ tsp ground turmeric
$^1/_2$ tsp red chili powder
salt and sugar, as needed
2 green chilies, stem removed and quartered
$^1/_2$-in (1-cm) piece fresh ginger root, julienned
2 tbsp chopped cilantro leaves
juice of $^1/_2$ lemon

METHOD

First make the dumplings. Whisk the yogurt and 2 cups water with the chickpea flour, salt, turmeric, sugar, garam masala, and ginger in a bowl. Set aside.

Heat the ghee in a heavy pan, add the fennel seeds and sauté briefly, then add the asafetida and stir for 30 seconds. As the flavors are released, add the yogurt mix and cook, stirring constantly, for 20–25 minutes or until the mixture becomes thick and acquires the consistency of a soft dough. Remove from the heat and transfer to a greased 6-in (15-cm) square cake pan. Chill in the refrigerator for about 30 minutes or until set like a cake.

To make the sauce, heat the oil in a saucepan over moderate heat and add the asafetida, cumin, and cloves. When they begin to crackle, add the onion and cook for 5–8 minutes or until soft.

Meanwhile, whisk the yogurt with the ground coriander, turmeric, red chili powder, and salt. Add to the onions, stirring constantly, and keep stirring as the mixture comes to the boil again, to prevent the yogurt from separating. Once boiling, add the green chilies and $^3/_4$ cup water. Bring back to a boil, then cook for about 5 minutes. Check the seasoning and add salt and sugar to balance the taste, if required. Finish with the fresh ginger, cilantro, and lemon juice. Keep hot.

Cut the dumpling "cake" into 1-in (2.5-cm) squares. Heat some oil in a frying pan and, when hot, add the dumplings, a few at a time. Fry for a couple of minutes, until the dumplings have a crust. Serve on top of the hot sauce, or mix into the sauce and bring to a simmer before serving.

Serves 6

thin and sour

Panchmael daal Five lentils mix

Panchmael means a mix of five, hence the name of this dish. It can be made with just three types of lentils—those most easily obtainable in large supermarkets and health food stores are red, *moong*, and *chana*. A visit to an Asian grocery store will enable you to find the others, but you can even make the dish with just one type.

INGREDIENTS

2 heaped tbsp split green lentils (*moong dal*)
2 heaped tbsp split yellow lentils (*toor dal*)
2 heaped tbsp split gram lentils (*chana dal*)
2 heaped tbsp split and husked black lentils (*urad dal*)
2 tbsp split red lentils (*masoor dal*)
1¹/₂ tsp salt
¹/₂ tsp ground turmeric
2 tbsp ghee
1 large onion, finely chopped
¹/₂ tsp red chili powder

1 tsp ground garam masala
1 tomato, chopped
1 tbsp chopped cilantro leaves
squeeze of lemon juice

Tadka
1 tbsp ghee
1 dried red chili
¹/₂ tsp cumin seeds
4 cloves
2 garlic cloves, finely chopped

METHOD

Mix all the lentils together, then wash under running water. Leave to soak in enough cold water to cover for about 20 minutes.

Put the lentils in a saucepan with 2¹/₂ cups water, 1 tsp salt, and half of the turmeric. Bring to a boil, skimming off the white scum from the surface whenever necessary. Cover and simmer over low heat for 20–25 minutes or until the lentils, except the *chana dal*, are very soft and broken down.

Meanwhile, heat the ghee in a frying pan and, when hot, add the onion and cook until golden brown. Add the remaining salt and turmeric, the chili powder, and the garam masala and sauté for a minute, then add the tomato and cook until soft.

Pour the onion and tomato mixture over the lentils and bring to a boil. If the lentils begin to thicken too much, add some boiling water and keep stirring, to ensure that they don't stick to the pan. Finish with the fresh cilantro and lemon juice. Remove from the heat and keep hot.

For the *tadka*, heat the ghee in a large ladle (or small pan) until smoking. Add the whole red chili, cumin seeds, cloves, and garlic, in that order and in quick succession as the garlic begins to turn golden, then pour the contents of the ladle over the lentils and cover the pan with a lid. Leave covered for 2 minutes, to let the smoke and flavors be absorbed by the lentils. Remove the lid, stir well and serve immediately.

Serves 4

Spicy, aromatic, and light

Lahsun ki chutney Garlic chutney

This is a fine example of one of the very hot chutneys and pickles that are consumed in the region of Rajasthan. These chutneys and pickles are often made from dried and preserved vegetables or fruit—here, *kachri*, a sour, tomato-like fruit, is used, adding texture as well as acidity and sharpness—and the heavy-handed spicing means that the chutney has a better keeping quality. In the old days, travelers would take these chutneys on their journeys and make a really tasty but simple meal of chutney and bread. This delicious chutney can be stored in the pantry for a week as long as it's covered by oil on top. It will keep for up to 2 weeks in the refrigerator. If you are unable to find *kachri*, you can increase the garlic by the same amount (9 oz/250 g). The result will be a much hotter chutney. Balance the flavor with 1 tbsp ketchup if it's too hot for your liking.

INGREDIENTS

1 cup vegetable or corn oil
1 tsp cumin seeds
5 oz (125 g) garlic, roughly chopped
$2^1/_2$ oz (75 g) dried red chilies, soaked in
   1 cup water, drained and made into a paste
$^1/_3$ cup malt vinegar

2 tbsp salt
1 tbsp red chili powder
9 oz (250 g) *kachri* (see above), coarsely
   pounded
3 tbsp sugar, or to taste
1 tbsp chopped cilantro leaves (optional)

METHOD

Heat the oil in a saucepan, add the cumin seeds, and, when they crackle, add the garlic. Fry until it begins to turn golden.

Add the chili paste, vinegar, salt, and chili powder. Cook, stirring constantly, for 5–6 minutes. Add the *kachri* if you have some and cook the chutney for a further 12–15 minutes or until the fat separates out and comes to the top.

Check the seasoning and add the sugar, if required. Remove from the heat and allow to cool. This chutney can be eaten cold or hot. If you decide to heat it up before serving, add the fresh cilantro to liven it up.

Makes about
1 lb (450 g)

hot, spicy,
and sharp

Missi roti Chickpea bread

This rustic, spiced bread uses two different flours along with spices and seasoning, which gives it a unique flavor. It was a favorite for travelers, who would carry some of this bread to have with small quantities of very spicy garlic chutney for a light meal during their journey. Chickpea flour increases water retention in the body, which is particularly useful when traveling in the desert. The bread can be served either as an accompaniment to any Rajasthani recipe in this chapter or as a snack with a chutney or pickle of your choice.

INGREDIENTS

$2^1/_2$ cups chickpea flour
$1^2/_3$ cups all-purpose flour
4 tsp salt
1 tsp finely chopped fresh ginger root
2 green chilies, seeded and finely chopped
1 tbsp finely chopped cilantro leaves
1 tsp carom seeds

$^1/_2$ tsp red chili powder
$^1/_2$ tsp ground turmeric
2 tbsp vegetable oil
1 red onion, finely chopped
1 green onion, finely chopped
3 tbsp melted ghee for brushing and basting

METHOD

Mix together the chickpea flour and all-purpose flour in a large bowl. Transfer 3–4 tbsp of the flour mix to a small bowl and set aside to use later if needed. Add the salt, ginger, green chilies, chopped cilantro, carom seeds, red chili powder and turmeric to the large bowl and mix well to combine with the flours.

Add the oil and 200ml (7fl oz) water and knead to obtain a stiff dough. If the dough feels slightly soft add some of the reserved flour. Gather the dough into a mound, cover with a clean, damp dishcloth, and set aside for 15–20 minutes.

Divide the dough into 8 pieces and shape into balls. Top each of the balls with chopped red onion and spring onion, then roll out using a rolling pin into a round 6–8 in (15–20 cm) in diameter.

Place a large frying pan over a low to moderate heat. When hot, cook the breads on the dry pan, one at a time, for 3–4 minutes on each side or until they start to dry out and color.

When both sides are done, brush with some melted ghee and turn the bread over, then brush the other side with melted ghee. Serve the breads hot.

Makes 8

Murgh makhani Old Delhi-style chicken curry

In Old Delhi in the 1950s, the legendary Moti Mahal restaurant created the dish that for millions of people around the world (especially in Britain) defines Indian food. "Butter Chicken," as Moti Mahal calls it, is the father and mother of chicken tikka masala. In the West, this dish is much interpreted, but in fact it has been enjoyed by Punjabis for decades. This is exactly how it is prepared in Old Delhi. Ideally, the chicken should be cooked in a *tandoor* on skewers, to give a smoky flavor, but an oven or barbecue grill are good enough alternatives. The chicken should be cooked two-thirds of the way through and then simmered in the sauce. Collect the juices from the cooking chicken, strain, and add them to the sauce, too.

INGREDIENTS

1 tsp ginger paste
1 tsp garlic paste
1^1/$_2$ tsp salt
1^1/$_2$ tsp chili powder
juice of ^{1}/$_2$ lemon
1^3/$_4$ lb (800 g) boned chicken thighs, skinned and cut in half
3^1/$_2$ oz (100 g) plain Greek-style yogurt
^{1}/$_4$ tsp ground garam masala

Sauce

2^3/$_4$ lb (1.25 kg) tomatoes, cut in half
1-in (2.5-cm) piece fresh ginger root, crushed

4 garlic cloves, peeled
4 green cardamom pods
2 cloves
1 cinnamon leaf or bay leaf
1^1/$_2$ tbsp Kashmiri chili powder
^{1}/$_2$ stick (^{1}/$_4$ cup) butter, cut into small pieces
1-in (2.5-cm) piece fresh ginger root, finely chopped
2 green chilies, quartered lengthwise
^{1}/$_3$ cup heavy cream
1 tsp salt
1 tsp ground dried fenugreek leaves
^{1}/$_4$ tsp ground garam masala
2 tsp sugar (optional)

METHOD

Prepare the barbecue grill or preheat the oven to 450°F (220°C).

To make the marinade, mix together the ginger paste, garlic paste, salt, chili powder, and lemon juice in a large bowl. Add the chicken and, using your hands, coat the pieces with the mixture. Set aside for 20 minutes. Mix the yogurt with the garam masala and apply to the marinated chicken. Set aside for another 10 minutes if you have time.

Serves 4–6

Thread the chicken onto skewers. Cook on the barbecue grill or in the oven for 15–18 minutes, turning the skewers after 10 minutes or so, to cook evenly on both sides.

rich, smooth, and fragrant

While the chicken is cooking, make the sauce. Place the tomatoes in a pan with ^{1}/$_2$ cup water and add the crushed ginger, garlic, cardamom pods, cloves, and cinnamon leaf. Cook until the tomatoes are completely broken down and soft.

Remove the pan from the heat and, using a hand-held blender, purée the mixture (or do this in a blender or food processor). Press through a sieve to make a very smooth purée.

Return the purée to the pan and bring to a boil. Stir in the chili powder. Cook until the purée starts to thicken, then slowly incorporate the butter, little by little, stirring constantly. The sauce will become glossy.

Add the chicken (off the skewers) and the strained juices from roasting. Simmer for 5–6 minutes. As the sauce begins to thicken, add the chopped ginger, slit green chilies, and cream. Continue simmering until the sauce is thick enough to coat the chicken.

Remove from the heat before the fat separates out and comes to the surface of the dish. (If that does happen, simply stir in 1–2 tbsp water and 1 tbsp more cream and remove immediately from the heat.) Add the salt, ground fenugreek, and garam masala and mix well. Check the seasoning and add the sugar, if needed.

Serve the chicken curry with hot naan (p50) or pilau rice.

Kadhai paneer Stir-fry of paneer cheese with peppers

A *kadhai*, or *karahi*, is the Indian wok, and this is the Indian answer to a stir-fry. The recipe here is probably the most popular of all *kadhai* dishes in India, by far the easiest, tastiest, and most colorful of the various different versions. This style of cooking is very versatile and quick if you've done some of the basic preparation—make a basic sauce in advance, and then it's simply a question of choosing your meat, fish, or vegetables and degree of spiciness. You may want to keep a jar of this basic *kadhai* sauce in your refrigerator. The *kadhai* method is becoming particularly popular with youngsters and people who are learning to cook and want to try out different things without spending a lot of time in the kitchen.

INGREDIENTS

1 tbsp ghee or corn oil
1/2 tsp crushed dried chilies
2 red or yellow peppers, seeded and cut into strips, 1/2 x 1 1/4 in (1 x 3 cm)
1 red onion, sliced 1/2 in (1 cm) thick
1 lb 5 oz (600 g) paneer, cut into batons, 1/2 x 1 1/4 in (1 x 3 cm)
2 tbsp finely chopped cilantro leaves
1/2 tsp dried fenugreek leaves, crumbled
juice of 1 lemon
2-in (5-cm) piece fresh ginger root, peeled and cut into julienne

Basic kadhai sauce

1/3 cup ghee or corn oil
1 oz (30 g) garlic cloves, finely chopped
1 tbsp coriander seeds, coarsely pounded
8 red chilies, coarsely pounded in a mortar
2 onions, finely chopped
2-in (5-cm) piece fresh ginger root, finely chopped
3 green chilies, finely chopped
1 lb 10 oz (750 g) fresh ripe tomatoes, finely chopped
2 tsp salt
1 tsp ground garam masala
1 1/2 tsp dried fenugreek leaves, crumbled
1 tsp sugar (optional)

METHOD

To make the sauce, heat the ghee in a pan, add the garlic, and let it color. Stir, then add the coriander seeds and red chilies. When they release their aromas, add the onions and cook until they start turning a light golden color. Stir in the ginger, green chilies, and tomatoes. Reduce the heat to low and cook until all excess moisture has evaporated and the fat starts to separate out. Add the salt, garam masala, and fenugreek leaves and stir. Taste and add some sugar, if needed.

For the stir-fry, heat the ghee in a *kadhai*, wok, or large frying pan. Add the crushed chilies, pepper strips, and red onion. Stir and sauté over high heat for under a minute, then add the paneer and stir for another minute. Add the sauce and mix well. Once everything is heated through, check for seasoning, adding a touch of salt if required. Finish with the fresh cilantro, fenugreek leaves, and lemon juice. Garnish with the ginger and serve with naan (p50).

Serves 4–6

colorful, sweet and sour

Subz saag gosht Lamb cooked with winter vegetables and spinach

This recipe has its origins in Kashmir, the northernmost state of India, on the border of Pakistan, where the winters are severe. This is a simple yet warming everyday dish using turnips, carrots, spinach, and dill with lamb. It could have been the starting point of what the Western world knows as *saag gosht* minus the root vegetables, but try it with the vegetables and see the difference for yourself.

INGREDIENTS

$1/3$ cup ghee or corn oil
2 tsp cumin seeds
2 tsp cloves
2 large onions, finely chopped
$1^3/4$ oz (50 g) garlic, finely chopped
$1^1/2$ oz (40 g) fresh ginger root, finely chopped
2 tsp red chili powder
1 tsp ground turmeric
2 tsp salt
$2^1/4$ lb (1 kg) boned leg of lamb, cut into
   1-in (2.5-cm) cubes

4 green chilies, slit lengthwise
$5^1/2$ oz (150 g) each turnips and carrots, cut
   into $1/2$-in (1-cm) cubes
$1^1/4$ cups lamb stock or water
7 oz (200 g) tomatoes, finely chopped
14 oz (400 g) spinach leaves, finely chopped
$1^1/2$ tsp ground mixed spices (equal parts
   cloves, nutmeg, mace, and green cardamom)
2 tbsp finely chopped fresh dill leaves

METHOD

Heat the ghee or oil in a large, heavy pan and add the cumin seeds and cloves. When they crackle, add the onions and sauté until they become light golden in color. Add the garlic and ginger and sauté for a further 2–3 minutes or until the garlic begins to change color.

Sprinkle in the red chili powder, turmeric, and salt and stir for another couple of minutes until the spices begin to release their aromas and the fat starts to separate out. Now add the cubes of lamb and cook for 5–6 minutes, stirring constantly, until the lamb begins to brown around the edges.

When most of the liquid has evaporated and the lamb is getting browned, add the green chilies, turnips, and carrots and stir. Pour in the lamb stock. Reduce the heat to low, cover with a lid, and cook until the lamb is three-quarters done.

Remove the lid, add the tomatoes, and cook for a further 10–12 minutes or until the lamb is nearly cooked and the tomatoes are incorporated with the *masala*. Stir in the spinach and increase the heat again. Cook for 2–3 minutes. (You can cover with a lid if you wish, to speed up the cooking of the spinach.)

The lamb and spinach should be cooked by now, so check for seasoning and correct if required. To finish the dish, sprinkle with the ground mixed spices and dill, then cover the pan with the lid and remove from heat.

Remove the lid from the pan at the table and serve immediately, with chapatti or tandoori roti.

Serves 4

rich, spicy,
and rustic

Dahi wali machli Catfish in yogurt sauce

Northern India is not known for its fish dishes, but every region seems to have at least one standard recipe. Most of the fish used in northern India are river fish or are caught from lakes or ponds. Local fish include *rohu* or *katla* but elsewhere can be replaced by perch, barramundi, or prized varieties like halibut or monkfish.

INGREDIENTS

2$\frac{1}{4}$ lb (1 kg) fillet of catfish, perch, or carp, cut into 1$\frac{1}{2}$-in (4-cm) cubes
1 tsp salt
juice of 1 lemon
1$\frac{1}{2}$ tsp ground turmeric
1$\frac{1}{2}$ tsp red chili powder
1 tbsp carom seeds (optional)
2 tbsp chickpea flour
vegetable oil for deep frying

Sauce
3 tbsp ghee or corn oil
1 onion, finely chopped

1 tsp ground cumin
1 tsp ground turmeric
1 tsp red chili powder
1 tsp salt
1-in (2.5-cm) piece fresh ginger root, finely chopped
2 green chilies, slit lengthwise
16 oz (450 g) plain yogurt
$\frac{1}{3}$ cup chickpea flour
1 cup fish stock or water
$\frac{1}{2}$ tsp dried fenugreek leaves, crumbled
$\frac{1}{2}$ tsp ground garam masala

METHOD

Set the oven to 275°F (140°C) before you begin to cook. Place the fish in a large bowl and rub with the salt, lemon juice, and turmeric. Set aside to marinate for 20 minutes.

Sprinkle the fish with the chili powder, carom seeds, and chickpea flour. Using your hands, mix and rub well to ensure that all the cubes of fish are coated with the mixture.

Heat oil in a deep saucepan. When hot, add the fish and deep-fry for 2–3 minutes or until golden brown. Drain on paper towels, transfer to an ovenproof dish, and place in the oven to keep warm while you make the sauce.

Heat the ghee in a saucepan, add the chopped onion, and sauté until golden brown. Add the cumin, turmeric, chili powder, and salt and sauté until the spices begin to release their flavor. Stir in the ginger and green chilies and cook for a further 2 minutes.

Whisk the yogurt and chickpea flour together in a bowl, making sure there are no lumps. Slowly add the yogurt mixture to the pan, stirring constantly to prevent the yogurt from separating. When all the yogurt has been incorporated, increase the heat and bring to a boil. Pour in the stock and bring back to a boil, then simmer for 3–5 minutes.

Add the pieces of fried fish and continue to cook over low heat for another few minutes. Check the seasoning, then stir in the fenugreek and garam masala. Cover with a lid to retain the aromas of fenugreek and spices and remove from heat. Serve immediately, with steamed rice.

Serves 4

light, fresh, and slightly sour

Daal makhani Black lentils

This is an earthy, rich Punjabi dish that is typical of the region, the land of five rivers. It is not for the calorie-conscious—it requires large amounts of butter and cream. You will need to go to an Asian grocery store to buy the specific type of lentil. The dish normally takes a lot of time to prepare—traditionally, it is put onto the embers of the coals in the *tandoor* and left to simmer gently all night.

INGREDIENTS

9 oz (250 g) whole black lentils (*urad*), soaked in lukewarm water overnight
1 tsp ginger paste
1 tsp garlic paste
1^1/$_2$ tsp salt
2 tsp red chili powder

2 tbsp tomato purée
^{2}/$_3$ cup salted butter
1 tsp ground garam masala
^{1}/$_2$ tsp ground dried fenugreek leaves
^{1}/$_2$ tsp sugar
^{1}/$_4$ cup heavy cream

METHOD

Drain the lentils and transfer them to a saucepan. Pour on 1^1/$_2$ quarts (1.5 liters) water and bring to a boil. Simmer for about 1 hour or until the lentils are thoroughly cooked but are not completely broken down and mashed.

Add the ginger and garlic pastes, salt, and red chili powder and simmer for a further 10 minutes. Reduce the heat to low and add the tomato purée and butter. Cook for 15 minutes or until the lentils are thick, stirring frequently. Take care that the mixture does not separate—that is, the butter does not separate from the lentils.

Stir in the garam masala, fenugreek leaves, and sugar, and adjust the seasoning. Stir in the cream and serve immediately.

Serves 4

rich, earthy, and creamy

Naan Naan bread

This humble bread from Delhi and Punjab is probably one of the best gifts from the *tandoor* to humankind. It is widely available and popular the world over, and makes an excellent accompaniment for any curry. Naan is traditionally cooked in a charcoal-fired clay oven but will work as well in a regular oven or under the broiler. Use your imagination and you could soon be making naan sandwiches and wraps, or even using it as a base for canapés.

INGREDIENTS
2 heaping tbsp caster sugar
2 eggs
$1^2/_3$ cups whole milk
6 cups all-purpose flour
$1^1/_2$ tsp baking powder
1 tbsp salt
$3^1/_2$ tbsp vegetable oil

METHOD
Preheat the oven to 425°F (220°C). Place two nonstick baking sheets in the oven to heat up.

Whisk the sugar and eggs with the milk in a small mixing bowl, stirring until the sugar has dissolved. Put the flour in a large mixing bowl and mix in the baking powder and salt. Gradually pour the milk mixture into the flour, mixing with your hand, and knead lightly, just enough to make a soft dough. Take care not to knead too much or the dough will become too stretchy. Cover the bowl with a damp cloth and leave to rest for 15 minutes.

Add the oil and mix lightly to incorporate it into the dough. Divide the dough into 16 small pieces. Roll out each piece into a round about 4 in (10 cm) in diameter. To form into the traditional "teardrop" shape, lay a round over one palm and gently pull one edge down until it stretches a bit. Place the breads on the hot trays and bake for 4–5 minutes.

Makes 16

Serve warm (if not serving immediately, reheat in a 350°F [180°C] oven for 1–2 minutes).

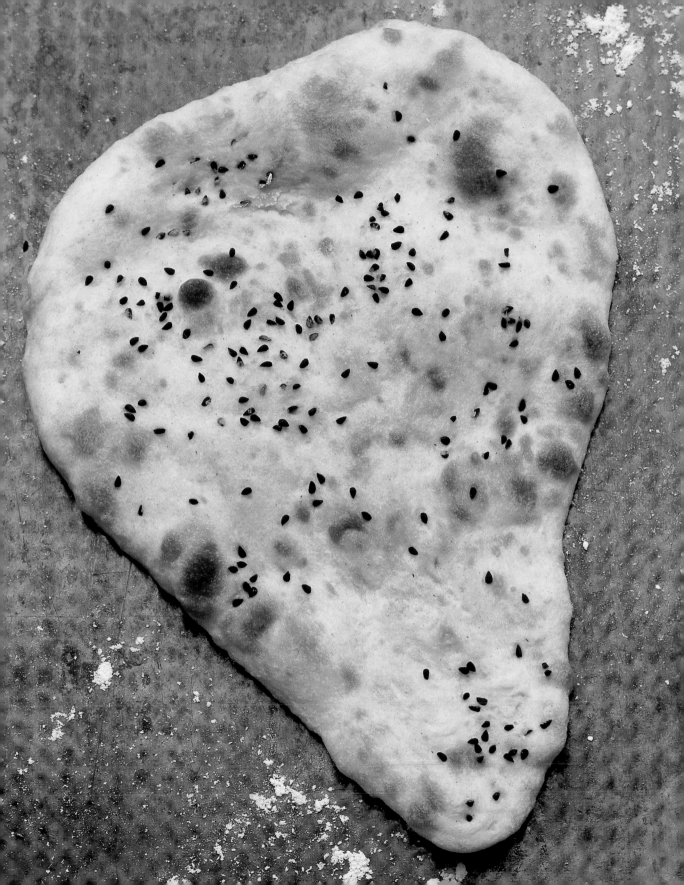

Nalli gosht Slow-braised lamb shank in saffron sauce

This is a very simple dish to make but is a great indicator of the level of finesse and sophistication in cooking that was reached during the reign of certain Mughal rulers in Lucknow. Slow cooking allows for maximum extraction of gelatin from the shanks, giving a shine and smoothness to the sauce that is unique.

INGREDIENTS

4 lamb shanks
3 tbsp corn oil
2 black cardamom pods, crushed
2 cinnamon sticks
2 large onions, finely chopped
1 tsp ginger paste
1 tsp garlic paste
$1^1/_2$ tsp chili powder
$^1/_2$ tsp ground fennel seeds
$^1/_2$ tsp ground coriander
1 tsp ground ginger

2 tbsp plain yogurt
5 tomatoes, puréed
$1^1/_2$ tsp salt
$2^1/_2$ cups lamb stock or water

To finish

$^1/_4$ tsp ground garam masala
generous pinch of saffron threads
3 drops of rose water (optional)
2 tbsp heavy cream

METHOD

First blanch the lamb shanks: place them in a large saucepan of boiling water, cover, and cook for 20 minutes. Drain. When cool enough to handle, cut away all the gristle from the meat.

Heat the oil in a pan large enough to hold the shanks. Add the cardamoms and cinnamon sticks, and when they crackle, add the onions. Cook until golden brown. Add the ginger and garlic pastes and cook for 2 minutes, stirring constantly. Add the ground spices and cook for 3 more minutes.

Slowly whisk in the yogurt and stir until the sauce reaches simmering point. Stir in the fresh tomato purée and bring the sauce to a boil. Season with the salt.

Add the lamb shanks to the simmering sauce. Cover with a tight-fitting lid and cook over low heat for $1^1/_2$–2 hours or until the lamb is very tender and the meat is almost falling off the bone. Add some stock from time to time: you will need the extra liquid to cook the shanks completely.

Alternatively, you can cook the lamb shanks in the oven. Put them in a braising tray, cover with the sauce and stock, and braise in a preheated 350°F (180°C) oven for $2^1/_2$–3 hours. Keep checking the shanks after 2 hours.

Remove the shanks and arrange them on a serving tray or plate. Cover and keep warm in a warm oven while you finish the sauce.

Skim any excess fat or oil from the sauce, then strain the sauce into a smaller saucepan and return to the heat. Add the garam masala powder, saffron, and rose water, if using. Bring to a boil again, adjust the seasoning, and stir in the cream. Remove the shanks from the oven and pour the sauce over them. Serve immediately.

Serves 4

smooth and
warmly
spiced

Kachhi mirch ka gosht Lamb shoulder with green chilies, mint, and yogurt

Shoulder of lamb is very good for braising, which is one of the cooking techniques used to make this dish. It is similar to a North Indian *korma*, but it has a sharp kick or bite and freshness from the green chilies and mint as well as great texture and "mouth feel" resulting from adding onions and more chilies at the end.

INGREDIENTS

$2^{1}/_{4}$ lb (1 kg) boned shoulder of lamb, cut into $1^{1}/_{2}$-in (3.5-cm) cubes
10 oz (300 g) plain yogurt
$1^{1}/_{2}$ tsp black peppercorns, coarsely crushed
2 tsp coriander seeds, roasted and coarsely pounded
2 tsp cumin seeds, roasted and coarsely pounded
2 tsp salt
$^{1}/_{3}$ cup ghee or corn oil
1 blade mace

5 black cardamom pods
9 oz (250 g) white onions, finely chopped
$^{3}/_{4}$ oz (20 g) fresh ginger root, finely chopped
6 green chilies, slit lengthwise
3 cups lamb stock or water
$1^{1}/_{2}$ oz (40 g) cashew nut paste
$2^{1}/_{2}$ tbsp heavy cream
1 red onion, cut into $^{1}/_{2}$-in (1-cm) cubes
1 tbsp finely chopped mint leaves
juice of 1 lemon
1 tsp ground roasted fennel seeds

METHOD

Wash the diced lamb in running cold water for 10 minutes to remove any blood. Dry using paper towels. Put the lamb in a bowl with the yogurt, peppercorns, roasted pounded coriander and cumin, and salt. Toss to mix, then set aside to marinate.

Reserve 1 tbsp of the ghee for later use and heat the rest in a heavy-based pan. Add the mace and black cardamoms and stir for a few seconds. Add the white onions and cook them over moderate heat until soft and translucent but not brown. As they begin to turn slightly golden, add the ginger and 4 of the green chilies.

Add the marinated lamb and stir. Cook for 12–15 minutes, stirring constantly, making sure that the lamb does not brown in the process. Pour in the stock, reduce the heat to low, and cook, covered, until the lamb is almost done.

Stir in the cashew nut paste and cook for a further 5–7 minutes. Add the cream and adjust the seasoning, if required. Leave to simmer gently.

In a separate pan, heat the remaining ghee and briskly sauté the red onion and the remaining green chilies until the onion is soft and translucent. Add to the simmering lamb, sprinkle on the mint and lemon juice, and stir in the fennel powder. Serve immediately, with paratha (p62) or pilau.

Serves 4

sharp, hot, and fresh

Rezala Bhopal-style goat curry

This is a fascinating recipe that comes from the kitchens of a very wealthy *maharani* in central India. I like it because it's very easy to remember and very simple to make. It strangely resembles a pound cake recipe from the medieval era, where you put in equal quantities of everything, mix it up, and pop it in the oven. In this case, just mix together all the ingredients and cover the pan. Cook either in the oven or on the stovetop over very low heat. The recipe here uses goat, but feel free to replace it with lamb or mutton—both work just as well.

INGREDIENTS

$2^{1}/_{4}$ lb (1 kg) boned leg of goat, cut into 1-in (2.5-cm) cubes
$^{3}/_{4}$ cup corn oil or ghee
7 oz (200 g) green chilies, slit lengthwise and seeded
7 oz (200 g) crisp-fried onions, crushed coarsely
2 tbsp pineapple, blended to a paste
7 oz (200 g) plain Greek-style yogurt
2 tbsp finely chopped fresh ginger root
1 tbsp garlic paste
3 tbsp roasted chickpea flour
1 tbsp salt
1 tsp whole allspice

2 tsp royal cumin or black cumin seeds
2 tsp red chili powder
2 tsp ground cumin
2 tsp ground garam masala
Layered paratha dough (p62), or a flour and water dough, to seal

To finish

$^{1}/_{3}$ cup heavy cream
2 oz (50 g) fried cashew nuts, pounded or blended to a paste
$^{1}/_{2}$ cup chopped cilantro leaves
2 tbsp chopped mint leaves

METHOD

If cooking in the oven, preheat it to 350°F (180°C).

Mix the meat with all the other ingredients except the paratha dough, and set aside to marinate for 10–15 minutes.

Transfer the marinated meat to an ovenproof earthenware casserole dish or ovenproof pan with a tight-fitting lid. Seal the lid using paratha dough. If need be, place a weight on the lid to prevent steam from escaping during cooking.

Put the casserole in the oven or the pot over low heat. Cook for 2 hours or until the meat is tender. If cooking in the oven, reduce the heat to 250°F (110°C) after 25–30 minutes.

Stir the sauce, then finish by adding the cream and cashew nut paste. Bring back to a boil. Taste and adjust the seasoning, if required. Sprinkle with the chopped cilantro and mint, and serve.

Serves 4

hot, spicy, and rich

Subz miloni *Seasonal vegetables in spinach and garlic sauce*

Vegetables such as mushrooms and baby corn were not available in the past, but are now more widely seen. Since this is a dish of mixed vegetables, feel free to use whatever you like. Just remember to cut all of the vegetables to more or less the same shape and size. Also, parboil hard vegetables beforehand and add the delicate and green vegetables later in the cooking.

INGREDIENTS

6 oz (150 g) carrots, cut into $1/2$-in (1-cm) cubes
6 oz (150 g) cauliflower, trimmed into
   $1/2$-in (1-cm) florets
4 oz (100 g) fine green beans, cut into
   $1/2$-in (1-cm) lengths
$2^{1}/4$ lb (1 kg) young spinach leaves
$1/3$ cup ghee or vegetable oil
2 tsp cumin seeds
$1^{1}/2$ oz (40 g) garlic, finely chopped
1 large onion, finely chopped
1-in (2.5-cm) piece fresh ginger root,
   finely chopped
6 green chilies, finely chopped
$1^{1}/2$ tsp ground coriander

2 tsp salt
4 oz (100 g) button or chestnut mushrooms,
   cut into $1/2$-in (1-cm) cubes
2 oz (50 g) baby corn, cut into $1/2$-in (1-cm)
   lengths, or canned sweetcorn (optional)
2 oz (50 g) broccoli florets, trimmed into
   $1/2$-in (1-cm) pieces (optional)
2 oz (50 g) frozen peas, thawed
1 tbsp chickpea flour
2 tbsp butter
4 tbsp heavy cream
1 tsp dried fenugreek leaves, crumbled
1 tsp ground garam masala

METHOD

Parboil the carrots, cauliflower, and green beans until al dente (3 minutes for the cauliflower and green beans, 4 minutes for the carrots). Drain well and refresh in iced water; drain again.

Blanch the spinach in boiling salted water until wilted, then drain and cool in ice water. Squeeze dry. Blend in a food processor to make a smooth paste, adding a little water as needed to liquify.

In a heavy-based pan, heat the ghee over medium heat. Stir in the cumin seeds, and when they start to crackle, add the garlic and sauté until golden. Add the onion, reduce the heat to low, and cook until soft and golden brown. Add the ginger and chilies and sauté for 2–3 minutes.

Stir in the carrots and cauliflower and cook for 2–4 minutes. Add the coriander and salt, then the mushrooms, and sauté, stirring, for 2–3 minutes or until they soften up. Add the baby corn and sauté for 1–2 minutes. Next add the broccoli, beans, and peas. Mix together well. Add the chickpea flour and stir for 2–3 minutes, to cook off the flour. Add the spinach paste, then bring to a boil, stirring in the butter and cream.

As soon as the vegetables are boiling, check the seasoning and adjust if necessary. Finish with the fenugreek leaves and garam masala. Do not cook for too long after adding the spinach paste or it will discolor and make the dish unappetizing in appearance. Serve with paratha (p62) or chapatti.

Serves 4–6

fresh, light,
and
aromatic

Bateyr masala Quail in spicy curry

In the 1750s, when *bawarchis* (cooks) supplied prepared dishes to their wealthy patrons, the food was delivered in covered and sealed trays, to prevent any tampering. A dish such as this would have been cooked for special occasions. Served with a pilau, it could be the centerpiece of your dinner table. Other game birds such as partridge, pheasant, or grouse will also work well.

INGREDIENTS

6 quail, about 10 oz (300 g) each, skinned
scant 1 oz (25 g) ginger paste
scant 1 oz (25 g) garlic paste
2$\frac{1}{2}$ tsp red chili powder
1 tsp ground turmeric
2$\frac{1}{2}$ tsp salt
$\frac{3}{4}$ cup vegetable oil or ghee
1-in (2.5-cm) cinnamon stick
1 blade mace
2 black cardamom pods

1 tbsp black peppercorns
5 cloves
5 green cardamom pods
9 oz (250 g) onions, processed to a fine paste
2 tbsp ground coriander
1 lb (450 g) plain yogurt
1$\frac{1}{2}$ tbsp chickpea flour
1 tsp ground garam masala
$\frac{1}{3}$ cup finely chopped cilantro leaves

METHOD

Clean the quail inside and out by washing under running cold water; drain and pat dry using paper towels. Season them by rubbing with a mixture of 1 tbsp of the ginger paste, 1 tbsp garlic paste, 1 tsp red chili powder, $\frac{1}{2}$ tsp turmeric, and 1 tsp salt. Set aside to marinate for 10–15 minutes.

Choose a shallow but wide pan that can hold the quail in it comfortably and has a tight-fitting lid. Set the pan over medium heat and pour in the oil. When hot, place the quail in the pan, a few at a time, and cook until they are golden brown on all sides. Using a slotted spoon, transfer the quail to a dish and set aside.

Heat the juices and oil left in the pot and add the whole spices, stirring to release their aromas. Add the onion paste and the remainder of the ginger and garlic pastes and cook, stirring constantly to prevent the pastes from sticking to the bottom of the pan. After 5–6 minutes, add the remainder of the chili powder, turmeric, and salt and the ground coriander. Cook until the fat begins to separate out from the pastes.

Return the seared quail to the pot and spoon the sauce over them carefully, taking care not to break the birds. Whisk the yogurt with the chickpea flour, then pour over the birds and mix into the sauce. Cover with the lid, reduce the heat to low, and cook for 15–20 minutes.

Remove the lid and transfer the quail to a serving dish; keep warm. Whisk the sauce for a few minutes using a hand whisk or fork to emulsify the mixture. It will still separate a little but should have a coating consistency. Taste and adjust the seasoning if required and finish with the garam masala and fresh cilantro. Spoon the sauce over the quail and serve immediately.

Serves 6

slightly fatty and aromatic

Gucchi aur murgh kalia Chicken and morel curry

In the mid-18th century, competition between *rakabdars* (chefs) in Lucknow was at its peak. Each tried to outdo the others by creating ever more sophisticated dishes. Addition of gold leaf was, and still is, the ultimate luxurious adornment.

INGREDIENTS

1³/₄ oz (50 g) large dried morels
1 lb 2 oz (500 g) onions, finely sliced
vegetable oil for deep-frying
10 oz (300 g) plain yogurt
¹/₂ cup ghee or vegetable oil
1 tsp royal cumin seeds
1 tsp whole allspice
¹/₂ nutmeg
1 blade mace
4 green cardamom pods
¹/₂ tsp black peppercorns
2¹/₄ lb (1 kg) boned chicken thighs, excess fat
   removed and each cut in half lengthwise

2 tbsp ginger paste
2 tbsp garlic paste
2 tbsp Kashmiri red chili powder
2 tsp salt
1 cup chicken stock
¹/₃ cup heavy cream
pinch of saffron threads
¹/₂ tsp ground garam masala
few drops of rose water (optional)
2 sheets of gold leaf (optional)

METHOD

Wash the morels thoroughly to get rid of any grit. Soak in ³/₄ cup water for 30 minutes to rehydrate. Drain the morels, reserving the liquid, and pat dry with paper towels.

While the morels are soaking, deep-fry the onions until golden. Drain, then blend with 1³/₄ oz (50 g) of the yogurt and a little water to make a paste.

Heat 1 tbsp of the ghee in a heavy-based pan and add ¹/₂ tsp of the royal cumin. When it crackles, add the morels and sauté for a couple of minutes over moderate heat. Using a slotted spoon, remove the morels from the pan and set aside.

Heat the rest of the ghee in the pan and add the whole spices, together with the remaining royal cumin. Stir for 1–2 minutes, then add the chicken pieces. Saute for 2–3 minutes over high heat, then add the onion, ginger, and garlic pastes and mix together. Stir for another 2–3 minutes. Add the red chili powder and salt and cook for 2–3 minutes. Stir in the remaining yogurt, little by little. Cook for 5 minutes, then add the stock and the reserved morel soaking liquid. Reduce the heat, cover the pan, and simmer gently until the chicken is cooked.

Remove the chicken pieces with a slotted spoon and set aside. Pass the sauce through a sieve, then return to the pan and bring back to a boil. Boil until reduced to a saucelike consistency.

Reduce the heat to low and stir in the cream, saffron, and garam masala. Add the chicken pieces and simmer briefly to heat up. Lastly, just before serving, add the morels and finish with the rose water, if using. Transfer to a shallow dish and garnish with the optional gold leaf.

Serves 4–6

aromatic
and spicy

Mutter pulao Green pea pilau

This is one of the simplest pilau rice preparations that you will ever come across. Traditionally in Lucknow and central states, pilaus were of many varieties and often used several ingredients together. In fact, pilaus were considered to be more exotic and special than biryanis, which were thought to be "rough and ready." The basic difference between boiled rice and pilau rice is not the use of spices but the method of cooking. Boiled rice may be cooked with spices, but the cooking liquid is drained away at the end, similar to when cooking pasta. For pilau rice, it is important to use just the right quantity of water, since it should all be absorbed when the rice is done. Rice has more flavor and nutrients when cooked by the pilau method.

INGREDIENTS

14 oz (400 g) basmati rice
$1/3$ cup ghee
1 tsp cumin seeds
$1/2$ tsp cloves
1 cinnamon leaf or bay leaf
4 green cardamom pods
1 cinnamon stick

2 red onions, finely sliced
4 oz (100 g) frozen peas, thawed
1 tbsp salt
2 tsp shredded mint leaves
2 tsp chopped cilantro leaves

METHOD

Wash the rice in cold running water, then soak in enough cold water to cover for 20–25 minutes. Soaking the rice reduces the cooking time and prevents the grains from breaking while cooking.

Heat the ghee in a heavy-based dutch oven over medium heat and add the whole spices. When they crackle, add the sliced onions and sauté until they are golden brown. Add the peas and sauté for 2–3 minutes. Pour in $3^1/2$ cups water. Add the salt, cover, and bring to a boil.

Drain the soaked rice and add to the casserole pot. Cover again and bring back to a boil. Cook, covered, for 8–10 minutes over moderately high heat. From time to time, remove the lid and gently stir the rice, keeping in mind that too much handling can break the rice grains.

When the water is nearly all absorbed and you can see small holes on the surface of the rice, sprinkle the mint and the cilantro over it. Cover the casserole dish tightly and reduce the heat to low. Cook for a further 10 minutes. Alternatively, finish cooking the rice in a preheated 250°F (130°C) oven for 10 minutes.

NOTE To make the pilau in a microwave, follow the recipe up to the stage of adding the peas. Then add the salt and the soaked rice and mix lightly for a couple of minutes, until the grains of rice are coated with oil. Transfer to a microwave container. Pour the measured quantity of water over the rice, cover with plastic wrap and prick it to make a few holes. Place in the microwave and cook for 18–20 minutes. Allow the rice to rest for 5 minutes, then transfer to a serving dish.

Serves 4

deliciously perfumed

Tawa paratha Layered paratha

These triangular breads are prepared in thousands of households across northern India almost every morning, to eat for breakfast, lunch, and dinner. You can add different spices, chilies, pastes, and so on to create your own unique paratha.

INGREDIENTS

4 cups chapatti flour
2 tsp salt
1 tbsp vegetable oil
1/2 cup chapatti flour to dust

3 tbsp melted ghee or vegetable oil
1 tbsp carom seeds or black onion
  seeds (optional)

METHOD

Step 1
Mix the chapatti flour with the salt, oil, and 1 cup plus 2 tbsp water in a large bowl, to make a smooth dough. Cover with a damp cloth or plastic wrap and leave to rest for 15 minutes.

Step 2
Divide the dough into 8 equal portions and shape each into a smooth ball. Take one ball at a time and flatten it. Dust with some of the extra flour and, using a rolling pin, roll it out into a disk 2^1/$_2$–3 in (6–8 cm) in diameter. Spread a little ghee on the surface of the disk, sprinkle with some seeds (if using), and dust with a little flour. Fold the disk in half to form a half-moon.

Step 2

Step 3
Repeat the same process of ghee, seeds, and flour on the surface of the half-moon, then fold into a triangle. Now flatten the triangle carefully, using the rolling pin, until it is about ^{1}/$_8$ in (3 mm) thick.

Step 4
Heat a dry tawa, griddle, or frying pan and fry each bread for a couple of minutes, until the surface is dry and it starts to get specks of brown. Turn it over and cook for a further 2 minutes. While the second side is cooking, brush the first side lightly with ghee. Turn the bread over again and brush the other side with ghee. You should see the steam opening up the layers as the bread cooks.

Step 3

Step 5
Remove from the heat once both sides are golden and crisp. Serve the breads hot from the pan.

Makes 8

Step 5 >

Chingri malai curry *Jumbo shrimp in coconut curry sauce*

This is one of the all-time favorite Bengali dishes, reserved for very special guests, big celebratory buffets, and weddings. I still have memories of the curry being served inside a green coconut. As a child I was told the term *malai* referred to the creamy flesh inside the coconut. It made sense then and it makes sense now, as this is how most people think of the dish. While traveling and working as a chef, it surprised me no end to see the similarity between Chingri Malai Curry and a Malaysian *laksa*. I often wonder if the Bengali name that we use has its origins in the "Malaya," which is how Malaysia is known in India.

INGREDIENTS

2-in (5-cm) piece fresh ginger root, roughly chopped
10 garlic cloves, roughly chopped
6 onions, roughly chopped
1 cup vegetable oil
1³/₄ lb (800 g) jumbo shrimp, the largest you can find, peeled and deveined
1 tbsp ground turmeric
1 tbsp salt

3 cinnamon leaves or bay leaves
2 tbsp ground cumin
4 green chilies, slit lengthwise
³/₄ cup thick coconut milk (p213)
1 tsp sugar (optional)
5 green cardamom pods, seeds removed and finely ground in a mortar
2 tbsp ghee

METHOD

Blend the ginger and garlic together in a food processor to make a fine paste. Remove and set aside. Blend the onions to a fine paste with ¹/₃ cup of the oil.

Season the shrimp with ¹/₂ tsp each of turmeric and salt. Heat 2 tbsp of the oil in a nonstick frying pan and sear the shrimp briefly, then remove and set aside.

Heat the remaining oil in a heavy frying pan and add the onion paste with the cinnamon leaves. Sauté over medium heat for 10 minutes or until light brown, stirring occasionally. Mix together the cumin, remaining turmeric, ginger-garlic paste and ²/₃ cup water, then add to the onions. Reduce the heat to low and cook for a further 5–8 minutes, stirring regularly. Stir in the remaining salt, the green chilies, and the shrimp and cook for 2–3 minutes.

Mix in the coconut milk and simmer for 2–3 minutes or until the shrimp are just cooked, adding a little more water if necessary. Adjust the seasoning with salt and sugar, sprinkle with the cardamom powder, and stir in the ghee. Serve immediately, with steamed rice.

Serves 4

rich, creamy, sweet, and spicy

Bhapa lobster Steamed lobster with coconut, ginger, and chili

This would make a great party dish, one sure to impress your guests. In India it is reserved for special occasions and intimate gatherings, when important guests and relations arrive. The use of coconut, mustard, chili, and ginger creates an interesting interplay of flavors. The sweetness of lobster and coconut is balanced by the heat from chili and ginger and the pungency of the mustard oil.

INGREDIENTS

$2^{1}/_{2}$ oz (75 g) yellow mustard seeds
scant 2 tbsp white vinegar
6 raw lobsters, about 1 lb (450 g) each
1 cup thick coconut milk (p213)
$3^{1}/_{2}$ oz (100 g) plain Greek-style yogurt
6 green chilies, slit lengthwise
2-in (5-cm) piece fresh ginger root, cut into
    julienne strips
5 garlic cloves, blended to a paste with a
    $^{1}/_{2}$-in (1-cm) piece fresh ginger root

2 tsp salt
$1^{1}/_{2}$ tsp caster sugar
$^{1}/_{3}$ cup mustard oil
1 tsp black mustard seeds

To finish
$^{1}/_{4}$ cup finely chopped cilantro leaves
1 tsp ground garam masala
1 tbsp shredded fresh ginger root

METHOD

Soak the yellow mustard seeds overnight in the white vinegar, then drain and blend to a paste.

Preheat the oven to 350°F (180°C). Slice each lobster lengthwise in half, leaving the head and shell on. Clean the lobster halves and dry on paper towels. Arrange the lobsters, shell side down, side by side in a casserole or roasting tin.

Whisk together the coconut milk, yogurt, chilies, ginger julienne, garlic and ginger paste, yellow mustard paste, salt, and sugar.

Serves 4–6

Heat the mustard oil in a pan to smoking point, then remove from heat and allow to cool. Reheat the oil and add the black mustard seeds. Once the seeds crackle, add the coconut-spice paste and bring to a boil over low heat, whisking constantly. Be careful not to let the mixture separate. Simmer gently for 2–3 minutes, then remove from heat.

sweet, hot, and creamy

Pour the sauce over the lobster and cover with foil. Cook in the oven for 15–18 minutes. Remove from the oven, sprinkle with the chopped cilantro, garam masala, and shredded ginger, and serve immediately, with steamed rice.

BENGAL

Bekti jhal deya Perch in Bengali mustard and onion sauce

Bekti is a freshwater fish commonly eaten in India. There are two varieties. The Kolkata fish is smaller and has beautiful white flesh with a delicate flavor. It is considered far superior to its Bombay counterpart, which is much larger, fattier, and considerably cheaper. Lake Victoria perch is a very good alternative to Kolkata *bekti*, but any meaty white fish such as halibut or cod could work just as well. If you wish, you can substitute $^1/_3$ cup English whole-grain mustard for the mustard paste.

INGREDIENTS
$2^1/_4$ lb (1 kg) white fish fillet, cut into $1^1/_2$-in
  (4-cm) cubes
1 tsp salt
1 tsp red chili powder
1 tsp ground turmeric
vegetable or corn oil for deep frying
3 tbsp finely chopped cilantro leaves

Mustard paste
$2^1/_2$ oz (75 g) yellow mustard seeds
$^1/_3$ cup white vinegar
1 tsp salt
1 tsp caster sugar
1 tsp ground turmeric

Curry
$^1/_3$ cup mustard oil
1 tsp black mustard seeds
3 red onions, finely sliced
2 tsp ground cumin
1 tbsp red chili powder
$1^1/_2$ tsp salt
$1^2/_3$ cups fish stock or water
3 tomatoes, cut into quarters and deseeded
6 green chilies, slit lengthwise
pinch of caster sugar (optional)
$^1/_4$ cup coconut cream (p213)

METHOD
To make the mustard paste, soak the mustard seeds in the vinegar overnight. Drain, then grind to a fine paste. Mix together the salt, sugar, and turmeric and stir into the paste.

Rinse the fish under cold running water, then dry with paper towels. Season with the salt, chili powder, and turmeric. Deep-fry the fish in hot oil for 1–2 minutes or until golden brown, then drain on paper towels and set aside.

To make the curry, heat the mustard oil in a deep pan or flameproof dutch oven over moderate heat. When it starts to smoke, remove from heat and set aside to cool. Reheat the oil, then add the mustard seeds and allow them to crackle. Add the onions and sauté over medium heat for 5–8 minutes or until translucent.

Add the mustard paste and sauté for a further 5 minutes. Stir in the cumin, chili powder, and salt. Add the fish stock and bring to a boil. Reduce the heat to low and simmer for 2–3 minutes. Now add the fried fish, tomatoes, and green chilies, and simmer for a further 6–8 minutes. Adjust the seasoning with salt (and sugar) if required and gently stir in the coconut cream. Garnish with the chopped cilantro and serve with steamed rice.

Serves 6

sharp, hot, and crunchy

Kosha mangsho Lamb cooked in rich onion sauce

This is a lamb curry from West Bengal and is quite popular in Bihar and neighboring areas as well. The term *kosha* literally translated means "tightened," which refers to the thickening of the spices and sauce to give a rich finish. The curry is often served on a cold day with a soft *khichri*, the original kedgeree, the combination being both comforting and invigorating.

INGREDIENTS

$3^1/_2$ tbsp mustard oil
$3^1/_2$ tbsp ghee or vegetable oil
3 cinnamon leaves or bay leaves
5 black peppercorns
3 black cardamom pods
4 dried red chilies
3 blades mace
6 large red onions, blended to a paste
2 heaped tbsp ginger paste
2 heaped tbsp garlic paste
$^1/_4$ cup red chili powder
2 tbsp ground cumin
2 tbsp ground coriander

$2^1/_4$ lb (1 kg) boned leg of lamb, cut into
   1-in (2.5-cm) cubes
5 large tomatoes, puréed
$1^1/_2$ tbsp salt
$1^2/_3$ cups lamb stock or water
1 tsp caster sugar

To finish
2 tsp each cinnamon stick, green
   cardamom pods, and coriander seeds,
   roasted and ground to a powder (p322)
finely chopped cilantro leaves

METHOD

Heat the mustard oil in a deep pan and bring to smoking point, then add the ghee, followed by the whole spices. When they start to crackle, stir in the onion paste and fry until it is light brown, stirring constantly to prevent it from sticking to the bottom of the pan and burning.

Add the ginger and garlic pastes and mix into the onions along with the chili powder and ground cumin and coriander. Fry for 2–3 minutes, then add the cubes of lamb. Cook over medium heat for 15–20 minutes, stirring frequently.

Add the puréed tomatoes and salt and cook for a further 15 minutes. Pour in the stock, reduce the heat to low, and cover the pan. Simmer until the lamb is tender. Uncover the pan, increase the heat, and reduce the sauce until it becomes thick and coats the lamb.

Adjust the seasoning with salt, if required, and stir in the sugar to balance the spiciness of the dish. Finally, stir in the ground roasted spices and sprinkle generously with chopped cilantro. Serve immediately with paratha, or even with a kedgeree.

Serves 4

rich, spicy, and slightly sweet

Pork chop bhooni Masala pork chops

Until the late 18th century, pork was not used much in Indian cooking. Although most of the country was Hindu, and consumption of pork was not barred, a large proportion of the population was vegetarian. It was only in Anglo-Indian cooking and in the hills in the eastern part of the country that pork was consumed. This recipe originates from Darjeeling, a hill station very popular with the British when they lived in India. The term *bhooni* refers to the dry, almost coating consistency of the spices that remain on the pork chops when the dish is finished.

INGREDIENTS

8 pork chops, about 4 oz (100 g) each, excess fat trimmed
1 tsp salt
1 tsp red chili powder
1 tbsp corn oil

Masala
$1^1/_2$ tbsp mild chili powder
1 tsp ground turmeric
1 tbsp ginger paste
1 tsp garlic paste
3 tomatoes, finely chopped
$^1/_4$ cup corn oil
$^1/_2$ tsp fenugreek seeds

20 curry leaves
2 large onions, finely sliced
2 tbsp tomato ketchup
1 tsp salt
1 tsp caster sugar
1 tsp ground garam masala

To garnish
2 large potatoes, peeled and cut lengthwise
$^1/_2$ tsp salt
$^1/_2$ tsp ground turmeric
2 tbsp corn oil
2 tbsp chopped cilantro leaves

METHOD

Sprinkle the pork chops with the salt and chili powder and rub in well. Heat the oil in a large, heavy pan and sear the pork chops for 2 minutes on each side or until they are colored. Remove from the pan and set aside.

For the *masala*, mix together the chili powder, turmeric, ginger and garlic pastes, and tomatoes in a bowl. Set aside.

Serves 4

Heat the $^1/_4$ cup corn oil in the pan, add the fenugreek seeds, and stir for a minute. As the seeds begin to brown, add the curry leaves and onions and sauté for 6–8 minutes or until the onions begin to turn golden brown. Add th tomato mixture to the pan and sauté for a further 3–5 minutes or until the spices are fragrant.

hot and fatty

Return the seared chops to the pan, and stir in the tomato ketchup, salt, and sugar. Spoon the spice mixture over the chops to coat them evenly. Reduce the heat to low and add $^3/_4$ cup water. Simmer, covered, for 15–20 minutes or until the chops are cooked through and tender.

While the chops are cooking, prepare the garnish. Cook the potatoes in boiling water seasoned with the salt and turmeric for 6–8 minutes or until they are just tender but still firm. Drain. Heat the oil in a frying pan, add the potatoes, and cook until crisp and golden. Keep hot.

Remove the chops from the pan, transfer to a serving platter, and keep warm. Continue to cook the sauce, uncovered, for a few more minutes, until it has a thick coating consistency. Finish by stirring in the garam masala.

Pour the sauce over the pork chops. Arrange the crisp potatoes around the edge and sprinkle with the chopped cilantro. If you like, serve with chapatti, rice, or even some crusty bread.

Murgir jhol Home-style chicken curry

The basic chicken curry differs from household to household. Every cook has his or her own recipe, and each swears by theirs. *Jhol* refers to the thin curry—or "gravy," as it's called in India—that makes it so special. This is quite a simple and rustic method of cooking—true home-style. You could use boneless chicken if you prefer, or even a whole bird cut up into small pieces. Or you could use quail, partridges, or even pheasants for this recipe; just adjust the cooking times.

INGREDIENTS

1/3 cup corn or vegetable oil
1/2 tsp cumin seeds
2 cinnamon leaves or bay leaves
3 green cardamom pods
4 black peppercorns
4 large red onions, finely chopped
4 medium potatoes, peeled and cut into quarters (optional)
2 tsp salt
2 1/4 lb (1 kg) chicken thighs with bone, skinned and cut in half

1 tbsp ginger paste
1 tbsp garlic paste
2 tbsp ground coriander
2 tbsp ground cumin
1 tbsp chili powder
1 tbsp ground turmeric
4 tomatoes, chopped or blended to a purée
1 2/3 cups chicken stock or water
3 green cardamom pods, roasted and ground
2-in (5-cm) cinnamon stick, roasted and ground
1 tbsp finely chopped cilantro leaves

METHOD

Heat the oil in a large pan and add the whole spices. When they crackle, add the onions and fry over medium heat until golden brown. Stir in the potatoes, if using, and cook for 5 minutes. Add 1 tsp of the salt, then add the chicken and cook for 5–8 minutes or until lightly browned.

Add the ginger and garlic pastes, the ground coriander and cumin, remaining salt, chili powder, and turmeric. Cook for a further 10 minutes, stirring constantly, until the spices begin to release their aromas. Stir in the tomatoes and cook for 5 minutes, then pour in the stock. Bring to a boil. Reduce the heat to low and simmer until the chicken is cooked.

Taste and adjust the seasoning, if required. Top with the roasted cardamom and cinnamon powder and finish with the chopped cilantro. Serve with steamed rice.

Serves 4–6

rustic, fresh, and spicy

Ghee bhaat *Ghee rice*

This is a basic dish of boiled basmati rice enriched with the addition of ghee. The nuttiness of ghee combined with the texture of sea salt is simple cooking at its very best. Normally you will find cooking times on the packaging of basmati rice, so follow these if they are given.

INGREDIENTS
1 lb 2 oz (500 g) basmati rice
3 tbsp ghee
1 tbsp flaked sea salt

METHOD
Wash the rice in running cold water, then leave to soak in enough cold water to cover for 20–25 minutes. Soaking the rice reduced the cooking time and prevents the grains from breaking while cooking.

Meanwhile, bring 2 quarts (liters) water to a boil in a large saucepan. When the water is boiling, add the drained rice. Bring back to a boil, then cook, uncovered, over medium-high heat for 10–14 minutes or until the rice is just cooked. It should not be al dente, like pasta, but neither should it be overcooked so that it disintegrates.

Drain the rice in a colander and, while the rice is still hot, add the ghee and sea salt and mix well. Serve immediately. If the rice gets cold, you can reheat it in the microwave for 1–2 minutes.

Serves 8–10

Poories Deep-fried puffed breads

Poories, or *luchis* as they are called in Bengal, are an excellent accompaniment to dry curries, as well as being very popular with children as a snack or even as picnic bread. In Bengal they sometimes use a tad more oil or ghee when making their dough, which produces a shorter and crisper bread, and they also use refined white flour more than whole-wheat flour, which is the norm in the rest of India. In addition, the Bengalis like to add some onion and carom seeds, which makes the bread dramatic in appearance, more flavorsome, and easier to digest.

INGREDIENTS

1 lb 2 oz (500 g) chapatti flour, all-purpose flour, or a mixture of the two (half of each)
2 tsp salt
1 tsp sugar
1 tsp carom seeds
1 tsp black onion seeds
1 tbsp ghee or oil
vegetable oil for deep-frying
2 tbsp vegetable oil for rolling

METHOD

Step 1
Mix together the flour, salt, sugar, and seeds in a bowl. Rub in the ghee with your fingers until it is thoroughly blended with the flour.

Step 2
Make a well in the center of the flour and pour in 1 cup water little by little, mixing to make a stiff dough. Work the dough well with your hands, then cover with a damp cloth and set aside for 15 minutes.

Step 3
Divide the dough into 20 pieces and cover once more with the damp cloth. Work with one piece at a time, keeping the rest covered.

Step 5

Step 4
While oil is heating in your deep-fryer or wok to about 350°F (180°C), roll each piece of dough into a smooth ball: apply a little oil to each dough ball, then, using a rolling pin, roll out into a disk about 4 in (10 cm) in diameter.

Step 5
Deep-fry the breads in the hot oil for 1–2 minutes or until they have puffed up and are crisp and golden on both sides. Drain on paper towels and serve hot.

Makes 20

Freshly made Poories >

SOUTH INDIA

< **Fishing boat, Kerala**

Southern India's ancient and deep-rooted cultural essence has been retained despite invasions, traders, religious conversions, and modernization. As with the rest of India, it originally consisted of many kingdoms whose Hindu and Muslim rulers fought wars to control the land and its resources. Many foreigners first touched Indian soil in the south, starting with the early Christians, and continuing over the centuries with the Portuguese, Dutch, Arabs, French, and, finally, the British toward the end of the 17th century.

After independence from Britain, southern India was divided on a linguistic basis into four different states: Andhra Pradesh, Tamil Nadu, Karnataka, and Kerala. The population was and is predominantly Hindu, just as in other parts of India, and as a result the cooking tradition is primarily vegetarian. Ayurveda (the ancient Indian medical system and way of life) has also had a great influence on the cooking culture. South Indians have great respect for the therapeutic value of food, and people follow Ayurvedic principles in their everyday eating. A traditional meal is more or less the same in most of the region: a large heap of rice on a banana leaf, with a variety of colorful vegetarian or meat dishes and pickles around it, arranged to balance flavors and provide nutritional richness.

New cultures and religions added new dimensions to South Indian cooking. For example, meat cookery was introduced by the Muslims in northern Kerala and Hyderabad and the Christian communities in Mangalore, Kochi, and central Kerala. Hyderabadi Muslim biryani is still the favorite biryani preparation for the majority of Indian people.

The cuisine in each of the four states has its own unique characteristics. Andhra food is considered to be the spiciest. Hot and spicy Andhra lamb and chicken curries are hugely popular with lovers of traditional Indian food.

The temple state of Tamil Nadu is renowned for its traditional vegetarian food and the most amazing variety of delicious snacks. The rice pancakes called *dosas*, steamed rice and lentil cakes called *idlis*, and popular train snacks like *vadais* and *bondas* are all contributions of the rich Brahmin (upper-class Hindu caste) community of Tamil Nadu. In the southern areas like Chettinad, meat and spicy-hot chicken curries are very popular, even though the majority of the people still keep to a strict vegetarian diet. The tangy flavor of *sambar*, spicy, peppery soups like *rasam*, and wonderful rice preparations with yogurt and sour tamarind are all examples of fine Tamil cooking.

Karnataka, home to the garden city of Bangalore, has a distinct culinary identity of its own. It is predominantly vegetarian, except for its border areas like Mangalore. There, the Christian and Anglo-Indian communities enjoy meat, just like people in the neighboring state of Kerala. Udupi, on the coast near Mangalore, is known for the cooking of its Hindu community, particularly famous for their *dosas* and other crispy pancakes. They also make tasty rice dishes like Bisi Bela Bhath (p116) and Chitra Anna, which are finished with fresh colorful garnishes and savory tempering.

Kerala, on the southwest coast, is the most beautiful part of southern India. This lush, fascinating state is known as the spice capital of the country and has a strong tradition of Ayurvedic practice. It's no surprise that Keralan cooking is so healthy, colorful, and light compared to the rest of India. Kerala has a solid base of Christians and Muslims in addition to Hindus, plus a few surviving families from the Jewish community, and all these faiths add to the culinary diversity. In the north of Kerala, you find excellent Muslim meat cooking, whereas Travancore, in central Kerala, has wonderful Christian chicken and lamb curries. Delicious seafood delicacies are prepared in the fishing communities along the coast, and the ancient Nair community is renowned for its vegetarian cooking.

In almost all the South Indian states, people prefer to use fresh ingredients like ginger, curry leaves, and coconut in their cooking, and these, as well as many spices, are grown in home gardens, as well as commercially to be exported to other parts of the world. Unlike northern India, where breads are often eaten with curries, people in this region like rice, preferring the local red rice to basmati for everyday meals.

In the villages, food is cooked in clay and earthenware pots, whereas affluent families use brass and silver utensils for everyday cooking (these metals are deemed to be auspicious and to offer medicinal value). Most of the dishes are stir-fried or boiled first and then cooked in coconut-based *masala* pastes. The final touch is to "temper" the dish with aromatic curry leaves, fragrant mustard seeds, and the sexy flavor of dried red chilies. The combination of these magical flavors is what makes South Indian curries so special.

Das Sreedharan

Roasting fresh coconut >
Brown it with ginger, garlic,
and whole spices

The Taste of South India

1. coconut
2. fenugreek seeds
3. cumin seeds
4. black mustard seeds
5. basmati rice
6. fennel seeds
7. coriander seeds
8. black peppercorns
9. split black lentils
10. cashew nuts
11. fresh green chilies
12. dried red chilies
13. tamarind pulp
14. curry leaves
15. limes
16. fresh ginger root

The raw materials

Indian cooking is often thought to use a lot of spices and combinations of very intense flavors. But South Indian cuisine employs a much simpler collection of spices and flavorings. More than in the cooking of the north of the country, in southern India great importance is given to the balancing of flavors. Subtle variations are created and layering of spices makes the food lighter.

Tamarind

This sweet and sour fruit is commonly used in South Indian cooking as a souring agent, and it brings a tangy contrast to mild coconut sauces. It's also used for chutneys and drinks. Tamarind pulp is sold in dried blocks and needs to be soaked in hot water to soften, then strained to yield tamarind water (p322).

Ginger

This rhizome (underground stem) is used extensively in Indian cooking, and many people grow their own ginger so they will have it fresh whenever it is needed. Dried ground ginger is sometimes acceptable, but the fresh root is always preferred.

Chilies

In the traditional cooking of this region, there are several kinds of chilies used, including fresh green ones about 3 in (7 cm) long and dried red chilies, which can range in size from tiny and very hot to those that are larger and less hot. Chilies are famously known for their fiery power and people feel wary of using them, but you can control their heat by using them whole so they don't lose their seeds in the sauce. Or, if chopping chilies, split them and remove the seeds first.

Curry leaves

This is the most widely used herb in South Indian cuisine. As the name suggests, it smells and tastes like curry. While the flavor is spicy, it is also nutty, a quality brought out when the leaves are lightly fried in oil until crisp. Curry leaves can also be added to a dish just like any other fresh herb, whole or torn. Buy them whenever you find them fresh, as they can be stored in the freezer wrapped in foil or sealed in a plastic bag.

Black pepper

Known as "black gold," pepper is one of the most widely used spices all over the world. Kerala is considered to be its birthplace, because the plant from which the spice comes (*Piper nigrum*) is native to Tranvancore. Black peppercorns are the dried, almost ripe berries of the plant. Keralan pepper markets are attractive places to visit—the spicy aroma of the crowded markets is carried a long way. Black peppercorns can be used whole or ground for garnishing dishes.

Black mustard seeds

Black or brown mustard seeds are used in most savory dishes, providing a flavor that is typical of South Indian cooking. When the mustard seeds are fried in oil, often with curry leaves and dried red chilies, they release a most delicious aroma. Most recipes can be made without them, but they bring a special magic.

Coriander seeds

Coriander seeds are part of most of the *masala* preparations in southern India, either dry-roasted or fried in oil. They have a very distinctive, strong flavor. Usually combined with fenugreek seeds, black peppercorns, and dried red chilies, they flavor many vegetarian and seafood dishes.

Fenugreek seeds

This very bitter spice provides the earthy, musky curry aroma in many South Indian dishes, both

Curry leaves >

meat and vegetarian. The seeds, which are angular in shape and yellowish in color, are added to pickles and chutneys, too. Use them in small quantities.

Cumin seeds

This popular spice has a delicate character. Its mild pungency makes it a perfect component of many spice mixtures, including garam masala (p28). Cumin seeds are also dry-roasted to sprinkle over rice dishes.

Fennel seeds

In flavor, fennel seeds are similar to anise, and they look like slightly plumper, greener cumin seeds. They have a very strong flavor, so use them carefully and in small quantities or they will overpower lighter spices.

Coconut

Coconut is a very important ingredient all over the world, but most particularly in South Indian cooking. Freshly grated coconut is often ground with spices or dry-roasted for curries, as well as being used in savory snacks and many sweets. Unsweetened

desiccated coconut can be used as a replacement, although it is drier in texture. Coconut milk and cream (p213) are also much used in South Indian curries, adding creaminess and sweetness.

Limes

Lime juice (and lemon juice) is used all over India to give an instant sour flavor to stir-fries and other dishes. The Indian lime is small and very aromatic with a strong citrus flavor.

Split black lentils

Black lentils are very popular in many parts of India. In the north, they are used whole to make famously rich dishes, whereas in southern India, the lentils are usually skinned and split (*urad dal*). In many recipes, split black

lentils are used as a spice, giving the dish a nutty flavor and crunchy texture. Their name is a bit confusing, since they are in fact creamy in color.

Rice

The traditional rice in South India is a red variety with a short, thick grain. It is not often found outside India. Fragrant basmati rice is considered to be the supreme variety and is reserved for special dishes. Mild-flavored rice flour is the main ingredient for making batters and doughs.

Cashew nuts

Cashews are cultivated in South India and are often added to savory dishes, as well as being used in many snacks and almost all sweets.

Madras meen kolambu Tamarind fish curry

Giant tamarind trees grow everywhere in southern India, offering shade from the sun and their fruits for cooking. The sweet and sour flavor of tamarind is found in all kinds of dishes, from the fruity sweets loved by schoolchildren to curries such as this one. Fish cooked in terra-cotta pots with red chilies and tamarind is eaten by millions of people in the fishing communities. Serve this curry with plain rice.

INGREDIENTS
2 tbsp vegetable oil
1 tsp mustard seeds
10 curry leaves
pinch of fenugreek seeds
2 garlic cloves, chopped
2 onions, chopped
$1/4$ tsp ground turmeric
$1/2$ tsp chili powder
3 tomatoes, chopped
1 tsp tomato paste
sea salt
$1/2$ cup tamarind water,
    made with $1^3/4$ oz (50 g) pulp and
    $1/2$ cup water (p322)
$1^1/4$ lb (500 g) lemon sole fillets

METHOD
Heat the oil in a large saucepan. Add the mustard seeds and, when they begin to pop, add the curry leaves, fenugreek seeds, and garlic. Sauté for 1–2 minutes or until the garlic turns brown. Stir in the onions and cook over moderate heat, stirring occasionally, for 10 minutes or until they are golden.

Add the turmeric and chili powder and mix well, then add the chopped tomatoes, tomato paste, and some salt and cook for a further 2 minutes. Pour in the tamarind water and $3/4$ cup water. Bring the mixture to a boil and simmer for 12 minutes, stirring occasionally, until the sauce thickens.

Cut the fish fillets into pieces and carefully mix into the sauce. Lower the heat and cook gently for 4–5 minutes or until the fish is just cooked through. Serve immediately.

Serves 6

sweet
and sour

Arachu vecha curry Coconut fish curry

This is a traditional fish curry from the region of Travancore, in southern Kerala, one of the most beautiful parts of southern India, where the coastal lowlands on the Arabian Sea are surrounded by lagoons. This is a fantastic dish for people who like mild curries. The creamy smooth flavor will balance spicier dishes. Serve with plain rice or any Indian bread.

INGREDIENTS

2 tbsp vegetable oil
7 oz (200 g) shallots, chopped
10 curry leaves
1¼ lb (500 g) tilapia or other white fish
   fillets, skinned
1 tbsp lemon juice

Spice paste

4 oz (100 g) freshly grated coconut
1 tsp ground coriander
½ tsp chili powder
large pinch of ground turmeric

METHOD

To make the spice paste, put the coconut, ground coriander, chili powder, and turmeric in a blender. Pour in ¾ cup water and process for 2–3 minutes to make a smooth paste. Set aside.

Serves 6

mild, creamy,
nutty and
aromatic

Heat the oil in a large frying pan, *karahi*, or wok. Add the shallots and curry leaves and cook over moderately low heat for 5 minutes or until the shallots are soft. Stir in the coconut spice paste together with ¾ cup water and bring the mixture to a boil. Cook for about 5 minutes, stirring occasionally, until the sauce has thickened.

Cut the fish fillets into 1-in (2.5-cm) pieces and add to the sauce. Pour in the lemon juice and mix carefully. Cook gently for 4–5 minutes or until the fish is cooked through. Remove the pan from the heat and serve immediately.

Nadan meen kootan Kingfish curry

Eating a fish curry at least once a day is a must for the majority of South Indians who live on the coast. Kingfish is very popular and versatile. Its rich flavor works well with the tamarind and coconut milk combination here, which is typical of the region. Many of the fish dishes are simple, prepared for daily meals, whereas this curry would be made for a festival or other special occasion.

INGREDIENTS
2 tbsp vegetable oil
$^1/_2$ tsp mustard seeds
10 curry leaves
pinch of fenugreek seeds
1 large onion, chopped
1-in (2.5-cm) piece fresh ginger root,
   thinly sliced
$^1/_2$ tsp ground turmeric
$^1/_2$ tsp chili powder
1 tsp ground coriander
2 tomatoes, chopped
sea salt
3 tbsp tamarind water, made with
   1 tbsp pulp and 3 tbsp water (p322)
$1^1/_4$ lb (500 g) kingfish fillet, skinned
   and cut into $1^1/_2$-in (4-cm) pieces
$^3/_4$ cup thick coconut milk (p213)
pinch of crushed black peppercorns

METHOD
Heat the oil in a large saucepan, *karahi*, or wok. Add the mustard seeds, and when they start to pop, add the curry leaves and fenugreek seeds. Sauté for 1 minute or until the fenugreek seeds turn golden, then add the onion and cook for 5 minutes over moderate heat, stirring occasionally.

Add the ginger, turmeric, chili powder, and ground coriander. Mix well, then add the tomatoes and salt to taste. Cook for 5 minutes, stirring constantly. Stir in the tamarind water and water and slowly bring to a boil.

Lower the heat under the pan, then add the fish cubes and simmer for 5–6 minutes or until the fish is just cooked through.

Turn the heat as low as possible and pour in the coconut milk. Add the pepper. Simmer gently for 2 minutes, then remove the pan from the heat. Serve immediately with boiled rice or potatoes.

Serves 4–6

sour and
spicy

Meen porichathu Shallow-fried masala sardines

For a feast, this dry curried fish makes a fantastic combination with wetter chicken and meat dishes. It's crunchy and has a delicious spicy flavor. Serve it as a dry side dish or with plain rice or a green salad as a main dish. Pomfret or any flat fish can be used instead of sardines.

INGREDIENTS

4 sardines, about 10 oz (300 g) in total
5 tbsp vegetable oil
1 small onion, finely sliced
small handful of chopped cilantro
    leaves
wedges of lemon

½-in (1-cm) piece fresh ginger root,
    finely chopped
10 curry leaves
10 black peppercorns
½ tsp chili powder
½ tsp ground turmeric
2 tbsp wine or cider vinegar
1 tsp lemon juice
salt

Spice paste

1 onion, chopped
2 green chilies, chopped

METHOD

Place all the ingredients for the spice paste in a food processor or blender. Process for 2–3 minutes to make a fine paste. Set aside.

Wash the fish under cold running water, then pat dry with paper towels. With a very sharp knife, make some slashes about 1 in (2.5 cm) apart along the whole length of the fish, on both sides. Don't cut too deeply, just enough to break the skin and cut slightly into the flesh.

Place the fish on a baking sheet and spread the spice paste all over the fish, ensuring that it penetrates well into the cuts. Leave to marinate for 15–20 minutes.

Heat 2 tbsp of the oil in a large frying pan. Add the onion and cook for 5–6 minutes over very high heat until the onion is well browned and crisp. Remove the onion from the pan and drain on paper towels.

Heat the remaining oil in the same pan over low heat. Carefully place the fish in the pan, cover, and cook for about 6 minutes on each side. Turn the fish once only during cooking to avoid breaking it up. Cook until the skin is brown and the flesh is cooked through.

Carefully remove the fish and place on a large serving dish. Sprinkle the crisp onions over the fish and garnish with cilantro and lemon wedges.

Serves 2–4

fragrant,
spicy,
and dry

Meen kari Sri Lankan fish stew

In Sri Lanka, as along the South Indian coast, fish is more popular than meat or chicken, and many of the dishes and cooking techniques on this beautiful island are similar to those in southern India. A wide variety of fresh seafood can be found in the markets. This tasty curry is common to many communities in Sri Lanka. It goes well with tamarind rice (p118) or a simple bread like Akki Rotti (p119).

INGREDIENTS
1 tbsp ghee or butter
12 shallots, cut into wedges
1$^1/_2$ tsp all-purpose flour
3 tbsp tomato paste
$^1/_2$ tsp chili powder
$^1/_2$ tsp ground coriander
$^1/_4$ tsp ground turmeric
salt
14 oz (400 g) kingfish or salmon fillet, skinned
   and cut into small pieces
1 cup thick coconut milk (p213)
1 tbsp wine or cider vinegar
pinch of crushed black peppercorns

METHOD
Heat the ghee or butter in a large saucepan, add the shallots, and fry for 5 minutes or until brown. Remove the pan from the heat and sprinkle the flour over the shallots. Mix well, then return to low heat.

Slowly add 2 cups water, mixing well to avoid lumps. Stir in the tomato paste, chili powder, coriander, turmeric, and some salt. Bring to a boil, stirring well, then add the fish. Simmer gently, covered, for 20 minutes or until the fish is cooked, stirring occasionally.

Remove the pan from the heat. Pour in the coconut milk and stir for 2 minutes. Add the vinegar and sprinkle with the crushed black pepper. Serve immediately.

Serves 4

deliciously
spiced

Koyilandi konju masala Boatman's shrimp masala

Jumbo shrimp dishes are a treat in coastal southern India, as shrimp are not easily affordable for ordinary people unless they live near beaches or areas where you can buy it fresh-caught. Kerala has its own distinctive ways of cooking shrimp and lobsters. This is a very popular dish in the local bars, which are well known for excellent spicy dishes. Eat this with breads like paratha, or plain rice.

INGREDIENTS
3 tbsp vegetable oil
pinch of cumin seeds
10 curry leaves
3 onions, sliced
$1/2$ tsp ground turmeric
1 tsp chili powder
1 tsp tomato paste
4 tomatoes, sliced
1-in (2.5-cm) piece fresh ginger root,
  thinly sliced
sea salt
$1^{1}/_{4}$ lb (500 g) raw jumbo shrimp,
  peeled but last tail section left on
chopped cilantro leaves to garnish

METHOD
Heat the oil in a large frying pan, *karahi*, or wok. Add the cumin seeds, curry leaves, and onions and cook over moderately low heat for 10 minutes, stirring occasionally, until the onions are golden.

Add the turmeric, chili powder, tomato paste, tomatoes, sliced ginger, and a little salt to taste. Cook for 5 minutes, stirring occasionally.

Add the shrimp and simmer for a further 5–6 minutes or until they turn pink and are just cooked.

Serve sprinkled with chopped cilantro leaves.

Serves 4–6

vibrant
and spicy

Konju pulungari *Jumbo shrimp and pumpkin curry*

Pumpkins are festival vegetables in most of the states in southern India. They are grown abundantly in almost every household garden and cooked in all kinds of ways. There are many varieties, with a range of colors, flavors, sizes, and seasons. White pumpkin has a particularly delicious and refreshing flavor, which goes amazingly well with coconut and shrimp in this subtle curry. Serve with tamarind rice (p118) or breads such as paratha.

INGREDIENTS
2 tbsp vegetable oil
$^1/_2$ tsp mustard seeds
pinch of cumin seeds
10 curry leaves
1-in (2.5-cm) piece fresh ginger root,
    cut into strips
2 green chilies, slit lengthwise
2 onions, sliced
6 oz (150 g) peeled pumpkin flesh,
    thinly sliced
$^1/_2$ tsp ground turmeric
salt
1$^2/_3$ cups thick coconut milk (p213)
1$^1/_4$ lb (500 g) raw jumbo shrimp,
    peeled but last tail section left on
1 tsp white vinegar

METHOD
Heat the oil in a large frying pan. Add the mustard and cumin seeds, and when they start to pop, add the curry leaves, ginger, chilies, and onions. Cook over moderately low heat for 10 minutes, stirring occasionally, until the onions are golden.

Add the pumpkin, turmeric, and a little salt and mix well for 1 minute, then pour in the coconut milk and $^3/_4$ cup water. Bring the mixture to a boil, stirring constantly.

Add the shrimp to the pan and cook, stirring, for 5 minutes or until the shrimp and pumpkin are cooked. Add the vinegar and mix well. Serve hot, with rice or bread.

Serves 4–6

subtle
and light

Njandu thengapal Crab in coconut milk

In most of southern India, crabs are not often cooked at home, mainly because it is hard to handle them. Crab would more likely be prepared in homes in fishing communities or in the traditional toddy bars. Unlike the usual spicy dry preparation, for this curry the crabs are cooked in a nicely spiced coconut milk sauce. Eat this with tamarind rice (p118) or a bread such as chapatti or paratha.

INGREDIENTS

3 tbsp vegetable oil
7 oz (200 g) shallots, finely sliced
10 curry leaves
3 garlic cloves, chopped
1-in (2.5-cm) piece fresh ginger root,
   finely sliced
$1/2$ tsp chili powder
$1/2$ tsp ground turmeric
1 fresh, uncooked crab, about 14 oz (400 g),
   cleaned and quartered
$1^{1}/_4$ cups coconut milk (p213)
2 tomatoes, quartered
salt
1 tsp lemon juice
$1/2$ tsp black pepper

METHOD

Heat the oil in a large frying pan and fry the shallots for 5 minutes or until they are soft. Add the curry leaves, garlic, and ginger and cook for a further 5 minutes over moderate heat.

Add the chili powder and turmeric, then slowly pour in 1 cup of water, stirring. Bring the mixture to a boil, then lower the heat and simmer for 10 minutes, stirring occasionally.

Add the crab pieces and continue simmering the curry over moderate heat for 10 minutes or until the crab is cooked.

Stir in the coconut milk and tomatoes and heat through gently for 2–3 minutes. Add salt to taste. Remove the pan from the heat, cover, and set aside for a few minutes, then add the lemon juice and sprinkle with the black pepper. Serve immediately.

Serves 4

creamy and
refreshing

Koonthal ullathiyathu Squid curry

Squid is enjoyed in both southern India and Sri Lanka, cooked as a curry, stuffed, or fried. If you go out on a boat to fish, the fishermen cook the freshly caught squid onboard with the minimum of spices and offer them as a special treat. Squid must be cooked for a short time or long simmered, otherwise it will be rubbery. Try this with breads such as paratha or chapatti or any flavored rice.

INGREDIENTS
3 tbsp vegetable oil
$1/2$ tsp mustard seeds
2 large onions, sliced
3 green chilies, slit lengthwise
1-in (2.5-cm) piece fresh ginger root,
    finely sliced
$1/2$ tsp chili powder
$1/2$ tsp ground coriander
2 large tomatoes, sliced
14 oz (400 g) cleaned squid,
    cut into $1/2$-in (1-cm) pieces
    and tentacles reserved
1 tbsp chopped cilantro leaves

METHOD
Heat the oil in a large frying pan and add the mustard seeds. When they begin to pop, add the onions and cook for 5 minutes or until they are golden brown.

Stir in the green chilies and ginger, then add the chili powder and ground coriander. Mix well and add the tomatoes. Cook over moderate heat for 5–10 minutes or until the tomatoes break down to give a thick sauce.

Add the squid pieces and tentacles and mix thoroughly. Cover and continue cooking over low heat for 15 minutes, stirring occasionally to prevent burning and sticking. If the dish becomes dry very quickly, stir in a few spoonfuls of water. Serve hot, garnished with the cilantro.

Serves 4

warm and colorful

Kerala lamb

This is a restaurant specialty, famously known as Malabar mutton curry, cooked all over southern India in Malabari restaurants. Muslims in Calicut are very fond of this dish, as it is easy to cook and has an extraordinary taste. The roasted coconut base and peppercorn flavor are typical of Keralan cooking. Plain rice or paratha are the best accompaniments.

INGREDIENTS

3 tbsp vegetable oil
7 oz (200 g) shallots, chopped
1 tbsp ground coriander
$1/2$ tsp ground turmeric
$1/2$ tsp chili powder
salt
$1^1/4$ lb (500 g) boned lamb,
 cut into cubes

Spice paste

4 oz (100 g) freshly grated coconut
 or desiccated coconut
1-in (2.5-cm) piece fresh ginger root, sliced

3 garlic cloves, chopped
1-in (2.5-cm) cinnamon stick
3 cloves
2 bay leaves
10 curry leaves
5 black peppercorns

For tempering

2 tbsp vegetable oil
$1/2$ tsp mustard seeds
10 curry leaves
2 green chilies, slit lengthwise

METHOD

First, make the spice paste. Roast the coconut with the ginger, garlic, cinnamon stick, cloves, bay leaves, curry leaves, and peppercorns in a dry pan until the coconut is browned. Allow to cool, then grind in a food processor, gradually adding about 1 cup water to make a fine paste.

Heat the 3 tbsp of oil in a frying pan, add the shallots, and fry for 5 minutes or until soft. Add the spice paste, the ground coriander, turmeric, chili powder, some salt, and $1^2/3$ cups of water. Bring to a boil. Add the lamb, then reduce the heat and cook, covered, for 30 minutes or until the lamb is well cooked.

Now prepare the tempering mixture. In a separate frying pan, heat the oil and add the mustard seeds. Once they start popping, add the curry leaves and green chilies. Stir-fry for 1 minute.

Pour the tempering mixture over the lamb curry and continue cooking for about 10 minutes or until the curry is very dry and thick. Serve hot.

Serves 4

exquisite
and
aromatic

Attirachi koot Hyderabadi mutton

Hyderabad is known for its spicy meat and chicken dishes, and even more for its meat biryanis. The traditional Islamic community there has introduced lot of new cooking combinations and delicacies to modern Indian cuisine. Mutton is the favorite meat. This dish was once called a royal dish and relished only by rich people, but today it is found on Indian restaurant menus all over the world. Serve with tamarind rice (p118) or chapattis.

INGREDIENTS

1¼ lb (500 g) boned mutton,
    cut into ½-in (1-cm) cubes
¼ cup vegetable oil
2 cloves
2 cardamom pods
½-in (1-cm) piece of cinnamon stick
1 bay leaf
1 onion, finely chopped
salt
cilantro leaves to garnish

Marinade

1 tsp ginger paste
1 tsp garlic paste
2 tomatoes, finely chopped
1 onion, finely chopped
½ tsp ground turmeric
½ tsp chili powder
1 tsp ground coriander
2 tbsp cilantro leaves

METHOD

Serves 4

spicy

Mix together the ingredients for the marinade in a bowl. Add the cubes of mutton and toss to coat with the marinade. Set aside for 20 minutes.

Heat the oil in a large saucepan and add the cloves, cardamom pods, cinnamon stick, and bay leaf. Sauté for 1 minute, then add the onion and cook until it is golden.

Add the marinated mutton to the pan with salt to taste and mix well. Cover and cook over low heat for about 30 minutes or until the mutton is tender. Garnish with cilantro leaves and serve.

Ethakka attirachi curry Lamb and plantain curry

A contribution from my head chef Prasad, this is a specialty from his home village. Lamb dishes are very popular with Keralans, and they like to experiment by adding unusual ingredients like plantain. Lamb is an expensive meat for home cooks, so this is a special occasion dish. Breads like chapatti and paratha are good with it.

INGREDIENTS

$1/4$ cup vegetable oil
1 tsp mustard seeds
10 curry leaves
1-in (2.5-cm) piece fresh ginger root, chopped
5 garlic cloves, chopped
2 green chilies, chopped
2 onions, sliced
2 tsp ground coriander
$1/2$ tsp ground turmeric
$1/2$ tsp chili powder
3 tomatoes, sliced
14 oz (400 g) boned lamb,
   cut into cubes
1 plantain, peeled and cut into
   small pieces
salt

METHOD

Heat the oil in a large frying pan. Add the mustard seeds and, when they start to pop, add the curry leaves. Then add the ginger, garlic, and green chilies and sauté for 3 minutes. Add the onions and cook for a further 10 minutes or until the onions are brown.

Stir in the ground coriander, turmeric, chili powder, and tomatoes, mixing well, then add the lamb and $1^2/3$ cups water. Bring to a boil, then cover and cook over low heat for 15 minutes.

Now stir in the plantain pieces together with some salt. Leave to cook for another 15 minutes or until the lamb is cooked through and the plantain is tender, stirring occasionally. Serve hot.

Serves 4

spicy
and rich

Pork vindaloo

Vindaloo (from the Portuguese *vindalho*) originates from Goa, where the cooking combines Portuguese influences with fiery Indian flavors. Vindaloo dishes are made by families in Goa for their Christmas celebrations. What makes a vindaloo dish unusual is the combination of curry spices and vinegar. This is an elaborate dish but worth the effort. If you can handle spicy food, be more generous with the chili. This is traditionally eaten with red rice, although plain rice is good too.

INGREDIENTS

2 lb (900 g) boned pork, cut into
   2-in (5-cm) cubes
4 tbsp vegetable oil
5 garlic cloves, finely chopped
2 onions, chopped
1 tsp ground turmeric
1/2 tsp chili powder
1/2 tsp tomato paste
3 tomatoes, chopped
3 tbsp wine or cider vinegar
salt
pinch of crushed black peppercorns
1 tbsp chopped cilantro leaves

Spice paste

1 tsp cumin seeds
4 cardamom pods
4 cloves
1-in (2.5-cm) cinnamon stick
5 black peppercorns
1 green chili, chopped
1-in (2.5-cm) piece fresh ginger root,
   chopped
4 garlic cloves, peeled
3 tbsp lemon juice

METHOD

To make the spice paste, grind the cumin seeds, cardamom pods, cloves, cinnamon stick, and peppercorns to a fine powder in a clean coffee grinder or spice mill. Blend the spice powder with the green chili, ginger, garlic, and lemon juice in a food processor to make a fine paste.

Mix the pork with the spice paste in a large bowl. Cover it with plastic wrap, then leave to marinate in a cool place for 1 1/2 hours.

Heat the oil in a frying pan, add the garlic, and sauté for 1 minute. Add the onions and cook until they are golden, stirring occasionally. Add the turmeric, chili powder, tomato paste, chopped tomatoes, and vinegar and stir well.

Add the marinated pork and salt to taste. Cook for 10 minutes, stirring occasionally. Pour in 1 cup water and bring to a boil, then reduce the heat and simmer for 30 minutes or until the meat is cooked through and the sauce is thick.

Add the black pepper, then serve hot, garnished with the chopped cilantro.

Serves 4

fiery hot
and sour

Kozhy kuruma South Indian chicken korma

Simple, mild chicken curries are typical of home cooking in the region, and in the Christian communities, chicken dishes are prepared for celebrations and special occasions, to be eaten with popular breads like *appams*. Home-grown chickens are preferred for their outstanding flavor.

INGREDIENTS

3 tbsp vegetable oil
1-in (2.5-cm) cinnamon stick
3 cloves
2 bay leaves
3 cardamom pods, crushed
2 onions, chopped
1 tsp ground coriander
$^1/_2$ tsp ground turmeric
$^1/_2$ tsp chili powder
2 tsp tomato paste
$1^1/_4$ lb (500 g) boneless, skinless
  chicken breast, cut into cubes

pinch of black pepper
salt
$1^1/_4$ oz (40 g) cashew nuts, ground with
  a little water to make a paste
cilantro leaves to garnish

Ginger-garlic paste
1-in (2.5-cm) fresh ginger root, chopped
4 garlic cloves, peeled

METHOD

For the ginger-garlic paste, put the ginger, garlic, and a little water in a small food processor or blender and grind to make fine paste. Set aside.

Heat the oil in a large frying pan. Add the cinnamon stick, cloves, bay leaves, and crushed cardamom pods and sauté for 2 minutes. Add the onions and stir well, then cook for 5 minutes or until the onions are soft.

Add the ginger-garlic paste, ground coriander, turmeric, chili powder, and tomato paste. Mix well, then cook over a low heat for 5 minutes, stirring occasionally. Stir in the chicken, black pepper, salt to taste, and $^2/_3$ cup water. Bring to a boil, then cover and simmer for 15–20 minutes or until the chicken is well cooked.

When the chicken is cooked, add the cashew paste and blend well. Simmer for a further 3 minutes. Serve hot, garnished with cilantro leaves.

Serves 4

aromatic,
nutty, and
mild

Kukul mus kari Sri Lankan chicken curry

Chicken curry is one of the highlights of weekend lunches in Sri Lanka. As in Keralan cooking, a special aroma is imparted with the use of coconut, and the layering of the spices makes it very easy to distinguish their various flavors. This dish comes from our friend Raj from Colombo. It is his favorite recipe from his grandmother. In return, I had to teach him some traditional vegetarian cooking from Kerala. Serve this with rice or bread.

INGREDIENTS
3 tbsp vegetable oil
2 onions, finely sliced
1-in (2.5-cm) piece fresh ginger root, chopped
2 garlic cloves, chopped
$1/2$ tsp ground turmeric
1 tsp chili powder
2 tsp ground garam masala
14 oz (400 g) boneless, skinless chicken breast,
   cut into bite-sized pieces
$3/4$ cup coconut milk (p213)
2 tomatoes, quartered
salt

METHOD
Heat the oil in a medium saucepan, add the onions, and cook until golden brown. Add the ginger, garlic, and ground spices. Mix well for 1 minute, then add the chicken. Cook, stirring, over medium heat for 5 minutes.

Pour in $1^1/4$ cups water. Bring to a boil, then reduce the heat, cover the pan, and cook for 10 minutes.

Turn the heat down very low and add the coconut milk. Cook for a further 10 minutes or until the chicken is cooked through. Stir in the tomatoes and salt to taste. Cook for a final 5 minutes to blend the *masala* well. Serve hot.

Serves 4

very creamy
and lightly
spiced

Koli erachi molagu Chicken pepper fry

This dish comes from Tamil Nadu, where it is cooked for festivals like Diwali and other special occasions. In some of the villages, the dish is prepared as an offering to the goddess as part of worship. The spice combination and abundance of black pepper make this dish different from other Tamil chicken recipes. Enjoy its fiery savoriness and thick texture with Indian breads and a cold glass of beer.

INGREDIENTS
3 tbsp vegetable oil
$^1/_2$ tsp mustard seeds
10 curry leaves
1-in (2.5-cm) piece fresh ginger root, finely sliced
3 garlic cloves, chopped
3 green chilies, sliced
2 onions, chopped
2 tomatoes, diced
salt
$1^1/_4$ lb (500 g) boneless, skinless chicken breasts, cut into $^1/_2$-in (1-cm) cubes
large pinch of crushed black peppercorns

Spice paste
1 tbsp vegetable oil
4 oz (100 g) freshly grated coconut or desiccated coconut
2 cloves
2 cardamom pods
3 black peppercorns
$^1/_2$ in (1 cm) cinnamon stick
$^1/_2$ tsp chili powder
$^1/_2$ tsp ground turmeric
1 tsp ground coriander

METHOD
To make the spice paste, heat the oil in a frying pan and roast the coconut with the cloves, cardamom pods, peppercorns, and cinnamon stick until the coconut is brown. Add the ground spices and sauté for 1 minute. Leave to cool, then transfer to a food processor or blender. Add $^3/_4$ cup water and grind to make a fine paste. Set aside.

Heat the oil in a large saucepan and add the mustard seeds. As they begin to pop, add the curry leaves, ginger, garlic, and green chilies. Cook for 3 minutes. Add the onions and cook until they are golden brown. Add the tomatoes and cook for another minute, then pour in the spice paste and add some salt. Stir well.

Add the chicken cubes and 1 cup of water. Bring to the boil, then cover the pan and cook for 20 minutes or until the chicken is cooked. Serve hot, sprinkled with the black pepper.

Serves 4

peppery
and thick

Rasa kayi Mixed vegetable curry

A common preparation in Karnataka, mixed vegetables are beautifully cooked in a tomato *masala* that is flavored—unusually—with fennel seeds. It's much spicier than a lot of other South Indian vegetarian dishes, although coconut milk makes it creamy and slightly sweet. Serve this with paratha or chapatti, or as a side dish with meat and poultry curries.

INGREDIENTS

4 oz (100 g) carrots, scrubbed and cut
  into 1-in (2.5-cm) pieces
4 oz (100 g) potatoes, peeled and cut
  into 1-in (2.5-cm) pieces
4 oz (100 g) green beans (fresh or frozen),
  cut into 1-in (2.5-cm) pieces
3 tbsp vegetable oil
2 onions, cut into small pieces
1 green chili, slit lengthwise
$1/2$ tsp chili powder
$1/2$ tsp ground coriander
$1/2$ tsp ground turmeric
salt
4 oz (100 g) cauliflower,
  separated into florets
$1/2$ cup coconut milk (p213)

Spice paste

2 garlic cloves, peeled
$3/4$-in (2-cm) piece of fresh ginger root,
  finely chopped
1 green chili, finely chopped
$1/2$ tsp fennel seeds
4 oz (100 g) tomatoes, chopped

METHOD

Grind all the ingredients for the spice paste in a mortar and pestle, or a blender or small food processor, until fine. Set aside. and cut into 1-in (2.5-cm) pieces

Heat the oil in a large pan, add the onions and green chili, and cook until the onions are soft. Add the carrots, chili powder, ground coriander, turmeric, and salt to taste. Mix well. Lower the heat and add the potatoes. Cover and cook for 10 minutes.

Add the cauliflower and green beans together with the spice paste and mix well. Cook, covered, for a further 10–15 minutes.

Remove the pan from the heat and slowly add the coconut milk, stirring to blend well. Serve hot.

Serves 4

quite spicy
and slightly
sweet

Cheera moru curry Spinach and yogurt curry

All Keralan meals have two things in common: a yogurt curry and a *thoran* (dry stir-fried vegetable). A yogurt curry is a dish we look forward to, and it's one of the easiest to make, adding vegetables in season. Spinach is my favorite, while the red leaves in the beet family are very popular in our village. This is a mild dish, but can be made spicier if you prefer. Remember, though, not to heat it too much once you add the yogurt. A yogurt curry is always eaten with rice.

INGREDIENTS

2 tbsp vegetable oil
$1/2$ tsp mustard seeds
pinch of fenugreek seeds
2 garlic cloves, finely chopped
3 dried red chilies
10 curry leaves
4 oz (100 g) shallots, chopped
3 fresh green chilies, slit lengthwise
1-in (2.5-cm) piece fresh ginger root,
   finely chopped
2 tomatoes, finely chopped
$1/2$ tsp ground turmeric
salt
4 oz (100 g) spinach, chopped
10 oz (300 g) plain yogurt

METHOD

Heat the oil in a large saucepan and add the mustard seeds. As they begin to pop, add the fenugreek seeds, then add the garlic, dried chilies, and curry leaves and sauté for 1 minute. Add the shallots, green chilies, and ginger and cook, stirring occasionally, until the shallots turn brown.

Add the tomatoes, turmeric, and salt to taste. Mix thoroughly, then add the spinach and cook for 5 minutes, stirring occasionally.

Remove the pan from the heat and gradually add the yogurt, stirring slowly and constantly. Set the pan over low heat and warm gently for 3 minutes, stirring constantly. Serve warm.

Serves 4

lightly
spiced and
creamy

Thakkali payaru curry Black-eye beans with spinach and tomatoes

A refreshing and light tomato dish, this is easy to make, and it's very versatile in that you can make it with other beans. I like to use my all-time favorite, black-eye beans. Be sure not to overcook the tomatoes, so that they retain their freshness. You can serve this with plain rice or chapatti to make a meal.

INGREDIENTS
3 tbsp vegetable oil
$1/2$ tsp mustard seeds
2 garlic cloves, finely chopped
10 curry leaves
$2/3$ cup chopped onion
2 green chilies, slit lengthwise
$1/2$ tsp chili powder
1 tsp ground coriander
$1/2$ tsp ground turmeric
7 oz (200 g) tomatoes, cut into small pieces
2 oz (50) spinach, chopped
4 oz (100 g) cooked or canned black-eye beans
salt
10 oz (300 g) plain yogurt

Serves 4

fresh, light,
and creamy

METHOD
Heat the oil in a large saucepan and add the mustard seeds. When they start to pop, add the garlic, curry leaves, and onion. Cook over moderate heat for 5 minutes or until the onion is soft.

Add the green chilies, chili powder, coriander, and turmeric. Mix well, then add the tomato pieces. Stir well, then add the spinach. Cook over low heat for 5 minutes.

Now add the black-eye beans with salt to taste. Cook for a further 1 minute or until everything is hot. Remove the pan from the heat and slowly add the yogurt, stirring well. Serve warm.

Vendakka vazhuthananga masala Okra and eggplant spicy masala

Okra and eggplant are the favorite vegetables for many South Indians, but in this versatile dish you can replace them with your choice. I like the way the crunchy okra and juicy eggplant blend with the aromatic spices. This can be eaten as a main dish with paratha or as a fantastic side dish with meat and fish curries.

INGREDIENTS
3 tbsp vegetable oil
pinch of fenugreek seeds
pinch of fennel seeds
2–3 cardamom pods
$^3/_4$ in (2 cm) cinnamon stick
1 bay leaf
3 garlic cloves, chopped
2 onions, finely chopped
$^1/_2$ tsp ground turmeric
$^1/_2$ tsp chili powder
1 tsp ground coriander
1 tbsp tomato paste
2 tomatoes, finely chopped
6 oz (150 g) okra, cut into pieces
6 oz (150 g) eggplant,
    cut into pieces
salt
2 tbsp chopped cilantro leaves

METHOD
Heat the oil in a saucepan and add the fenugreek seeds, fennel seeds, cardamom pods, cinnamon stick, bay leaf, garlic, and onions. Cook, stirring occasionally, until the onions are golden brown.

Add the turmeric, chili powder, ground coriander, and tomato paste and stir well, then cook for a further 1 minute. Stir in the chopped tomatoes and 2 cups of water. Bring to a boil, then reduce the heat and simmer for about 10 minutes or until the sauce is thick.

Add the okra and eggplant to the sauce with salt to taste and stir thoroughly. Cover and cook over low heat for 5 minutes or until the eggplant and okra become tender.

Garnish with chopped cilantro and serve hot.

Serves 4

nicely
spiced
and dry

Kizhangu payaru stew Potato and green bean stew

This is a wonderful dish, so easy to make and with a divine flavor. At home, we always relished simple stews with potatoes, but my mother liked to experiment by adding seasonal vegetables. This one was my favorite. You can replace the vegetables according to availability and to make the dish more colorful. Stew dishes are traditionally eaten with *dosas* and paratha.

INGREDIENTS
2 tbsp vegetable oil
1 tsp mustard seeds
2 dried red chilies
a few curry leaves
2 onions, chopped
$1/2$ tsp ground coriander
$1/2$ tsp ground garam masala
$1/2$ tsp ground turmeric
$1/4$ tsp chili powder
2 tomatoes, quartered
10 oz (300 g) potatoes, peeled
  and cut into wedges or cubes
4 oz (100 g) green beans (fresh or
  frozen), cut into 1-in (2.5-cm) pieces
salt
$3/4$ cup coconut milk (p213)
pinch of crushed black peppercorns

METHOD
Heat the oil in a large saucepan and add the mustard seeds. When they begin to pop, add the dried chilies and curry leaves and sauté for 2 minutes. Stir in the onions and cook over moderate heat for 5 minutes or until the onions are soft.

Stir in the coriander, garam masala, turmeric, and chili powder. Add the tomatoes and cook for 5 minutes. Add the potatoes and mix well, then cook over gentle heat for a further 5 minutes.

Add the green beans and salt to taste. Cook for another minute, then reduce the heat to very low. Pour in the coconut milk and $1/2$ cup water. Stir well to combine. Cook for 15–20 minutes or until all the vegetables are tender. Garnish with the black pepper and serve hot.

Serves 4

slightly
sweet and
very light

Kootu sambar Vegetables with lentils

Sambar is the most famous accompaniment for the traditional pancakelike breads called *dosas*, and it is the curry always served first at any feast in southern India. Sambar is made in hundreds of ways in the different regions, using a variety of vegetables and different roasted spices. It is a dish of the common man. Enjoy it with rice, *dosas*, or Akki Rotti (p119).

INGREDIENTS

4 oz (100 g) split yellow lentils
   (*toor dal*)
1 tsp ground turmeric
1 tsp chili powder
2 onions, cut into small pieces
4 oz (100 g) carrots, peeled and
   cut into 1-in (2.5-cm) pieces
4 oz (100 g) green beans (frozen
   or fresh), cut into 1-in (2.5-cm) pieces
3 tomatoes, quartered
4 oz (100 g) potatoes, peeled
   and cut into cubes
1/4 cup tamarind water, made with
   1 tbsp pulp and 1/4 cup water (p322)
salt

Spice paste

4 oz (100 g) freshly grated coconut
   or desiccated coconut
2 tsp coriander seeds
1 dried red chili

For tempering

1 tbsp vegetable oil
1 tsp mustard seeds
10 curry leaves
3 dried red chilies

METHOD

For the spice paste, roast the coconut and spices until brown. Leave to cool, then grind in a food processor, gradually adding about 1 cup of water to make a fine paste.

Bring 1 1/4 cups of water to a boil in a saucepan and add the lentils, turmeric, chili powder, and onions. Simmer until the lentils are well cooked.

Add the carrots, beans, tomatoes, and potatoes and stir well. Cover and cook for 10 minutes or until the vegetables are tender. Add the tamarind water and salt to taste. Cover and cook for a further 5 minutes.

Stir in the spice paste. Bring to a boil, then reduce the heat to moderate and cook, uncovered, for 5 minutes, stirring occasionally.

For tempering, heat the oil in a frying pan and add the mustard seeds. As they begin to pop, add the curry leaves and dried red chilies. Pour this over the curry and gently stir through. Serve hot.

Serves 4

hot and
tangy

Bissi bela bhath Mixed vegetable rice

In this typical dish of the Brahmin community of southern India, mixed lentils are cooked with basmati rice to introduce a nutty, aromatic flavor. It's a rich dish and can be eaten as complete meal.

INGREDIENTS

6 oz (150 g) split yellow lentils (*toor dal*)
2 tbsp vegetable oil
2$\frac{1}{2}$ oz (75 g) freshly grated coconut
7 dried red chilies
2 tsp coriander seeds
1 tsp split gram lentils (*chana dal*)
1 tsp split black lentils (*urad dal*)
1 tsp ground turmeric
$\frac{1}{2}$ tsp fenugreek seeds
pinch of asafetida
1 lb 2 oz (500 g) basmati rice
salt
$\frac{1}{2}$ cup tamarind water, made
    with 1$\frac{3}{4}$ oz (50 g) pulp and
    $\frac{1}{2}$ cup water (p322)

For tempering

2 tbsp vegetable oil
1 tsp mustard seeds
10 curry leaves
1 tbsp chopped raw cashew nuts

METHOD

Bring 2 cups water to a boil in a large saucepan. Add the yellow lentils and simmer until tender. Drain and set aside.

Heat the oil in a frying pan and add the coconut, red chilies, coriander seeds, split gram and black lentils, turmeric, fenugreek seeds, and asafetida. Fry until fragrant. Allow to cool, then grind to a fine powder in a clean coffee grinder or spice mill.

Clean the rice in cold running water, then place it in a large saucepan. Add 1 quart (liter) water and a little salt. Bring to a boil, then simmer for about 20 minutes.

Add the yellow lentils, tamarind water, and spiced coconut powder. Cook for a further 5 minutes. Add just a little more water if the mixture becomes very dry too quickly.

Meanwhile, for the tempering, heat the oil in a frying pan and add the mustard seeds. As they begin to pop, add the curry leaves and cashew nuts and cook, stirring, until the nuts turn golden brown. Pour the mixture over the cooked rice, mix together, and serve hot.

Serves 4

nutty, aromatic, and rich

Puli choru Tamarind rice

Rice preparations are very common in Tamil Nadu and Karnataka. The addition of nuts and lentils and careful spicing make this rice dish very savory and colorful. It goes well with all kinds of curries, be they meat, fish, poultry, or vegetable.

INGREDIENTS

1³/₄ oz (50 g) tamarind pulp
1¹/₄ cups long-grain or basmati rice
salt
2 tbsp vegetable oil
1 tsp mustard seeds
1 onion, finely chopped
³/₄ oz (20 g) raw peanuts
1 tbsp split gram lentils (*chana dal*)
  or split yellow lentils (*toor dal*)
10 curry leaves
3 dried red chilies
1 tsp fenugreek seeds
1 tsp asafetida
1 tsp chili powder
1 tsp ground coriander
1 tsp ground turmeric
1 tbsp chopped cilantro leaves

METHOD

Bring ¹/₂ cup water to a boil in a small saucepan. Add the tamarind pulp and simmer for 10 minutes, stirring occasionally. Strain the thick tamarind water into a bowl and set aside.

In a large saucepan, bring 2 cups of water to a boil. Add the rice and a little salt to taste. Allow to cook for 20–25 minutes or until the rice is tender. Drain and keep warm.

Rinse the saucepan, then heat it and pour in the oil. When the oil is hot, add the mustard seeds. As they begin to pop, add the onion, peanuts, lentils, curry leaves, dried chilies, and fenugreek seeds. Cook, stirring frequently, until the onions are soft.

Add the asafetida, chili powder, ground coriander, turmeric, and some salt. Cook over moderate heat, stirring, for 2–3 minutes. Pour in the tamarind water. Mix well and cook for 15 minutes.

Add the rice and stir to combine, then transfer to a bowl. Garnish with the chopped cilantro.

Serves 4

fragrant, rich, and savory

Akki rotti *Savory rice breads*

Unlike in northern India, where wheat flour is used, breads in the south of the country are made with rice flour. This is my friend Vidya's recipe, which she made for me many times. It's a very light bread, spiced for a delightful change. Unlike many other breads, this can be made very quickly.

INGREDIENTS
2 cups rice flour
$1^3/_4$ oz (50 g) freshly grated coconut
  or desiccated coconut
2 tbsp chopped cilantro leaves
10 curry leaves, chopped
2 green chilies, chopped
$2^1/_2$ oz (75 g) shallots, finely sliced
10 cashew nuts, roasted and ground
salt
vegetable oil for frying

METHOD
Put all the ingredients in a large bowl and mix well. Make a well in the center and gradually stir in about 2 cups of water to make soft dough. With floured hands, knead the dough to mix and shape it into small balls.

Roll out the balls on a surface dusted with rice flour to make disks as thin as possible. Leave to rest for 10 minutes.

Heat a large frying pan and coat the bottom with oil. Place one disk of dough in the pan and cook for 2–3 minutes or until golden brown. Turn over and brown the other side. Remove from the pan and keep hot while you cook the remaining breads. Serve hot.

Serves 4

PAKISTAN

< **Fruit and vegetable market, Karachi**

PAKISTAN

Pakistan is a country of over 160 million people and an area of almost 350,000 square miles (900,000 sq km). Through various invasions and occupations and through trade, it has been greatly influenced by its neighbors—India on the east, Iran and Afghanistan to the west, and China in the north, through the ancient Silk Road—and its culture, traditions, and cuisine have evolved accordingly over time.

The four provinces of the country, which range in terrain from very high mountains to the coastlines of the Arabian Sea and Indian Ocean, provide a great diversity of meat, game, poultry, fruits, and vegetables.

If given a choice, every Pakistani would eat meat every day. Lentils and beans are also sometimes used as the main part of a curry, but this is mainly for economic reasons, meat being more expensive. The favorite meats are lamb and mutton, although veal and beef are also eaten. Because Pakistan is a Muslim country, pork is never consumed. Various breeds of sheep and goats are reared in different parts of the country, most of them in a natural environment eating wild plants and herbs. Because they are pastured and organic, their meat has an excellent flavor. Chicken is the most popular poultry, while game birds such as quail, pigeons, and partridges are also occasionally enjoyed.

First-time visitors to Pakistan are always surprised to find so many fruits and vegetables. From the mountains to the plains, there is an abundance of cherries, apples, peaches, apricots, mangoes, oranges, and lychees, and from the coastal area come bananas and papayas. The array of vegetables includes potatoes, tomatoes, onions, carrots, peas, cauliflower, and many local varieties.

For everyday meals, Pakistanis add vegetables to meat—or meat to vegetables—whichever way you want to look at it. This is primarily to help the household budget, as it stretches the same amount of meat to feed more people. Meat is also added to beans and lentils, but to a lesser extent. One very popular dish is "chickpeas with chicken."

In Pakistan, the word "curry" is alien. *Salan* is probably the closest word for what is called a curry in India and the rest of the world. What makes a Pakistani curry different from an Indian curry is the regular use of meat and a limited use of spices. And unlike Thai curries, in Pakistan there is no added sourness or sweetness in the seasoning.

A very important rule to follow in making a good Pakistani curry is "less is more." Nothing ruins a curry faster than adding too many ingredients. Each ingredient is used for a particular purpose, and is not duplicated with a similar ingredient. For example, if lemon is added, then vinegar is not required. Similarly, if fresh cilantro is used for flavoring, fresh mint is not needed. Each flavor can then be appreciated for its individual characteristics.

Another vital aspect of a good Pakistani curry is the freshness of the ingredients. Food is purchased each morning and eaten by the evening. At home, cooking is mostly done by women, and the recipes are passed verbally from mother to daughter. This makes Pakistani curries all the more interesting, since the same dish will taste quite different from house to house and region to region.

Traditionally, the curry cooking pot was made of earthenware, but today this has been replaced by a saucepan (without a handle). The first step in making a curry is almost always preparing the *massalla*—cooking onions, ginger, garlic, and tomatoes with spices until the oil separates out. This is the basic foundation for most Pakistani curries.

Food colorings are not generally used in Pakistani curries, nor in tikkas and barbecued meats. Red color from red chilies and yellow from turmeric is all that is needed. Only rice dishes such as biryanis and some desserts are tinted with food colorings.

The predicament of a Western curry-lover is often heartburn—when you eat a curry for dinner in a restaurant anywhere else in the world, it will still be with you for breakfast. However, this is not the case with a Pakistani curry. It is unique: fresh in flavor, based on seasonal ingredients for the very best taste, carefully spiced, nutritious, and economical to make. A Pakistani curry can be enjoyed every day and for every occasion.

Mahmood Akbar

Making the massalla >
Fry onions, garlic, ginger and tomatoes in hot oil.

The Taste of Pakistan

1. rock salt
2. cloves
3. black peppercorns
4. fresh ginger root
5. onions
6. garlic
7. tomatoes
8. star anise
9. mint leaves
10. fresh green chilies
11. cinnamon sticks
12. cilantro leaves
13. basmati rice
14. fenugreek leaves
15. four seeds
16. ground red chili
17. ground cumin
18. ground turmeric
19. ground coriander

The raw materials

The key flavoring ingredients for a Pakistani curry can be divided into four groups. The first consists of the components of the *massalla* base: onions, garlic, fresh ginger, and tomatoes. Second is spices, followed by fresh herbs and aromatics, and then salt, which is an essential seasoning for any curry. Careful balancing of these flavorings creates a foundation for the meat, legumes, and vegetables to be added.

Onions

The purplish-red variety of onion commonly cultivated in Pakistan is more pungent and lower in water content than European onions and is also less sweet, so onions do not impart a sweet flavor in Pakistani curries.

Garlic

Because Pakistan has such hot weather, our garlic is more pungent than that grown in Europe. For all curries, garlic is pounded to a paste—usually with a mortar and pestle—to extract its full flavor and aroma. Garlic paste (and ginger paste, see below) can be made in larger quantities in a food processor, and kept in an airtight jar in the refrigerator for 2 weeks. The pastes can also be frozen for up to 3 months; pack into an ice cube tray lined with plastic wrap and cover with more plastic wrap.

Ginger

Where onions and garlic are the basic ingredients in curries everywhere—and in much European cooking—almost no Pakistani curry can be made without adding ginger to this foundation, too. Ginger not only infuses curries with a warmth and earthy aroma, it also contributes positive medicinal properties. Only fresh, raw ginger is used, including for garnishing. It should be young, with a thin skin—older ginger has fibrous flesh. The skin is best scraped, not peeled. For many curries, ginger is pounded to a paste with a mortar and pestle; if very young ginger is used, the skin can be left on.

Tomatoes

The Portuguese introduced the tomato to the Indian subcontinent via Goa, and it took more than a hundred years for the tomato to spread from there and be accepted in the rest of the region. The Italian-type plum tomato is the variety most commonly grown in Pakistan, and it is in season from mid-spring until late fall. Although a staple in curries and every salad, tomatoes are not much used otherwise, except as a garnish. If tomatoes are not in season, you can substitute canned Italian plum tomatoes in the recipes.

Spices

The base (*massalla*) of most Pakistani curries consists of fresh aromatics and tomatoes cooked with black pepper, red chili powder, turmeric, coriander, cumin, and salt. These spices are always added in small quantities, and each fulfills a unique requirement in the blend: black pepper provides the aroma and the bite, red chili the heat, turmeric the color, cumin the flavor, coriander the earthiness, and salt, of course, the savor. They don't duplicate each other, nor do they overwhelm each other. Other spices are added for particular dishes. For example, star anise adds an aromatic anise-licorice flavor to biryanis and other rice dishes.

While fennel, cumin, mustard, and fenugreek seeds are grown locally, most of the other spices associated with curries, like cloves, cardamom, cinnamon, nutmeg, mace, and so on, are imported from neighboring countries. In everyday home cooking, these spices are used only occasionally, and mainly whole rather than ground.

Fresh fenugreek leaves >

Herbs

In Pakistani cuisine, mostly fresh ingredients are used, and so it is with herbs, which have been used here for centuries. Cilantro, mint, and fenugreek leaves are among the most popular fresh herbs, to add extra flavoring to curries and to garnish them.

Chilies

The Dundicut is the most popular chili in Pakistan. Bright red to deep ruby red in color, it has a strong aroma and—Pakistanis think—a hot, pungent flavor (although in comparison with Thai and Scotch bonnet chilies, Dundicuts are quite mild). The heat level varies, ranging from 30,000 up to 150,000 Scoville units (the higher the number, the hotter the chili).

Dundicuts are commercially cultivated in Sindh Province. The total consumption of red chilies in Pakistan is about 400,000 lb (180,000 kg) per year, and over three-quarters of this is the Dundicut variety.

Red Dundicut chilies are rarely used fresh, but are usually dried and then ground into a powder.

Red chili powder is considered indispensable for many dishes. As with other spices, chilies should be freshly ground, if possible. If you are buying red chili powder, choose small packets and do not keep for more than 2–3 months.

Hot and pungent green chilies are available fresh throughout the year. Their size varies according to the season and where they are grown, but they are generally 3–5 in (7–12 cm) long.

Rock salt

For seasoning curries, rock salt is preferred for its unique flavor, which is not overly salty or pungent. Rock salt is mined in abundance in Pakistan.

Yogurt

Thick plain yogurt is added to curries to give a slightly sour flavor and to make them milder. Coconut milk and cream are never used in Pakistani curries.

Basmati rice

Probably the best rice in the world, basmati is the one to use for all Pakistani rice dishes, especially in biryanies.

Four seeds

This combination of dried, peeled seeds from various melons, pumpkin, and summer squash is used in chutney recipes (see pp148–149) as well as in halwas, sweetmeats, and desserts.

Palak gosht Spinach and lamb curry

No wedding meal or special dinner is considered complete without this curry. It is almost always made with mutton or lamb, although some people prefer to use chicken. The vast popularity of this dish is due to the fact that it is pretty indestructible—whichever way you cook it, it still somehow comes out tasting good. You can make it ahead and reheat it, serve it for lunch or dinner, and eat it with any kind of rice—plain boiled to chickpea pilau (p140)—or with nan or roti, plus some onion raita (p152). It is loved by people of all ages, in all seasons, and is the ultimate comfort food.

INGREDIENTS

$^1/_4$ cup sunflower oil
2 large onions, finely sliced
1 tsp garlic paste
2 medium tomatoes, peeled and chopped
1 tsp red chili powder
1 tsp ground turmeric
1 tsp cumin seeds
salt

$1^1/_4$ lb (500 g) boned leg of lamb,
  cut in small pieces
$1^1/_4$ lb (500 g) fresh spinach leaves
  or well-drained frozen spinach

To garnish
chopped green chilies
slivers of fresh ginger root

METHOD

Heat the oil in a saucepan, add the onions, and cook until slightly browned. Add the garlic paste and tomatoes and stir for a minute. Add the chili powder, turmeric, cumin seeds, and salt to taste and stir. If necessary, add a tablespoon or two of water to prevent the mixture from sticking to the bottom of the pan and burning. Stir until the oil separates out.

Now add the lamb pieces together with $1^1/_2$–2 cups water. Put the lid on and leave to cook over moderately low heat for 30–40 minutes. Add the spinach and continue cooking, covered, for 12–15 minutes or until the lamb is tender.

Remove the lid and simmer for a further 10–15 minutes or until excess liquid has evaporated and the oil separates out. Garnish with chopped green chilies and slivers of ginger, and serve.

NOTE: The curry can be made in advance (it's great for freezing) and reheated in the pan over low heat, or in a microwave.

Serves 4–5

spicy and
fragrant

Tamatar gosht Lamb and tomato curry

Make this curry when tomatoes are in peak season and full of flavor—Tamatar Gosht is simply pieces of lamb and lots of tomatoes cooked into a curry. Lamb (or mutton) works well with the slightly sharp taste of tomatoes; however, beef or veal shoulder or rump can be substituted for the lamb, as can chicken, quail, fish, or even squid. Serve with plum chutney (p148) and leavened roti (p146) or nan.

INGREDIENTS

$1/4$ cup sunflower oil
1 large onion, finely chopped
1 tsp ginger paste
$1/2$ tsp garlic paste
$1^1/4$ lb (500 g) tomatoes, peeled and chopped
salt
1 tsp red chili powder
1 tsp cumin seeds
3 black cardamom pods

5 cloves
1 bay leaf
$1^1/4$ lb (500 g) boned lamb leg or shoulder,
   cut into small pieces
$1/4$ cup chopped cilantro leaves

To garnish
slivers of fresh ginger root
chopped green chilies

METHOD

Heat the oil in a saucepan, add the onion, and fry until slightly browned. Add the ginger and garlic pastes and stir, then add the tomatoes. Add some salt, the chili powder, cumin seeds, cardamoms, cloves, and bay leaf. Stir until the oil separates out.

Add the lamb and fry, stirring, for 5 minutes. Pour in 1 cup water and stir well, then put the lid on the saucepan and reduce the heat to moderately low. Cook for 45–60 minutes or until the lamb is cooked and tender.

Remove the lid and keep cooking gently, stirring, until the oil separates out. Stir in the chopped cilantro leaves. Garnish with the ginger and green chilies, and serve.

NOTE: The curry can be made in advance (it's good for freezing) and reheated in the pan over low heat, or in a microwave.

Serves 2–3

tangy and
slightly
sweet

Gurda keema Ground lamb and kidney curry

Keema, or ground meat, is the staple food in every household, every roadside restaurant, and every cafeteria in Pakistan, and *keema* is probably the first curry to be mastered and consumed over and over again by every Pakistani student in the US or UK. The meat was traditionally beef; then mutton or lamb became popular. Nowadays among the urban population, ground chicken is picking up. Vegetables, such as potatoes, peas and onions, lentils, and beans are often added for flavor and to extend the dish. But kidneys lift ordinary *keema* to a higher status, making this curry worthy to be served to a special guest. Instead of including kidneys, you can, of course, add potatoes or peas. Serve this with plain yogurt and pratha (p146).

INGREDIENTS

6 lamb's kidneys, sliced
$1^1/_2$ tsp garlic paste
1 tsp ground turmeric
$^1/_4$ cup sunflower oil
2 large onions, finely sliced
1 tsp ginger paste
4 medium tomatoes, peeled
   and chopped
1 tsp red chili powder

1 tsp cumin seeds
1 tsp ground coriander
salt
$1^1/_4$ lb (500 g) coarsely ground lamb
4 tbsp chopped cilantro leaves

To garnish
green chilies cut into julienne
fresh ginger root cut into julienne

METHOD

Pour 1 cup water into a small saucepan. Layer the sliced kidneys in the pan, cut side down. Add $^1/_2$ tsp of the garlic paste and $^1/_2$ tsp turmeric. Bring to a boil, then drain the kidneys. This helps to remove their strong smell.

Heat the oil in a saucepan, add the onions, and cook until golden brown. Add the remaining garlic paste, the ginger paste, and tomatoes and stir well, then add the chili powder, remaining turmeric, the cumin seeds, ground coriander, and salt. Cook, stirring, until the oil separates out.

Add the ground lamb and stir to mix with the *massalla*. Add the kidneys and mix them in. Put the lid on the saucepan and cook for 30–35 minutes over low heat.

Remove the lid and cook for a further 8–10 minutes or until excess liquid has evaporated and the oil separates out.

Stir in the chopped cilantro. Garnish with green chilies and ginger, and serve.

NOTE: The curry can be made in advance (it's good for freezing) and then reheated in the pan or in a microwave.

Serves 4–5

meaty
and spicy

Passanda curry Sliced beef curry

The word *passanda* means a thin slice of meat, usually beef or veal, although lamb is also sometimes used. Prepared like this, a simple piece of meat is transformed into a lavish dish. The curry is ideal for any occasion, and is best served with mint raita (p152) and roti or nan. A less expensive cut of beef or veal can be used, as long as it is very lean and tender.

INGREDIENTS
1¼ lb (500 g) fillet of beef
3 tbsp sunflower oil
2 large onions, finely chopped
1 tsp garlic paste
1 tsp ginger paste
1 large tomato, peeled and finely chopped
5–6 tbsp chopped cilantro leaves

Marinade
7 oz (200 g) plain Greek-style yogurt
1 tsp red chili powder
½ tsp ground turmeric
1 tsp ground black pepper
1 tsp cumin seeds
1 tsp ground coriander
salt

METHOD
Cut the beef into ¼-in (5-mm) slices. With a meat mallet, beat the slices until they are even thinner. Mix together the yogurt, spices, and salt to taste. Add the slices of beef and turn to coat with the spiced yogurt. Leave to marinate for 2–3 hours.

Heat the oil in a saucepan, add the onions, and cook until lightly browned. Stir in the garlic and ginger pastes, then immediately add the tomato. Stir for a few minutes. Add the marinated beef with all the spiced yogurt. Stir around for 1 minute, then put the lid on the saucepan and turn the heat to low. Cook for 15–20 minutes or until the beef is very tender.

Remove the lid and stir for a few more minutes or until the oil separates out. Stir in ¼ cup of the chopped cilantro. Garnish with the remaining chopped cilantro and serve.

NOTE: The curry can be made in advance (it's good for freezing) and reheated in the pan over low heat or in a microwave.

Serves 4–5

thick and warmly spiced

Desi murgh curry Special chicken curry

In the fifties and sixties, if you were invited to dinner and served this curry, it would show that your hosts had spared no expense or effort in your honor, and you would have been duly thankful. Thus was the status of a "Desi Murgh" curry, when chickens were hard to obtain, quite expensive, and difficult to cook. Farmed chicken changed all this and turned a glorious curry into an ordinary one. To get the real taste of the original, you have to use a *desi murgh*—a young, male, organic pasture-raised chicken. It should be slowly cooked until tender to allow all the herbs and spices to penetrate and release the full flavor of the chicken. If necessary, a regular chicken can be used instead of a pasture-raised organic bird; however, you will probably need to reduce the amount of water for cooking. Serve with mango pickle (p150) and nans or boiled or pulao rice.

INGREDIENTS

$1/4$ cup sunflower oil
2 large onions, finely sliced
2 tsp garlic paste
2 tsp ginger paste
4 tomatoes, peeled and finely chopped
2 oz (50 g) plain Greek-style yogurt
$1^1/2$ tsp red chili powder
1 tsp ground turmeric
1 tsp cumin seeds

2 tsp ground coriander
3 large black cardamom pods
6 cloves
1 bay leaf
salt to taste
1 pasture-raised organic chicken, about $2^3/4$ lb (1.2 kg), cut into 8 pieces, skinned if preferred
5–6 tbsp chopped coriander leaves

METHOD

Heat the oil in a large saucepan, add the onions, and cook until dark golden brown. Remove the onions with a slotted spoon. Allow to cool, then chop them finely in a food processor. Set aside.

Add the garlic and ginger pastes to the hot oil in the saucepan and stir for a few minutes. Add the tomatoes and stir in well, then stir in the yogurt. Cook for 5–6 minutes. Add the browned onion paste and stir to mix, then add all the spices, the bay leaf, and salt to taste. Cook, stirring, until the oil separates out.

Put the chicken pieces in the pan and spoon the spice mixture over them. Add 2 cups water. Put the lid on the pan and cook over low heat, stirring occasionally, for 40–50 minutes or until the chicken is cooked through and tender. Add more water if needed.

Remove the lid and continue cooking for 10 minutes or until the oil in the sauce separates out. Stir in $1/4$ cup of the chopped cilantro. Garnish with the remaining chopped cilantro and serve.

NOTE: The curry can be made in advance and reheated in the pan over low heat, or in a microwave.

Serves 4

flavorful
and wet

Subzi biryani Vegetable biryani

If you want a rice dish that is more than a rice dish, if you want one that is versatile and colorful, if you want it to be a centerpiece on your table and a dish to show your masterly skills, then this is the one to make. It is appropriate with any curry or condiment, great for picnics and barbecues, can be eaten hot or cold, and is loved by children. You can use any vegetables that are in season.

INGREDIENTS

1¼ lb (500 g) basmati rice
½ cup sunflower oil
2 large onions, sliced
1 tsp ginger paste
1 tsp garlic paste
8 oz (225 g) peeled and
   finely chopped tomatoes
1 tsp red chili powder
1 tsp ground turmeric
1 tsp ground coriander
2 cinnamon sticks
4 black cardamom pods

1 tsp cumin seeds
1 tsp black peppercorns
1 tsp cloves
4 star anise
2 bay leaves
salt
9 oz (250 g) plain Greek-style yogurt
9 oz (250 g) potatoes, peeled and diced
6 oz (150 g) shelled fresh or frozen peas
6 oz (150 g) carrots, peeled and diced
4 tbsp finely chopped cilantro leaves
fried brown onions to garnish (p140)

METHOD

Thoroughly wash the rice in running cold water, then leave to soak in enough water to cover for at least 1 hour. Drain the rice and cook in plenty of boiling salted water until it is 90 percent cooked. Drain the rice and set aside.

Heat the oil in a saucepan, add the onions, and fry until golden brown. Add the ginger and garlic pastes and cook for 1 minute, then stir in the tomatoes, all the spices, the bay leaves, some salt, and the yogurt. Cook for about 10 minutes or until the oil separates out.

Add the potatoes, fresh peas, and carrots with ½ cup water and cook for 5–8 minutes or until the vegetables are tender. (Add frozen peas when the potatoes and carrots are almost done.) Remove from the heat.

Spread half the cooked rice over the bottom of a large saucepan. Put the cooked vegetables on this layer of rice and sprinkle with the chopped cilantro. Cover with the remaining rice.

Dampen a clean, thick dishcloth with water and cover the saucepan. Put the lid tightly on the cloth and set the saucepan on a very low heat. (You can place the saucepan in a heavy frying pan to further reduce the heat.) Cook like this for about 30 minutes.

Mix the rice gently with the vegetables, then spoon into a large, flat dish. Garnish with fried brown onions and serve.

Serves 4–5

colorful
and
aromatic

Batair dahi wala Quail in yogurt curry

Until a few years ago, quail (*batair*) were only available as wild game and were considered a great delicacy, deemed fit only for *nawabs* and *maharajas*. Now, however, quail are farmed and easily available to everyone. This combination of quail and yogurt is ideal, as the yogurt tenderizes the birds and the tartness highlights their flavor. Other game birds like partridges can be cooked in the same way—use 6 partridges and increase the cooking time slightly. Serve with fresh cilantro chutney (p150) and chickpea pilau (p140) or nans.

INGREDIENTS

$1/4$ cup sunflower oil
1 large onion, finely sliced
salt
12 red chilies
$1/2$ tsp red chili powder
2 cinnamon sticks
4 black cardamom pods
8 cloves

20 black peppercorns
2 bay leaves
1 tsp cumin seeds
12 quail, about 3 oz (75 g) each,
    skinned if preferred
10 oz (300 g) plain Greek-style yogurt
cilantro leaves to garnish

METHOD

Heat the oil in a large saucepan, add the sliced onion, and cook until lightly golden brown. Add some salt, the whole chilies, and all the spices and stir for a few minutes. Add the quail and stir for a few more minutes to be sure they are well coated with the spice mixture.

Add the yogurt and stir to mix, then reduce the heat to moderately low and cook, uncovered, for 20–25 minutes, stirring occasionally.

With the tip of a sharp knife, check that the quail are fully cooked and tender. Then continue stirring gently until all excess liquid has evaporated and the oil separates out. Garnish with cilantro leaves and serve.

NOTE: The curry can be made in advance and reheated in a microwave.

Serves 4

light and
gamy

Jhinga curry Shrimp curry

Shrimp (*jhinga*) are found abundantly in the warm waters of the Arabian Sea, which lies to the south of Pakistan. White-shelled shrimp, which are delicate in flavor, are the most common variety, followed by tiger shrimp. If available, use white-shelled shrimp for this curry, as they blend beautifully with the aromatic, spicy *massalla*. The *massalla* can be cooked in advance; however, the shrimp must be added and cooked just before serving. Cumin raita (p153) and vegetable biryani (p138) are good accompaniments.

INGREDIENTS

1¼ lb (500 g) raw jumbo or tiger shrimp
3 tbsp sunflower oil
1 onion, chopped
1 tsp garlic paste
1 tsp ginger paste
1 medium tomato, peeled and
  finely chopped
8 oz (225 g) plain Greek-style yogurt
1 tsp red chili powder

½ tsp ground black pepper
½ tsp ground turmeric
½ tsp cumin seeds
½ tsp ground coriander
salt
2 tbsp coarsely chopped green chilies
¼ cup chopped cilantro leaves
cilantro leaves to garnish

METHOD

Peel the shrimp, leaving the last tail section on. Devein the shrimp, then set aside.

To make the *massalla*, heat the oil in a saucepan, add the onion, and fry until light golden brown. Add the garlic and ginger pastes and stir for 1–2 minutes. Add the tomato and yogurt and cook, stirring, for another few minutes. Add the chili powder, black pepper, turmeric, cumin seeds, ground coriander, and salt to taste, and cook, stirring, until the oil separates out.

Add the shrimp and cook over moderately high heat, stirring frequently, for 4–5 minutes or until the shrimp turn pink. Make sure you don't overcook them. Stir in the green chilies and chopped cilantro, and garnish with cilantro leaves. Serve hot.

Serves 4–5

fragrant
and spicy

Subzi biryani Vegetable biryani

If you want a rice dish that is more than a rice dish, if you want one that is versatile and colorful, if you want it to be a centerpiece on your table and a dish to show your masterly skills, then this is the one to make. It is appropriate with any curry or condiment, great for picnics and barbecues, can be eaten hot or cold, and is loved by children. You can use any vegetables that are in season.

INGREDIENTS

1¼ lb (500 g) basmati rice
½ cup sunflower oil
2 large onions, sliced
1 tsp ginger paste
1 tsp garlic paste
8 oz (225 g) peeled and
    finely chopped tomatoes
1 tsp red chili powder
1 tsp ground turmeric
1 tsp ground coriander
2 cinnamon sticks
4 black cardamom pods

1 tsp cumin seeds
1 tsp black peppercorns
1 tsp cloves
4 star anise
2 bay leaves
salt
9 oz (250 g) plain Greek-style yogurt
9 oz (250 g) potatoes, peeled and diced
6 oz (150 g) shelled fresh or frozen peas
6 oz (150 g) carrots, peeled and diced
4 tbsp finely chopped cilantro leaves
fried brown onions to garnish (p140)

METHOD

Thoroughly wash the rice in running cold water, then leave to soak in enough water to cover for at least 1 hour. Drain the rice and cook in plenty of boiling salted water until it is 90 percent cooked. Drain the rice and set aside.

Heat the oil in a saucepan, add the onions, and fry until golden brown. Add the ginger and garlic pastes and cook for 1 minute, then stir in the tomatoes, all the spices, the bay leaves, some salt, and the yogurt. Cook for about 10 minutes or until the oil separates out.

Add the potatoes, fresh peas, and carrots with ½ cup water and cook for 5–8 minutes or until the vegetables are tender. (Add frozen peas when the potatoes and carrots are almost done.) Remove from the heat.

Spread half the cooked rice over the bottom of a large saucepan. Put the cooked vegetables on this layer of rice and sprinkle with the chopped cilantro. Cover with the remaining rice.

Dampen a clean, thick dishcloth with water and cover the saucepan. Put the lid tightly on the cloth and set the saucepan on a very low heat. (You can place the saucepan in a heavy frying pan to further reduce the heat.) Cook like this for about 30 minutes.

Mix the rice gently with the vegetables, then spoon into a large, flat dish. Garnish with fried brown onions and serve.

Serves 4–5

colorful
and
aromatic

Chana pulao Chickpea pilau

This is a great combination of protein and carbohydrates, and makes a complete meal if served with a salad and yogurt. It can be made spicy or mild, according to your taste. A rice dish like this is a good way to introduce people—including children—to the wonderful world of curries. It can be packed into lunchboxes to take to school or work and is perfect eaten outdoors on a warm summer evening.

INGREDIENTS

1¼ lb (500 g) basmati rice
½ cup sunflower oil
4 oz (115 g) thinly sliced onion
1 tsp fresh ginger root, cut in slivers
3 cinnamon sticks
1 tsp black peppercorns
1 tsp cumin seeds
3 black cardamom pods

salt
4 oz (115 g) dried chickpeas, soaked overnight and cooked until tender, or 14 oz (400 g) canned chickpeas, drained

Fried brown onions
2 tbsp sunflower oil
1 large onion, thinly sliced

METHOD

Thoroughly wash the rice in running cold water, then leave to soak in a bowl with enough water to cover for at least 1 hour. Drain.

Heat the oil in a saucepan, add the onion, and fry until golden brown. Add the ginger, all the spices, and salt to taste and stir for about 1 minute. Add 3 cups water and bring to a boil. Add the soaked rice and cooked or canned chickpeas. Cover the saucepan, reduce the heat, and simmer for about 15 minutes or until the rice is about 90 percent cooked.

Dampen a clean, thick dishcloth with water. Remove the lid from the saucepan. Cover with the cloth, then put the lid back on tightly and set the pan over very low heat. (You can place the saucepan in a heavy frying pan to further reduce the heat.) Cook like this for 25–30 minutes.

Meanwhile, heat the oil in a large saucepan, add the onion, and cook until dark golden brown and crisp. Remove the onion with a slotted spoon and drain on paper towels.

Garnish the pilau with the fried brown onions and serve.

Serves 4–5

aromatic and hearty

Spice mountains, Lahore >

Lobia curry Black-eye bean curry

A typical family meal consists of a meat dish, a vegetable dish, and a dish of lentils or beans. This curry would be quite a common choice, since it is economical and ideal for winter or summer. It's also great for those who don't eat meat, because if served with garlic nan and a rice dish, plus cucumber raita (p153), it makes a whole meal. The closest equivalent to what we call *lobia* are black-eye beans, although you can also use other legumes such as red kidney beans (cooking time may vary, according to the bean you use).

INGREDIENTS

3 tbsp sunflower oil
2 onions, chopped
1 tsp ginger paste
1 tsp garlic paste
3 medium tomatoes, peeled and
   chopped
1 tsp red chili powder
$1/2$ tsp ground turmeric
1 tsp cumin seeds
2 tsp ground coriander
$1/2$ tsp ground black pepper

salt
10 oz (300 g) dried black-eye beans,
   soaked for 8–10 hours, then drained
$1/4$ cup chopped cilantro leaves

To garnish
chopped green chilies
cilantro leaves

METHOD

Heat the oil in a saucepan, add the onions, and fry until light golden brown. Add the ginger and garlic pastes and the tomatoes, and stir for a few minutes, then add the dry spices and salt to taste. Cook, stirring, until the oil separates out.

Add the black-eye beans and stir to blend with the spice mixture. Pour in 3 cups fresh water and bring it to a boil. Put the lid on the saucepan, reduce the heat to low, and cook for 45–50 minutes or until the beans are tender.

Serves 4–5

Remove the lid and simmer over gentle heat until excess liquid has evaporated and the oil separates out. Stir in the chopped cilantro and remove from the heat. Garnish with chopped green chilies and cilantro leaves, and serve.

warmly
spiced and
earthy

NOTE: The curry can be made in advance (it freezes well) and then reheated in the pan over low heat, or in a microwave.

Subzi curry Mixed vegetable curry

Although Pakistan is a meat-eating nation, various *subzi* (vegetable) curries feature very frequently in everyday meals. This curry is eaten on its own by the poor or as part of a meal by the more affluent. For a lot of people, it is the curry of choice, preferred over meat for its healthiness and taste, excellent served with fresh cilantro chutney (p150) and roti. Almost any vegetable can be made into a curry, following the right technique and method. The key factors are to use very fresh vegetables and subtle spicing, and to eat the curry as soon as it is cooked.

INGREDIENTS
3 tbsp sunflower oil
1 large onion, finely chopped
1 tsp garlic paste
1 tbsp fresh ginger root cut in slivers
2 large plum tomatoes, peeled and chopped
$1/2$ tsp ground turmeric
1 tsp red chili powder
1 tsp cumin seeds
salt
$1^1/4$ lb (500 g) potatoes, peeled
   and diced
$1^1/4$ lb (500 g) cauliflower, cut into
   medium florets
5–6 tbsp chopped cilantro leaves

METHOD
Heat the oil in a saucepan, add the onion, and cook until slightly browned. Add the garlic paste and ginger slivers, then add the tomatoes, spices, and salt to taste and stir well. Add the potatoes and cauliflower together with $1/2$ cup water. Stir well, then put the lid on the pan. Cook for 15–20 minutes or until the vegetables are tender.

Remove the lid and continue cooking until the oil separates out. Stir in most of the chopped cilantro leaves. Garnish with the rest of the cilantro and serve.

NOTE: The curry can be made in advance and reheated in the pan over low heat, or in a microwave.

Serves 3–4

fresh and
fragrant

Alloo curry Potato curry

When you are not sure what to cook, or you have to prepare a meal in a hurry, potato curry is always the answer. It will never let you down. You can eat it for breakfast (serve it on toasted country bread, topped with a couple of fried eggs), lunch, or dinner, alone or as part of a meal, with any kind of bread or rice. It's great as a leftover, too. All varieties of potatoes can be used, even young new potatoes. This is true comfort food, delicious with apple chutney (p149) and plain nan.

INGREDIENTS
2 tbsp sunflower oil
1 large onion, finely chopped
2 large plum tomatoes, peeled and chopped
8 red chilies
$^1/_2$ tsp red chili powder
1 tsp cumin seeds
salt
$1^1/_4$ lb (500 g) potatoes, peeled and diced,
  or whole new potatoes
chopped cilantro leaves to garnish

METHOD
Heat the oil in a saucepan, add the onion, and cook until slightly browned. Add the chopped tomatoes, then stir in the chilies, chili powder, cumin seeds, and salt to taste. Add $^1/_2$ cup water and cook, stirring, until excess liquid has evaporated.

Serves 3–4

Add the potatoes together with another $^1/_2$ cup water. Stir well to coat the potatoes with the spice mixture, then put the lid on the pan. Cook for 15–20 minutes or until the potatoes are tender but not breaking up.

savory and
comforting

Remove the lid and continue cooking until the oil separates out. Garnish with chopped cilantro and serve hot.

NOTE: The curry can be made in advance and reheated in the pan over low heat, or in a microwave.

Khamiri roti Leavened roti

A roti spread with ghee or butter is a combination made in heaven. Serve these slightly puffy breads hot, straight from the oven.

INGREDIENTS

1 tsp dry yeast
$^1/_4$ tsp sugar
$1^1/_4$ lb (500 g) white or whole-wheat bread flour
1 tsp salt

METHOD

Dissolve the yeast and sugar in 2 tbsp warm water, then leave for 15 minutes to become frothy.

Sift the flour and salt into a large mixing bowl. Add the yeast mixture and more water (about 1 cup) to make a dough. Knead for 8–10 minutes or until pliable.

Divide the dough into equal portions and shape each into a ball. Leave in a warm place for 30 minutes. The dough will rise slightly.

Preheat the oven to 350°F (180°C).

Makes 5–6

With a rolling pin, roll out each ball of dough to a 9-in (23-cm) disk. Place on a nonstick baking sheet and bake for 3–5 minutes or until lightly browned and a bit puffy. Serve immediately.

Pratha Fried roti

The crisp, crackling texture and taste of a fried roti goes well with just about every curry ever created. They are best freshly fried, but can be frozen or refrigerated, then reheated in the oven (wrapped in foil), in the microwave, or in a frying pan.

INGREDIENTS

2 cups white bread flour
2 cups whole-wheat flour
$1^1/_4$ tsp salt

$2^1/_2$ tsp sunflower oil
1 cup sunflower oil for frying

METHOD

Sift the flours and salt into a large mixing bowl. Add $1^1/_2$ cups water and the $2^1/_2$ tsp oil, and knead to make a pliable dough. Leave to rest for 30 minutes.

Makes 4–5

Divide the dough into equal portions and shape into balls. Roll out into 8-in- (20-cm-) diameter disks. Heat the oil for frying in a large frying pan. Fry the breads over moderate heat for about 2 minutes on each side or until golden brown. Drain on paper towels and serve hot.

Leavened roti >

Alloo bukhara chatney Plum chutney

For this chutney we use dried round purple or black plums, which are a different variety from the plums that are dried to make prunes. Due to its high sugar content, the chutney can be kept in the refrigerator for 2–3 months.

INGREDIENTS

$3^3/_4$ cups sugar
$1^1/_4$ lb (500 g) dried plums, soaked
  for 30 minutes and drained
small pinch of salt

small pinch of red chili powder
$^1/_4$ tsp black peppercorns, crushed
good pinch of white cumin seeds
$^1/_4$ oz (5 g) four seeds (p129)

METHOD

Put the sugar and $1^1/_4$ cups water in a large saucepan and bring to a boil, stirring to dissolve the sugar. Add the dried plums and cook for 20 minutes over medium heat.

Stir in the salt, red chili powder, crushed pepper, and cumin seeds. Mix in the four seeds. Allow to cool before serving or storage.

**Makes 2¹/₂ lb
(1 kg)**

Lassan achar Pickled garlic

This *achar* (pickle) can be stored in a cool cupboard for 2–3 months or in the refrigerator for up to 6 months.

INGREDIENTS

$^1/_2$ cup white vinegar
3 tbsp salt
1 tbsp red chili powder
4 tsp ground turmeric
$^1/_2$ tsp black onion seeds

2 tbsp fennel seeds
1 tbsp fenugreek seeds
$1^1/_4$ lb (500 g) garlic cloves, peeled
2 cups mustard oil

METHOD

Combine the vinegar with the salt and all the spices in a large glass or ceramic jar. Add the garlic cloves. Leave in a cool place to marinate for 15 days.

Add the mustard oil and leave to marinate for a further 5–10 days or until the garlic cloves are slightly soft and have lost their pungent smell.

**Makes 2¹/₂ lb
(1 kg)**

Saib chatney Apple chutney

This can be kept in the refrigerator in an airtight container for up to 2 months.

INGREDIENTS
1$\frac{1}{4}$ lb (500 g) green apples
lemon juice
1$\frac{1}{2}$ cups sugar
$\frac{1}{4}$ tsp salt
small pinch of red chili powder
$\frac{1}{4}$ tsp black peppercorns, crushed
1$\frac{1}{4}$ tsp four seeds (p129)

METHOD
Peel and core the apples and cut into slices. Dip into a bowl of water acidified with lemon juice to prevent discoloration.

Put the sugar and $\frac{2}{3}$ cup water in a large saucepan and bring to a boil, stirring to dissolve the sugar. Add the drained apple slices and cook over medium heat for 15 minutes or until the apples have softened.

Stir in the salt, red chili powder, crushed pepper, and four seeds. Allow to cool before serving.

**Makes 1½ lb
(600 g)**

Aam ka acar Mango pickle

Use very unripe, green mangoes for this pickle. In a cooler climate, the marinating time may need to be extended—it can easily be doubled. All homemade pickles improve with age. Keep this in a cool place or the refrigerator.

INGREDIENTS
1¼ lb (500 g) small unripe mangoes
½ cup white vinegar
3 tbsp salt
1 tbsp red chili powder
4 tsp ground turmeric
½ tsp black onion seeds
2 tbsp fennel seeds
1 tbsp fenugreek seeds
2 cups mustard oil

METHOD
Cut the unpeeled mangoes lengthwise into quarters, leaving the pits in.

Combine the vinegar, salt, and all the spices in a large glass or ceramic jar. Add the mangoes and stir. Leave to marinate in a cool place for 10–15 days or until the mangoes are slightly softened.

Add the mustard oil. Leave to marinate for a further 5–10 days before using.

**Makes
2¼ lb (1 kg)**

Dhania chatney Cilantro chutney

Serve this chutney as soon as it is made, to preserve its fresh green color.

INGREDIENTS
5 oz (140 g) cilantro leaves
2 tbsp chopped green chilies
1 tsp red chili powder
salt

METHOD
In a food processor or blender, purée the cilantro leaves with the green chilies to make a fine paste. Add a little water, if necessary.

Stir in the chili powder and salt to taste, and serve immediately.

**Makes 12 oz
(350 g)**

Cilantro chutney, Apple chutney (recipe p149) and Mango pickle >

Podina raita Mint raita

Mint has a wonderful aromatic fragrance and flavor, and it gives yogurt a beautiful green color, which is why this is the most popular of all the raitas. It enhances the flavor of the food it is eaten with and also acts as a mouth-cleanser between each bite.

INGREDIENTS
8 oz (225 g) plain Greek-style yogurt
salt to taste
$1/4$ cup finely chopped mint leaves
1 tsp finely chopped green chili

Serves 4–5

METHOD
Whisk the yogurt in a bowl to be sure it is well combined and thick, then add the salt, chopped mint, and green chili, mixing well. Chill for at least 30 minutes before serving.

Piyaz raita Onion raita

With its sharp onion flavor, this raita is a good partner for curries made from vegetables, lentils, and beans. It also goes well with rice dishes.

INGREDIENTS
8 oz (225 g) plain Greek-style yogurt
$1/4$ cup finely chopped onion, squeezed dry
$1/2$ tsp crushed dried chilies
salt

Serves 4–5

METHOD
Whisk the yogurt in a bowl to be sure it is well combined and thick, then add the onion, crushed chilies, and salt to taste, mixing well. Chill for at least 30 minutes before serving.

Kheera raita Cucumber raita

Cucumber raita is very popular during the summer months, as it is known for its cooling properties. Serve it with vegetable and bean curries. It is also delicious eaten on its own with a fresh salad.

INGREDIENTS
8 oz (225 g) plain Greek-style yogurt
4 tbsp grated cucumber, squeezed dry
$1/2$ tsp red chili powder
salt

METHOD
Whisk the yogurt in a bowl to be sure it is well combined and thick, then add the cucumber, chili powder, and salt to taste, mixing well. Chill for at least 30 minutes before serving.

Serves 4–5

Zeera raita Cumin raita

Popular during the winter months, when fresh herbs and other vegetables are scarce, cumin raita has an aromatic, mildly spicy flavor. It's great with meat, fish, and seafood curries and goes well with all rice dishes, too.

INGREDIENTS
8 oz (225 g) plain Greek-style yogurt
$1/2$ tsp salt
$1/2$ tsp white cumin seeds

METHOD
Whisk the yogurt in a bowl to be sure it is well combined and thick, then add the salt and cumin seeds, mixing well. Chill for at least 30 minutes before serving.

Serves 4–5

SE ASIA

MYANMAR & MARITIME

< Rice terrace fields,
China borders

Almost everyone in Southeast Asia eats rice, and most people eat it two or even three times a day. With rice is eaten the best meat, fish, and vegetables that can be afforded, which not only provides a balanced diet, but also gives the pleasure of contrasting textures and tastes, among them the strong, aromatic flavors of herbs and spices. Sauces are also sometimes included in a dish, partly to blend and distribute the flavors of the ingredients, and partly to moisten the food. People in Southeast Asia have been cooking and eating in this way for centuries, but at some fairly recent date—perhaps around 200 years ago—these dishes became known as curries.

How much sauce must there be to make a dish a curry? It's hard to say. The sauce may be runny, or it may be reduced to make it thick; there may be more sauce than solids in the dish; or there may be very little liquid at all. At one extreme, it would be correct to speak of a curry soup, such as the Burmese chicken noodle soup called Ohno Kwautskwe (p172) or the lamb stew of central Java called Gulé Kambing (p194). *Gulé*, which in Indonesia and Malaysia is usually spelled *gulai*, is a general term for stews with plenty of sauce, and a *gulai* is simply a curry: the Malaysian Gulai Kepala Ikan (p184) translates into English as Fish-Head Curry. In Singapore this is considered a typical local dish, and most people call it by its English name.

In the four countries in this chapter—Myanmar (Burma), Malaysia, Singapore, and Indonesia—the flavoring ingredients that add zest to a curry are generally incorporated into a paste, which traditionally is made at home, fresh each day. This is hard work, and many modern cooks will not refuse commercial curry powders (Filipino curries are usually spiced with curry powder). There are many locally produced brands and varieties: powders for beef, lamb, or goat; for fish; for vegetables; or for well-known recipes like Vindaloo, all available in the local market. For meat, the mix usually contains more of the stronger spices and extra garlic, to counteract the smell and flavor of the meat. The names of the curry powders usually suggest an Indian connection, as of course does the word "curry" itself, even in its original Tamil form, *kari* or *karé*. For the Tamils, that meant either pepper, or a mix of water with hot spices.

In addition to the aromatics and spices, curries also need color: yellow from turmeric root, red from red chilies. Mixed, they tint the sauce an appetizing reddish-orange color.

A creamy texture is achieved with coconut milk, which is used in this part of the world just as Western cooks use dairy products. Coconut cream can be compared to heavy cream, coconut milk to light cream or milk.

In the Philippines, curries are particularly popular in Mindanao and other southern parts of the country. The people here broadly agree with their Malaysian and Indonesian neighbors on curry's Indian connections, on the fact that it should have sauce, and on how the sauce should be made. The shopping list is quite short and there are only minor differences between regional cuisines. Aromatics, such as lemongrass, galangal, and curry leaves or kaffir lime leaves are needed, as well as the three universal essentials: shallots or onions, ginger, and garlic. In addition, a curry must be seasoned with strong-tasting spices like ground coriander, nutmeg, cumin, cardamom, pepper, and, of course, chilies.

Filipinos have a unique cookery tradition in *adobo*, a stew of pork, beef, or chicken, whose dominant flavor is sourness. This comes from vinegar, following a long tradition of vinegar-making in the Philippines. Different vinegars produce different tastes: palm sugar and sugar cane vinegars make an *adobo* sweeter than other vinegars would. The late Doreen Fernandez, in writing on the food of the Philippines, showed that *adobo*-type dishes were popular long before the Spanish arrived, and one of these, called Adobo sa Gata, was (and still is) made with coconut milk. So it is fair to say that *adobo* recipes could represent curries from the Philippines.

Adobo is, in fact, the Filipino form of the word *adobado*, the name given by the Spanish conquistadores to a Mexican stew that they particularly liked. So there may be an ironic parallel in this naming of dishes: the Spaniards brought *adobado* to Manila and the islands just as the British—perhaps—brought "curry" to their colonies in Southeast Asia.

Sri Owen

Toasting peanuts >
Fry in hot oil to enhance
their nutty flavor

The Taste of Myanmar & Maritime SE Asia

1. candlenuts
2. kaffir limes
3. apple eggplants
4. green mango
5. green chilies
6. red chilies
7. galangal
8. turmeric root
9. shrimp paste
10. dried shrimp
11. lemongrass
12. dried shelled peanuts
13. blanched dried peanuts
14. peanuts in shell
15. asam gelugur
16. tamarind pods

The raw materials

The key ingredients used in the curry pastes or spice mixtures for Burmese, Malaysian, Singaporean, Filipino, and Indonesian curries provide the characteristic tastes and flavors of the cooking of this region. These ingredients are now generally available in the West, as are different types of shrimp paste and fish sauce, and the fruits, vegetables, and nuts described here.

Lemongrass

This aromatic ingredient is one of the first to come to mind when thinking about Southeast Asian cooking. Pieces of lemongrass may be added to a curry sauce whole (sometimes slightly bruised by pressing with the flat of a knife) and removed before serving. Alternatively, the outer, tougher leaves are stripped off (they can be added to a sauce as a flavoring) and the inner tender part is then chopped into rounds like green onion and blended into a curry paste.

Galangal

This pinkish rhizome, known as *laos* or *lengkuas* in Indonesia and Malaysia, resembles ginger, but it is not as hot, and it has a bitter taste. It is very tough and hard—a large piece can damage the blades of a food processor. So peel and dice galangal before blending it in a curry paste. Alternatively, you can put a ³/₄-in (2-cm) piece of galangal into a curry while it's cooking. Just remember to take it out before serving—if you bite on it, it can break a tooth.

Turmeric

Both red and white varieties of turmeric have been in popular use for a very long time all over Southeast Asia. As with galangal and fresh ginger, turmeric root needs to be peeled and chopped before use. If you can't get fresh red turmeric root, you can use ground turmeric instead—just ¹/₂–1 tsp is all you need in a curry paste if you are cooking for 4. Aromatic turmeric leaves are also used in Southeast Asian curries, but are rarely found in Europe.

Kaffir lime

Kaffir lime leaves are easily recognized by their figure-eight shape and their delicious fragrance. Though they are edible and have a refreshing taste, they are rather tough, even after being cooked for a long time. So it is best to discard them before serving. The zest of the kaffir lime is also used in cooking to add an appetizing perfume. If a recipe calls for lime juice (usually as a substitute for the souring agent, tamarind water), it will be the juice of ordinary lime, not kaffir lime, which isn't a very juicy fruit.

Chilies

Although chilies are very important in Asian cooking today, they were only introduced to this area in the 16th century, when seeds and plants were brought from Central America. There are many different varieties of chilies, ranging widely in their heat, but generally speaking, the larger the chili, the milder the taste. In Southeast Asian curries, all kinds of chilies are used, from large, long red chilies, which are not too hot, to tiny bird's-eye or bird chilies (in Malaysian, *chili padi*; *cabe rawit* in Indonesian), which are the hottest.

Tamarind

Tamarind, which has a sourness different from that of any citrus fruit, is important for giving depth to and balancing the sweetness of much Southeast and South Asian cooking. If available, fresh tamarind pods can be used in a curry sauce—simply crack the shell and take out the pod. More common is tamarind pulp, which is sold in a small compact block. This is used in the form of tamarind water,

Fresh red chili >

made by simmering or soaking tamarind pulp in water, then squeezing it and passing it through a sieve to extract the flavorful liquid (p322).

Asam gelugur

This souring agent is often sold with a misleading label that says "tamarind slices," "tamarind skins," or (the latest version) "assem skins." The shriveled, blackened contents of the bag are, in fact, slices of *asam gelugur* (*Garcinia atroviridis*). They are easy to use: rinse 2 slices under the cold faucet, then drop into the boiling curry sauce. The *asam* slices will expand, at the same time exuding their sour juice. Discard the slices before serving. *Asam gelugur* can also be used in any recipe to replace tamarind water (and save the work of making it): a slice equals 2 tbsp tamarind water.

Dried shrimp

The one ingredient the Burmese simply cannot do without is dried shrimp. They are the main ingredient in the Burmese relish called Balachaung (p170), which is normally eaten with curries in

Myanmar, and can be served as a relish or accompaniment to other curries eaten with rice. The tiny dried shrimp are usually roasted before being packaged for sale. Before use, soak them in hot water for 10 minutes, then drain and chop, crush with a mortar and pestle, or blend in a blender.

Shrimp paste

Another essential ingredient in the cooking of this region is shrimp paste, called *terasi* or *trassie* in Indonesia and *balachan* or *blachen* in Malaysia. In Myanmar they have their own fish paste (*ngapi*), but they also use *terasi* and *balachan*. Shrimp

paste is sold in hard blocks or individually wrapped slices, and is extremely strong-smelling and salty. Use it very sparingly.

Fish sauce

Another salty and strong-smelling condiment, fish sauce is used all over Southeast Asia. Various fish sauces are made in Myanmar, the Philippines, and Vietnam, but Thai fish sauce (*nam pla*) is the most widely available.

Coconut

Coconut oil is the traditional frying medium in Indonesia and Malaysia, and coconut milk and cream (p213) are used in curries all over the region. Another coconut preparation is *kerisik*, which is freshly grated coconut that is dry-roasted and then blended to make a brown, oily paste. It is used in the rich Malaysian beef rendang (p177).

Eggplant

Many kinds of eggplants, in all sizes, colors, and shapes, are used in Southeast Asian cooking. One popular variety is the apple eggplant, which is slightly bigger than a golf ball. Apple eggplants come in different shapes, but are typically globular or egg-shaped. They also come in different colors—purple, bright yellow, white, or shades of green ranging from light to intense—as well as multicolored, with whites and greens often delicately fading into each other.

Okra

Although more commonly found in Indian cooking, this vegetable is also much enjoyed in Southeast Asia. One popular use for okra is in the Singaporean dish known as Fish Head Curry (p184).

Mango

This tropical fruit has been cultivated in India for several thousand years and is now grown over almost all of South and East Asia. There are more than 40 varieties, but it is the green or unripe mango that is used as a souring agent in Southeast Asian curries. The Thai variety, which is used in this chapter's recipes, is normally larger than the Indian, and its sourness is checked by a pleasant slight sweetness.

Candlenuts

Resembling macadamia nuts in appearance, candlenuts, which are called *kemiri* in Indonesia and *buah keras* in Malaya, are used in many Indonesian and Malaysian dishes, as well as in Nonya cooking in Singapore. Candlenuts are always crushed or ground before being mixed with other ingredients and then blended to make a curry paste. Never eat candlenuts raw, because they are mildly toxic until they are cooked. Raw macadamia nuts make a satisfactory substitute. Another alternative is blanched almonds.

Peanuts

These are used all over Southeast Asia because they are cheap, filling, and nutritious. You can buy them in their shells, or already shelled in the form of dried nuts. Their thin outer skins range in color from pink to almost red or, if they have been blanched and dried, to an off-white color. Peanut sauce (p171) tastes and looks much better if you use pink or reddish peanuts. To bring out their nutty flavor and aroma, roast the peanuts first in a dry wok for 6–8 minutes, stirring constantly, or deep-fry them in hot oil for 4 minutes. Drain on paper towels and leave to cool before grinding finely.

Rice

Throughout Southeast Asia, rice is not just a staple food, it is a symbol of good living, and the foundation of every meal. To accompany any curry, plain boiled or steamed rice is always the best choice. Malaysians and Indonesians love compressed rice (p166). With no added flavoring, not even salt, rice absorbs the tastes and aromas of the curry, moderates and blends them. Cooking rice in an electric steamer will ensure perfect results without any effort.

To cook white, long-grain rice, such as basmati or Thai fragrant (jasmine) rice conventionally, use a thick-bottomed pan, preferably nonstick. Measure the rice in a cup, and use the same cup to measure the water (equal quantities of rice and water). Wash the rice in two or three changes of water, then put into the pan with the measured water and bring to a boil. Stir once with a wooden spoon, then leave the rice to simmer, without a lid, until it has absorbed all the water. Stir once more, then turn the heat to low and cover the pan tightly, using foil or a dishcloth, if necessary, to prevent the steam from getting out. Leave over low heat, undisturbed, for about 10 minutes, then serve.

Crushing dried shrimp >

Compressed rice Lontong

Lontong is always eaten cold. In Indonesia, Singapore, and Malaysia, it is cooked inside a rolled-up banana leaf, or in a container woven from a coconut frond (it is then called *ketupat*, but the taste and texture are the same). By being cooked in this confined space, the rice grains, as they absorb moisture, are pressed into a soft but solid mass. In most parts of the world, you can now buy boil-in-bag rice, and this saves you the trouble of rolling or weaving any containers. Make sure, though, that it is not "easy-cook" or "precooked," because these won't work for this method. Buy a plain long-grain rice, preferably basmati. Check, too, that the bags (made of a special plastic with tiny holes) are the right size—the rice should fill them one-third full, not much more or less. If the bags are too big, machine- or hand-stitch a seam across the bag to reduce the size.

INGREDIENTS
2 bags of boil-in-bag long-grain rice

METHOD

Step 1
Fill a large saucepan two-thirds full of cold water and bring it to a rolling boil. Put in the bags of rice and let them boil for 1¹/₄ hours, topping off the pan with very hot water when necessary to make sure the rice is always covered.

Step 1

Step 2
Pour off the water and take out the bags, which will now be plumped like small white pillows. Let them cool, then store them overnight (or longer) in the refrigerator.

Step 3
To serve, cut open and strip off the plastic bags, then cut the lontong into chunks and put these in a serving bowl.

Serves 4–8

Step 2

Step 3 >

Spiced tamarind relish

This relish can be used as a dipping sauce for crudités or plain cooked vegetables, or serve it in place of the chutney that would conventionally accompany a curry. Additionally, you can stir 1–2 tbsp of this relish into any curry while it is cooking, and it can take the place of plain tamarind water.

INGREDIENTS

2 tbsp peanut oil
4 shallots, finely chopped
2 tsp very finely chopped or grated fresh
  ginger root
1/2 tsp chili powder, or 1 large red chili,
  seeded and finely chopped

2 garlic cloves, crushed
1 tsp brown sugar
1 tsp ground coriander
1 tsp coarse sea salt
1 cup thick tamarind water (p322)

METHOD

Step 1
Heat the oil in a wok or saucepan, add the shallots, and stir-fry for 2 minutes to soften.

Step 2
Add the ginger, chili powder, and garlic, and stir-fry for 2 minutes. Stir in the brown sugar, ground coriander, and salt. Continue stirring over low heat until the mixture becomes quite sticky.

Step 3
Add the tamarind water and simmer for 5 minutes, stirring often. Taste and adjust the seasoning, adding more salt if necessary. Simmer, stirring, until the relish becomes quite thick.

Step 4
Leave the relish to cool, then transfer it to a jar with a tight-fitting lid, and refrigerate until needed.

**Makes about
1 cup**

Step 1

Step 2

Step 3 >

Balachaung Dried shrimp relish

This is a Burmese hot relish, made of dried shrimp with plenty of garlic and chilies. Once made, it can be kept in an airtight jar in the refrigerator for up to a month. It is worth making a good quantity. Among the recipes it appears in is the Burmese chicken curry with limes and tomatoes (p176).

INGREDIENTS
8 oz (225 g) dried shrimp, soaked in hot water
    for 10 minutes, then drained
3 tbsp peanut oil
4 shallots, finely chopped
4 garlic cloves, finely sliced
2 tsp toasted sesame oil
2–4 red chilies, seeded and finely chopped,
    or $1/2$–1 tsp chili powder
2 tsp finely chopped fresh ginger root
$1/2$ tsp ground turmeric
$1/2$ tsp salt, or more to taste
juice of 1 lime or lemon

METHOD
Finely chop the shrimp with a sharp knife, pound them in a mortar and pestle, or put them in a small blender and blend until fine. Set aside.

Heat the peanut oil in a wok or saucepan and fry the shallots and garlic for 2–3 minutes or until they are slightly colored. Remove with a slotted spoon and reserve.

Add the sesame oil to the wok or pan, heat, and then add the chilies, ginger, turmeric and salt. Fry for 2 minutes, stirring all the time.

Put in the ground shrimp and continue stir-frying for 1 minute. Now add 2 tbsp hot water and the lime or lemon juice. Stir until the liquid is absorbed by the shrimp. Mix in the reserved fried shallots and garlic.

The relish should be moist, not dry. Taste and add salt if you think it is needed. When cold, store in an airtight jar. Serve cold as a relish.

**Makes about
1 cup**

Sambal kacang Peanut sauce

This sauce is used in the Philippines Karé-karé (p198), and it is a very popular sauce with all kinds of satay, in Malaysia, Singapore, and Indonesia. It makes an excellent dipping sauce for crudités (called *lalab* in Indonesia), and it is the sauce for various cooked vegetable salads called *gado-gado*, which are claimed by Indonesians and Malaysians as among their national dishes.

INGREDIENTS
$^1/_2$ cup vegetable oil
8 oz (225 g) raw peanuts
2 garlic cloves, chopped
4 shallots, chopped
thin slice of shrimp paste (optional)
salt to taste
$^1/_2$ tsp chili powder
$^1/_2$ tsp brown sugar
1 tbsp dark soy sauce
2 tbsp tamarind water (p322) or lemon
   juice, or to taste

METHOD
Heat the oil in a wok or large, shallow saucepan and fry the peanuts over moderate heat for about 4 minutes, stirring them frequently. With a slotted spoon, transfer them to a colander lined with paper towels and leave them to cool. Then grind them in a blender or coffee grinder to a fine powder. Remove and set aside. Pour off all but 1 tbsp oil from the wok.

Put the garlic, shallots, shrimp paste (if using), and a little salt into the blender and blend to make a smooth paste.

Heat the oil in the wok, then add the garlic and shallot paste and fry for 1 minute. Add the chili powder, sugar, soy sauce, and $2^1/_2$ cups water and bring to a boil. Add the ground peanuts and stir to mix. Simmer, stirring occasionally, until the sauce has reduced to the thickness you want. This should take 8–10 minutes. Taste, and add the tamarind water and more salt, as needed.

This sauce can be stored for up to 1 week in an airtight jar in the refrigerator. It can also be frozen for up to 2 months. Thaw it out completely before reheating it in a saucepan. If it has become too thick, add water and continue heating until it reaches the right consistency.

**Makes about
2 cups**

Ohno kwautskwe Burmese chicken noodle soup

In Myanmar, this is a popular breakfast dish. Thick coconut milk and chickpea flour give the soup extra richness, and the flavors are delicious. My Burmese friend, who gave me the recipe, said that instead of round rice noodles, you can use the flat rice noodles called rice sticks. As an appetizer for 6–8, use only 2 oz (60 g) noodles.

INGREDIENTS

6 oz (175 g) round rice noodles
2 skinless, boneless chicken breasts, cut into
   bite-size pieces
1 tbsp fish sauce
1 small onion, chopped
2 garlic cloves, chopped
1 tsp chopped fresh ginger root
1 tsp chopped turmeric root
   or 1/2 tsp ground turmeric
1 large red chili, seeded and chopped
1 1/4 cups thick coconut milk (p213)
2 tbsp peanut oil

1 quart (liter) chicken stock
3–4 tbsp chickpea flour, dissolved in
   1/2 cup cold water

To garnish
hard-boiled eggs, quartered or sliced
1 red onion, thinly sliced, soaked in cold water
   for a few minutes, then drained
slices of lemon
deep-fried shallots (p211)
crushed dried chilies
chopped cilantro leaves

METHOD

Cook the noodles in boiling water for 2–3 minutes; drain and refresh under the cold faucet. Set aside in a colander. Just before serving, reheat the noodles by pouring boiling water over them while they are still in the colander and shake to drain as much water from them as possible.

Rub the chicken with the fish sauce, then set aside.

Blend together the onion, garlic, ginger, turmeric, and chili in a food processor or blender. When smooth, add 3 tbsp of the coconut milk or stock to make a paste.

Fry the paste in the peanut oil in a saucepan over moderate heat for 2–3 minutes, stirring constantly. Add the chicken and stir-fry for another 2–3 minutes. Add half of the stock and bring to a boil. Continue cooking the chicken for 8–10 minutes.

Heat the other half of the stock in another pan until starting to boil. Add the dissolved chickpea flour, stirring to prevent lumps. When thickened, pour the stock through a sieve into the pan containing the chicken mixture. Stir well. When the soup starts to boil, add the remaining coconut milk. Taste and adjust the seasoning by adding salt or more fish sauce, if necessary. Bring the soup back to a rolling boil.

At the same time, ask your guests to help themselves to the hot noodles, ready for the chicken soup to be ladled into their bowls. When everyone has soup, they should then help themselves to the garnishes, and eat while the soup is hot.

Serves 4

creamy
and rich

Wether hin lay Pork curry with mango

I think this is a really delicious curry. My Burmese friend, Kyu Kyu, suggested that I make a golden pork curry (Wet Thani) with bamboo shoots, not mango. For a pork curry with mango, she said that dried or pickled mangoes should be used. So it was a challenge for me to devise a new version. I decided to use a fresh green mango to give sourness to the sauce, as well as bamboo shoot, because it goes so well with pork. Instead of a fresh green mango, you can use a few slices of pickled mango. Another Burmese friend calls this a "sour stew of pork."

INGREDIENTS

$1^{1}/_{2}$ lb (675 g) pork fillet/tenderloin or
   boned pork chops, cut into
   1-in (2.5-cm) medallions
2 tbsp fish sauce
2 tsp lime juice
5 tbsp peanut oil
6 shallots, finely sliced
1 small, unripe Thai or Indian green mango,
   about 4–6 oz (115–175 g), peeled and
   cut into fine julienne strips
1 tbsp thick tamarind water (p322)

salt and pepper
7 oz (200 g) canned sliced bamboo shoots,
   drained and rinsed

Paste

4 garlic cloves, finely chopped
$^{1}/_{4}$-in (5-mm) piece shrimp paste
2 tsp grated fresh ginger root
2 large red chilies, seeded and
   finely chopped

METHOD

Marinate the pork medallions in a mixture of the fish sauce and lime juice for 20 minutes.

Meanwhile, make the paste by crushing the ingredients with a mortar and pestle until smooth.

Heat the oil in a wok or frying pan and fry half of the pork medallions over moderate heat for 3 minutes, stirring often. Using a slotted spoon, transfer these to paper towels to drain. Repeat this process for the rest of the pork, and set aside.

Serves 4

There should still be enough oil in the pan for the next step (if not, add another tbsp). Heat the oil again over moderate heat, then stir-fry the shallots for 2 minutes. Reduce the heat to low, add the paste from the mortar, and stir for 2–3 minutes. Add $1^{1}/_{4}$ cups hot water, stir, and bring to a boil. Put in the mango and tamarind water. Simmer for 10 minutes or until the sauce is reduced by half. Adjust the seasoning, adding salt if needed and a few twists of the pepper mill.

**savory
and sour**

Return the pork to the wok and add the sliced bamboo shoots. Stir to mix, then continue cooking for 3–5 minutes or until everything is very hot. Serve immediately, with rice or noodles.

Kye thar hin Chicken curry with lime and tomatoes

This curry is very popular all over the region, perhaps because, although it is an authentic Burmese curry, it is not made with coconut milk or yogurt, but with tomatoes. If you have an abundance of tomatoes during the summer in your garden, use them. They must be very ripe, however, otherwise your curry will be just as good made with the best canned chopped plum tomatoes you can get.

INGREDIENTS

2 tbsp peanut oil
2 onions, finely chopped
2 garlic cloves, finely chopped
1 tsp ground turmeric
1 tbsp ground coriander
2 cinnamon sticks
4 cloves
1 stalk lemongrass, cut into 2 pieces
4 kaffir lime leaves
2 boneless chicken breasts, each cut in half
8 chicken thighs, boned

1 lb (450 g) ripe tomatoes, peeled and chopped, or 14 oz (400 g) canned chopped plum tomatoes, drained
juice of 2–3 limes
3 tbsp Balachaung (p170)
$^{1}/_{2}$ tsp cayenne pepper (optional)
1 tbsp fish sauce
1 tbsp toasted sesame oil
salt, if needed

METHOD

Preheat the oven to 325°F (160°C).

Pour the peanut oil into a large saucepan. Place over high heat and, when hot, stir-fry the onions and garlic for 2–3 minutes, stirring often. Add the turmeric, ground coriander, cinnamon, cloves, lemongrass, kaffir lime leaves, and chicken pieces. Stir-fry for 6–8 minutes or until the chicken pieces are slightly browned.

Add the tomatoes, lime juice, balachaung, cayenne pepper (if using), and fish sauce, stirring well. Cover the pan and simmer for 3 minutes. Uncover and stir in $^{1}/_{4}$ cup hot water and the sesame oil. Continue cooking, covered, over medium heat for 20 minutes.

Using a slotted spoon, transfer the chicken pieces to an ovenproof dish and place in the oven. Bake for 20–25 minutes.

Meanwhile, continue cooking the sauce for 4–6 minutes or until it has become thick and oily. Spoon out some of the oil and discard it, at the same time removing the solid seasonings (lime leaves, cinnamon sticks, and lemongrass). Taste and adjust the seasoning, adding salt if needed.

Take the chicken from the oven and pour the curry sauce over it. Serve hot, with plain boiled rice.

Serves 4–6

pungent,
citrusy, and
spicy

Rendang daging Beef rendang

This is a long-cooked stew, with the beef simmered for 2–3 hours in coconut milk. Most of the liquid boils away, and you are left with a thick, rich-tasting, spice-laden sauce, in which the meat is no longer boiling but frying. Eventually all the sauce is absorbed into the meat, which becomes moist, almost black, and very tender. In Malaysia, the meat is usually either beef or chicken, but the other ingredients differ from one state to the next. In some areas, tamarind water is added, in others spices like cinnamon, cumin, and cardamom are used. My own favorite recipe is that of my grandmother, in whose home in West Sumatra I grew up. The recipe here is from Trengganu. It is almost the same as my grandmother's but with an additional ingredient that we don't normally use in rendang, called *kerisik*.

INGREDIENTS

3 lb 3 oz (1.35 kg) boneless beef, preferably brisket or good stewing steak, cut into $^3/_4$-in (2-cm) cubes
2 quarts (liters) thick coconut milk, made from 2 coconuts (p213)
8 shallots or 2 onions, finely chopped
$^1/_2$-in (1-cm) piece galangal
3 kaffir lime leaves
1 tsp salt
1 stalk lemongrass, cut in half crosswise

1 turmeric leaf (optional)
$^1/_4$ cup *kerisik* (p164)

Paste
6 garlic cloves, chopped
6 large red chilies, seeded and chopped
1 tbsp chopped fresh ginger root
2 tsp chopped turmeric root or
   1 tsp ground turmeric

METHOD

To make the paste, blend together the garlic, chilies, ginger, and turmeric in a blender or food processor until smooth.

Put the beef into a large saucepan and add the coconut milk, shallots, galangal, lime leaves, salt, lemongrass, and the paste. Bring to a boil over medium heat. Stir once, then leave to bubble gently for $1^1/_2$–2 hours, stirring occasionally. Taste and add more salt, if necessary.

When the mixture is thick, continue cooking slowly, stirring constantly. Add the turmeric leaf (if using) and the *kerisik*. By now the meat will getting brown and very tender. Continue stirring for perhaps 20 more minutes.

Take out the piece of galangal and the leaves, and serve the rendang hot, with rice. In many parts of Malaysia, it is the custom to eat rendang with compressed rice (p166).

Serves 8–10

meaty, rich, and spicy

Daging masak merah Red curry of beef

You will find this curry on the menu of many Malaysian restaurants, a slightly different version each time. Mine is from Pontianak, a town in West Kalimantan (Indonesian Borneo) near the Malaysian border. This recipe differs from the original only in the quantity of red chilies: instead of 40, I use only four.

INGREDIENTS

2 tsp chopped fresh ginger root
2 tsp chopped turmeric root, or
    1 tsp ground turmeric
$\frac{1}{2}$ tsp coarse sea salt
1–1$\frac{1}{2}$ lb (500–600 g) rump or sirloin
    steak, cut into pieces (2 per person)
3 tbsp peanut oil
3 tbsp thick tamarind water (p322)
6 ripe red tomatoes, peeled and chopped,
    or 14 oz (400 g) canned chopped tomatoes,
    drained
1$\frac{1}{4}$ cups coconut cream (p213), heavy
    cream, or (my own choice) plain yogurt
handful each of mint leaves and cilantro
    leaves, roughly chopped

Red paste

3 shallots, chopped
6–8 garlic cloves, chopped
4 large red chilies, seeded and chopped
1 red pepper, seeded and chopped (optional)
$\frac{1}{4}$ cup tomato paste
4 candlenuts, roughly chopped, then roasted
    until slightly colored (optional)
2 tbsp peanut oil

To garnish

4 tbsp deep-fried shallots (p211)
2 oz (60 g) unsalted cashew nuts, fried in
    a little oil until browned
2 oz (60 g) raisins, fried briefly in a little
    oil until plump

METHOD

Grind the ginger, turmeric, and sea salt in a mortar to make a paste. Rub the pieces of beef all over with this paste, and set aside for at least 30 minutes before cooking.

To m_ _ the red paste, blend all the ingredients together with 3 tbsp water until smooth. Transfer _ _aste to a large saucepan and simmer over moderate heat for 6–8 minutes, stirring often. _ _ove from the heat and set aside.

_ the oil in a frying pan and fry the pieces of beef, a few at a time, for 2 minutes on each side, _ _ing them over once only. Set aside.

Reheat the paste in the saucepan for 2 minutes, stirring well, then add $\frac{1}{2}$ cup hot water and the tamarind water. Bring to a boil. Put in the beef, stir, and cover the pan. Continue cooking over moderate heat for 6–8 minutes.

Add the tomatoes and stir to mix with the beef. Cook for 3 more minutes. Now add the coconut milk, or cream or yogurt, and continue cooking, turning the beef over several times, until the sauce is well reduced. This will take only a few minutes. For the final minute of cooking, put in the mint and cilantro leaves.

Serve hot, with the garnish of fried shallots, cashews, and raisins sprinkled over all.

Serves 2–4

spicy and
savory

Laksa lemak Laksa with shrimp and tofu

The original meaning of the word *laksa* is fine rice noodles or rice vermicelli, but nowadays a *laksa* is a spicy soup made with coconut milk and whatever noodles you choose, plus chicken, fish, shrimp, scallops, and so on. *Lemak* literally means "fat," but it should be understood here as "rich, lavish, and delicious." This will make a substantial one-bowl meal; a smaller bowl could provide an appetizer for 8.

INGREDIENTS

1 block Chinese tofu, about 14–16 oz
  (400–450 g)
2–3 tbsp peanut oil
16 raw jumbo shrimp, heads removed,
  peeled, and deveined
1 tsp salt
1¼ quarts (liters) chicken or vegetable stock
1¼ cups thick coconut milk (p213)
8–12 oz (225–350 g) rice vermicelli, soaked
  in hot water in a covered bowl for
  5 minutes, then drained
4–6 oz (115–175 g) bean sprouts
2 hard-boiled eggs, quartered

Paste

1–2 large red chilies, chopped
2 shallots, chopped
1 garlic clove, chopped
2 candlenuts, chopped, or 1 tbsp ground almonds
1 tsp chopped fresh ginger root
1 tsp chopped galangal
1 tsp ground coriander
1 tsp sea salt
2 tbsp tamarind water (p322)
2 tbsp peanut oil

To garnish

2 tbsp chopped green onions
handful of flat-leaf parsley
2 tbsp deep-fried shallots (p211)

METHOD

First make the paste by blending the ingredients together until smooth. Transfer to a small pan and cook over moderate heat for 4 minutes, stirring. Remove from the heat and set aside.

Cut the tofu into quarters, then cut each quarter into quarters again (handle these carefully—they break easily). Heat the oil in a nonstick frying pan and fry the tofu pieces, turning them over several times, until they are just slightly colored. Drain on paper towels and set aside.

Rub the shrimp with the salt and set aside. Bring the stock to a boil in a large saucepan. Stir in the paste and boil for 2 minutes. Add the shrimp and cook for 2 minutes, then remove them with a slotted spoon and keep them aside in a bowl.

Pour the coconut milk into the stock and bring back to a boil. Simmer for 4–5 minutes while you distribute the noodles, shrimp, and tofu pieces equally among the bowls. Then distribute the bean sprouts and quartered hard-boiled eggs, putting these on top of the shrimp and tofu.

Adjust the seasoning of the soup, and bring it to a rolling boil, then ladle the boiling soup into the bowls. Garnish with the green onions, parsley, and crisp-fried shallots. Serve immediately.

Serves 4

rich and
spicy

Kari kepiting pedas Chili crab

This is my variation on a well-known Singaporean dish. I ate an excellent version a few years ago in the Courtyard Restaurant of the newly renovated Raffles Hotel, made with live crabs brought in from Sri Lanka. Live crabs are recommended for this recipe, although you can use frozen uncooked crab claws (not frozen cooked claws). If you plan to use live crabs, my advice is not to buy one weighing less than $4^1/_2$ lb (2 kg). Under that weight, a crab probably has very little meat in it.

INGREDIENTS

6–9 lb (3–4 kg) frozen uncooked crab claws, thawed in the refrigerator (this may take up to 36 hours)
$2^1/_2$ cups chicken stock or hot water
$^1/_2$ cup peanut oil

Curry paste

6 shallots, chopped
4 garlic cloves, chopped
1 tbsp chopped turmeric root, or
   1 tsp turmeric powder
2–4 red bird chilies, chopped
6 large, dried red chilies, soaked in hot water for 5 minutes, drained, and chopped
2 tbsp yellow bean paste
1 tsp salt
1 tsp sugar
1 tbsp peanut oil

Ginger and tomato sauce

6 large red chilies, seeded and thinly sliced diagonally
5 tsp grated fresh ginger root
1 lb (450 g) ripe red tomatoes, peeled and chopped, or 14 oz (400 g) canned chopped plum tomatoes, drained
1 tsp salt
1 tsp paprika (optional)
2 tbsp white malt vinegar, wine vinegar or cider vinegar

To finish

2 egg yolks, beaten
1 tbsp light soy sauce
4 green onions, cut into thin rounds

METHOD

To make the curry paste, blend all of the ingredients together in a blender or food processor until smooth. Transfer the paste to a saucepan and simmer for 5–8 minutes, stirring frequently with a wooden spoon. Remove from the heat and leave to cool.

Mix all the ingredients for the ginger and tomato sauce in a glass bowl and keep aside.

Serves 4

Wash the crab claws thoroughly under cold running water, then dry on paper towels. Crack each claw with a mallet.

Put the cooked curry paste into a large saucepan and add the chicken stock. Bring to a boil.

chili-hot and rich

Meanwhile, heat 2 tbsp of the oil in a wok and stir-fry the crab claws, in several batches, for 3 minutes per batch. Add more oil if necessary. As they are fried, drain the fried claws on paper towels.

When all the claws are fried, stir the curry sauce in the saucepan, increase the heat, and put in the crab claws, stirring so that every claw is well coated. With a slotted spoon, transfer the claws to a large heated platter, leaving some sauce in the pan.

Pour the egg yolks and soy sauce into the bowl containing the ginger and tomato sauce and mix well. Then pour this into the curry sauce in the saucepan. Cook over low heat, stirring constantly, until the sauce is hot and slightly thickened. Be careful not to scramble the egg.

Pour the curry sauce over the claws on the platter. Sprinkle with the chopped green onion and serve immediately. You should, of course, eat this with your fingers, so provide finger bowls for everyone, plus French bread to soak up the sauce. I like to eat this curry with plain boiled white rice or with compressed rice (p166).

Gulai kepala ikan Fish head curry

On my first visit to Kuala Lumpur and Singapore, many years ago, I was instructed that whenever a curried fish is served whole, the most honored guest must receive the head. In his or her turn, this person must show great pleasure and acknowledge the privilege gracefully. There is not a great deal of meat on the fish head, but the cheeks and eyes are considered delicacies. If I were hosting such a party, I would make sure that the head is cut off with the neck and the shoulders, if fish can be said to have these. Joachin, my Singaporean friend who gave me this recipe, tells me that what is really good in this dish is the sauce, which penetrates both the fish and the vegetables, which are usually okra and eggplants. In West Sumatra, my grandmother used to put *pakis* (edible fern shoots) into her fish curry. If you cannot find fish curry powder, use a mixture of 1 tbsp ground coriander, 2 tsp ground cumin, 1 tsp ground turmeric, 1 tsp paprika, 1 tsp ground fennel seed, $^1/_2$ tsp freshly ground black pepper, and $^1/_4$ tsp chili powder.

INGREDIENTS
juice of $^1/_2$ lime (2–3 tsp)
$^1/_4$ tsp ground turmeric
$^1/_4$ tsp chili powder
1 tsp coarse sea salt
4 whole trout, with heads, $2^1/_4$–$2^3/_4$ lb
    (1–1.25 kg) in total
2 tbsp peanut oil
1 tsp cumin seeds
1 tsp fennel seeds
1 tsp black mustard seeds
4–6 curry leaves or kaffir lime leaves
2 large red chilies, seeded and
    sliced diagonally
8 small okra
8 apple eggplants or baby purple eggplants,
    cut into halves
6 ripe tomatoes, peeled and chopped

Curry sauce
6 garlic cloves, chopped
1 tbsp chopped fresh ginger root
3 tbsp peanut oil
6 shallots, finely sliced
3 tbsp fish curry powder
3–4 tbsp thick tamarind water (p322)
1 cup coconut milk (p213)
1 cup coconut cream (p213)
salt and pepper

Serves 4

sweet and sour

METHOD

Mix together the lime juice, turmeric, chili powder, and coarse salt. Rub the fish inside and out with this, then put them back in the refrigerator in a large bowl, covered with plastic wrap, until you are ready to cook.

Preheat the oven to 350°F (180°C). Arrange the fish in an ovenproof casserole dish or braising pan that will accommodate them tightly side by side.

To make the sauce, crush the garlic and ginger in a mortar until they are puréed and well mixed. Heat the oil in a wok or a large, shallow saucepan and fry the shallots, stirring often, until they are soft. Add the garlic and ginger and continue stirring, then add the fish curry powder. Stir in the tamarind water and coconut milk. Bring to a boil and let the sauce bubble gently for 15 minutes. Add the coconut cream and simmer for a further 10 minutes. Season with salt and pepper. (The sauce can be made ahead of time and refrigerated. If you do this, take it out of the refrigerator when you turn on your oven, and heat it for 5 minutes in a saucepan before pouring it over the fish.)

Pour half of the sauce over the fish in the casserole. Put it into the oven to cook for 25 minutes.

When the fish has been in the oven for about 15 minutes, start the vegetables. Heat the oil in another saucepan and, when it is hot, put in the cumin, fennel, and black mustard seeds. Stir until the seeds are popping, then add the curry leaves and the chilies. Keep stirring for a minute or so, then add $1/2$ cup hot water and $1/2$ tsp of salt. Bring to a boil. Add the okra and eggplants, cover, and cook for 4 minutes. Uncover the pan and put in the tomatoes. Continue cooking, uncovered, for 2 minutes, then adjust the seasoning, adding more salt if necessary.

Pour the rest of the curry sauce into the vegetable mixture. Stir gently to mix, then cook over high heat for 2–3 minutes.

Check to see if the fish are cooked. If they are, take the dish out of the oven. Place the curried vegetables on top of the fish and serve, with plain boiled rice or cold compressed rice (p166).

Ikan masak kuah belimbing Sour fish curry

Belimbing is the usual Malay word for carambola, also called star fruit, which is widely available in the West. However, the traditional souring agent in this fish curry is what in Indonesian is called *belimbing wuluh,* or *belimbing asam* in Malay. If you can get this, use 10–12 of the tiny fruits, thinly sliced. I've used *asam gelugur* (p163). Another alternative is 4 oz (115 g) thinly sliced unripe mango. My choice for this curry is a fresh halibut. Other suitable fish are pomfret, red snapper fillets, turbot fillets, or whole small trout.

INGREDIENTS

1/2 tsp sea salt
1/4 tsp ground turmeric
1 tsp lime juice
black pepper
4 good-sized halibut steaks, 6–9 oz
   (175–250 g) each
2 1/2 cups coconut cream (p213)
2 slices *asam gelugur*
1 stalk lemongrass, cut in half crosswise

Paste

6 shallots, chopped
4–6 large red chilies, seeded and chopped
2 tsp chopped turmeric root, or
   1/2 tsp ground turmeric
1 tsp coarse sea salt
2 tbsp peanut oil

METHOD

Mix together the sea salt, turmeric, lime juice, and a few twists of the pepper mill. Rub the fish with this mixture. Leave in a glass bowl in a cool place for 10 minutes or so.

Blend all the ingredients for the paste together with 2 tbsp water in a food processor or blender until smooth.

Put 3 tbsp of the coconut cream into a saucepan big enough to accommodate the fish. Heat over moderate heat until the oil comes to the top. Add the paste and cook, stirring, for 2–3 minutes. Put in the *asam gelugur* and stir, then add the lemongrass. Put in half of the remaining coconut cream, bring to a boil, and cook for 8 minutes or until the liquid has reduced by half.

Add the rest of the coconut cream and bring back to a boil, then add the fish steaks. Cook for 4–6 minutes, depending on the thickness of the fish.

Remove from heat. Adjust the seasoning, and take out the asam gelugur, if used, and the lemongrass. Cover the pan and leave the fish in the sauce for just another minute or two, then serve immediately with rice or noodles and a mixed green salad.

Serves 4

sweet and sour

Kelia itik Rich curry of duck

This is a West Sumatran dish. In Java, "duck" is *bebek*, but I use the Sumatran word *itik* here because this is the word for duck in Malaysia, where a variation of this dish is called Gulai Itik. Most Southeast Asians consider duck to be rather strong-smelling, so they cook it with plenty of garlic, or they use chicken instead— the chicken is simply chopped into ten pieces, and bones and all go into the pot. I prefer my duck with as few bones as possible—in fact, no bones at all—so I use boneless breasts. This dish will freeze well. Make sure that the sauce covers the duck when it is packed. To serve, thaw at room temperature for 2–3 hours, then put it into a pan or a wok and heat until the sauce is thick and hot.

INGREDIENTS
1 quart (liter) thick coconut milk, made
   from 2 fresh coconuts (p213), or
   3 cans (14 oz/400 g each) coconut milk
8–10 garlic cloves, chopped
4–6 large red chilies, seeded and chopped
1 tbsp chopped fresh ginger root
1 tbsp chopped turmeric root
2 tsp chopped galangal
6 shallots or 2 onions, finely chopped
3 kaffir lime leaves
1 stalk lemongrass, cut in half
4 duck breasts, skin and fat removed and each
   breast cut into 2 or 3 portions
1 tsp coarse sea salt

METHOD
If using canned coconut milk, heat it slowly in a large saucepan for 5 minutes or until the thick and thin parts of the "milk" are well mixed. Remove from the heat.

Put $1/4$ cup of the coconut milk into a blender and add the garlic, chilies, ginger, turmeric root, and galangal. Blend until smooth. Put this paste and the chopped shallots into the saucepan containing the rest of the coconut milk. Add the kaffir lime leaves, lemongrass, duck pieces, and salt.

Bring to a boil. Stir once, then leave to bubble gently over medium heat, without stirring, for at least 45 minutes. By this time the coconut milk will have become quite thick and oily. From this point on, you need to stir often, cooking until the sauce becomes really thick and very little oil is left on top of it. Taste and add more salt if needed. Serve hot, with rice.

Serves 4

garlicky,
rich, and
spicy

Bebek bumbu bali Duck breasts in Balinese spices

This recipe is an adaptation of a renowned traditional duck dish called Bebek Betutu. There are three reasons why I feel I can include it in a curry book. The first is that this was traditionally a long-cooked duck with a sauce, though the sauce was very much reduced because the duck was wrapped in a banana leaf and the meat absorbed much of it. Secondly, the spice paste, or *bumbu*, contained a long list of ingredients that would not be at all out of place in an Indian curry. And finally, this is an endangered recipe, like those of many traditional dishes. I hope that my modern version may help it to survive. Note that the duck breasts should be left to marinate in the refrigerator for at least 4 hours, and preferably overnight. The paste and marinade should be prepared a day in advance.

INGREDIENTS
2 cups thick coconut milk (p213),
   chicken stock, or water
6–8 duck breasts, with skin
1 lb (450 g) spinach leaves, finely shredded

Paste
6 shallots or 2 medium onions, chopped
4 garlic cloves, chopped
4–6 large red chilies, seeded and chopped,
   or 1 tsp chili powder
3 candlenuts or macadamia nuts, chopped,
   or 2 tbsp slivered almonds
1 tbsp coriander seeds
1 tsp cumin seeds
2 tsp chopped turmeric root, or
   1 tsp ground turmeric
1 small piece of shrimp paste (optional)
3 tbsp lime juice
1 tsp coarse sea salt

Spice mixture
3 cloves
2 green cardamoms
1-in (2.5-cm) cinnamon stick
1/4 tsp grated nutmeg
1/4 tsp black pepper
1/2-in (1-cm) piece galangal
1 stalk lemongrass, cut in half crosswise

Serves 6–8

**aromatic
and
savory**

METHOD

Blend all the ingredients for the paste together with $1/4$ cup water in a food processor or blender until smooth. Transfer the paste to a saucepan.

Combine all the ingredients for the spice mixture and add to the paste, stirring well to mix. Bring to a boil over medium and stir for 2 minutes.

Add about $1/4$ cup of the coconut milk, then continue cooking for 5–8 minutes, stirring often. Transfer to a large glass bowl and set aside to cool completely.

Score two deep incisions through the skin and fat of each duck breast (not cutting into the meat). Put the breasts into the cold spice mixture and turn each one once or twice to make sure it is well coated on all sides. Leave to marinate in the refrigerator for at least 4 hours, or overnight if possible.

There are two ways to cook the duck. To long-cook, preheat the oven to 325°F (160°C). Loosely wrap the duck breasts with half of the marinade in two layers of banana leaves or aluminum foil, making sure that the edges are tightly sealed. Cook in the oven for 30 minutes, then turn the heat down to 170°F (75°C) and cook for a further $1^1/2$–2 hours.

Alternatively, to short-cook the duck, preheat the oven to 400°F (200°C). Take the breasts out of the marinade and, with a knife or the side of a fork, scrape off all the marinade from the skin. Put the breasts, skin side up, on a rack in a roasting pan and roast for 25–30 minutes.

While the duck is cooking, take the lemongrass, cardamoms, cinnamon, and galangal out of the remaining marinade, then put 2–4 tbsp of the marinade, or the remaining half (depending on how strong you want the sauce to be), into a saucepan. Add the rest of the coconut milk. Bring to a boil and simmer for 10 minutes.

Add the spinach and continue cooking for 4–5 minutes. Adjust the seasoning and set aside until ready for use. Reheat for serving.

If you have long-cooked the duck breasts, skim off and discard the oil from the cooking juices, then mix the cooking juices into the spinach sauce. Cut each duck breast diagonally into several slices, and serve hot with the sauce and rice, potatoes, or pasta.

Gulai bagar West Sumatran mutton curry

In West Sumatra, this curry is made with a leg or shoulder of goat cooked on the bone, then cut up in big chunks, bones and all, for serving. I prefer to use a boned, rolled and tied shoulder of mutton, served in thick slices.

INGREDIENTS

1 boned shoulder of mutton, 3 lb (1.5 kg)
salt and pepper
6 tbsp freshly grated or desiccated coconut
1 tbsp coriander seeds
4–6 candlenuts, finely chopped, or
   3 oz (85 g) slivered almonds
3 tbsp peanut oil
8 shallots or 3 medium onions, finely sliced
2 tsp finely chopped fresh ginger root
4 large red chilies, seeded and finely
   chopped, or 1 tsp chili powder
4 garlic cloves, crushed

1 tsp ground turmeric
1 cinnamon stick
3 cardamom pods
2 cloves
$1/2$ tsp ground cumin
pinch of grated nutmeg
$1^1/4$ cups coconut milk (p213)
$1^1/4$ cups coconut cream (p213)
2 tbsp tamarind water (p322)
1 stalk lemongrass, cut into thirds
2 kaffir lime leaves
2 large purple eggplants, cut into large chunks

METHOD

Preheat the oven to 425°F (220°C). Rub the mutton joint with salt and pepper. Lay it on a rack in a roasting pan and roast for 20 minutes. Turn off the oven, but leave the meat inside.

In a frying pan, roast the coconut for 6 minutes over low heat, stirring constantly, until it turns brown. Add the coriander seeds and candlenuts and stir for 2 minutes. Transfer to a plate and cool, then process to a powder in a blender or food processor. Put back on the plate and set aside.

Heat the oil in a large saucepan and fry the shallots, ginger, chilies, and garlic for 3–4 minutes, stirring. Add the turmeric, cinnamon, cardamoms, cloves, cumin, nutmeg, and the powdered coconut mixture. Cook, stirring, for 2 more minutes. Pour in the coconut milk and bring to a boil. Simmer for 30 minutes. Put the mutton into the sauce, cover, and simmer for another 30 minutes.

Uncover the pan. Add the coconut cream, tamarind water, lemongrass, and kaffir lime leaves. Continue cooking, uncovered, over medium heat (the sauce should bubble gently) for 10–15 minutes longer, turning the mutton every 5 minutes or so. Taste and add more salt, if necessary.

By now the sauce will be quite thick. Take out the meat and leave it to rest on a plate or a wooden board for 10–15 minutes. Remove the cinnamon stick, cardamom, lemongrass, and leaves from the sauce. Put the eggplants into the sauce and cook them, on a high heat, for 8 minutes. Add a little hot water if you think the sauce is becoming too thick and is sticking to the bottom of the pan.

To serve, cut the meat into thick slices. Arrange these, with the eggplants, on hot serving plates and top with the sauce. Serve with plenty of rice.

Serves 4–6

rich and
spicy

Eating rice from banana leaves, Bali >

Udang asam pedas Hot and sour shrimp curry

This is one of the wide variety of shrimp curries that are popular all over Indonesia. There are hot and sour shrimp, shrimp *sambal goreng*, shrimp curry with potatoes, and many more cooked in coconut milk and tamarind. The hotness, of course, comes from chilies, so reduce the quantity of these if you prefer your food less hot. The sourness in this case comes from a combination of tamarind and tomatoes. There is no need to add any sugar, because the dish contains so much onion, and the tamarind itself is sweet as well as sour. For convenience, you can fry the shrimp and make the sauce ahead of time. Then, before serving, reheat the sauce and, when hot, add the shrimp to finish the cooking.

INGREDIENTS

12–16 raw jumbo shrimp or tiger shrimp, peeled, but last tail section left on, and deveined
1 tsp coarse sea salt
$1/2$ tsp ground turmeric
$1/2$ tsp chili powder
3 tbsp peanut oil

2–6 large green chilies, seeded and thinly sliced diagonally
1 tsp ground coriander
6–8 large, red and ripe tomatoes, peeled and chopped
3–4 tbsp tamarind water (p322)
salt

Sauce
3 tbsp peanut oil
3 large red onions, chopped
4 garlic cloves, finely sliced
1 tbsp finely chopped fresh ginger root

To garnish
chopped green onions
deep-fried shallots (p211)

METHOD

Rub the shrimp with the sea salt, turmeric, and chili powder, then set aside for 10–12 minutes. Heat the oil and, when hot, fry the shrimp, in two batches, for not more than 2 minutes per batch. They will not be fully cooked at this point. Drain on paper towels.

To make the sauce, heat the oil in a wok or large frying pan. Add the onions and fry, stirring often, for 8–10 minutes or until they are soft and just starting to color. Add the garlic, ginger, and chilies and stir-fry for a minute or so, then add the ground coriander and stir for another minute. Put in the chopped tomatoes and the tamarind water, stir them around, and cook over low heat for 3–4 more minutes. Adjust the seasoning.

Add the shrimp to the sauce and stir them around for 2 minutes or until hot and cooked through. Serve immediately, with the green onions and shallots scattered on top. As a main course dish, the accompaniment can be rice, noodles, or bread, with salad or plain cooked vegetables.

Serves 4

chili-hot
and sour

Gulé kambing Javanese lamb curry

This is a liquid stew, or a curry soup. When I was at school in central Java, this *gulé*, made with goat meat, was a treat that we bought at least twice a week from a street vendor whose stall was a block away from our house. For us, *gulé* was a one-bowl meal, with a small helping of boiled rice or compressed rice added to the piping-hot curry. You could also have rice noodles in your *gulé*.

INGREDIENTS

1 quart (liter) thick coconut milk (p213)
1 tbsp ground coriander
1 small stick of cinnamon, about 1¼ in (3 cm)
3 cloves
2 kaffir lime leaves
½-in (1-cm) piece galangal
1 stalk lemongrass, cut in half crosswise
3 tbsp tamarind water (p322)
salt and pepper
2¼ lb (1 kg) boneless lamb shoulder or leg, cut into 1-in (2.5-cm) cubes

1 bird chili, or ½ tsp cayenne pepper (optional)
4 garlic cloves, chopped
4 candlenuts, chopped, or 2 tbsp ground almonds
1 tbsp ground ginger
1 tbsp chopped turmeric root, or 1 tsp ground turmeric
2 tbsp peanut oil
1 tsp coarse sea salt

Paste

6–8 shallots or 2 onions, chopped
4–6 large red chilies, seeded and chopped, or 1 tsp chili powder

To garnish

2 tbsp deep-fried shallots (p211)
handful of chopped flat-leaf parsley

METHOD

First make the paste: put all the ingredients in a blender or food processor with 2 tbsp water and blend until smooth. Transfer the paste to a saucepan, bring to a boil over moderate heat, and simmer, stirring often, for 4–5 minutes. Add ¼ cup of the coconut milk and continue simmering and stirring for 4 minutes or until the oil from the coconut milk comes to the top.

Add the coriander, cinnamon, cloves, kaffir lime leaves, galangal, lemongrass, tamarind water, and salt and pepper to taste. Cook, stirring, for 2 minutes. Then add the lamb cubes and turn up the heat a little. Keep stirring with a wooden spoon until all the meat is coated with the spice paste. Stir in ¾ cup hot water. Cover the pan and continue cooking for 5–8 minutes. (The curry can be prepared to this point ahead of time; reheat before continuing.)

Pour in half of the remaining coconut milk and stir to mix. Bring to a boil, then leave to bubble gently for 10 minutes. Add the rest of the coconut milk, stir well, and bring back to a boil. Stir again, then cook for 2 more minutes so that the *gulé* is piping hot. Sprinkle with the shallots and parsley and serve immediately with rice or noodles.

Serves 4

aromatic and spicy

Adobong manok Chicken adobo

Although people in the Philippines prefer not to call *adobo* "curry," the sauce, when cooked, does closely resemble a curry sauce. (Note that this adobo is cooked with coconut milk.) My version of it adapts the traditional method and starts by cooking the chicken, whole, in vinegar; this gives the finished dish an attractive appearance.

INGREDIENTS

1 chicken, $2^{1}/_{2}$–3 lb (1.1–1.35 kg)
6–8 garlic cloves, finely chopped
1 cup sugar cane vinegar,
   white vinegar, or rice vinegar
1–2 kaffir lime leaves or bay leaves
$^{1}/_{2}$–1 tsp coarsely ground black pepper
   or chopped fresh red chilies

1 tsp salt
2 tbsp peanut oil
$^{1}/_{2}$–1 tsp ground turmeric
$^{1}/_{2}$–1 tsp paprika
$^{2}/_{3}$ cup coconut cream (p213)
2 tbsp light soy sauce

METHOD

Put the chicken into a large saucepan and add the garlic, vinegar, 1 quart (liter) water, the kaffir lime leaves, black pepper, and salt. Bring to a boil, then cover the pan, reduce the heat, and simmer for 30 minutes.

Transfer the chicken to a colander. Turn the heat up under the saucepan and boil the stock until it has reduced to half its original volume. This will take 20–25 minutes.

Heat the oil in another large saucepan, add the turmeric and paprika, and stir, then add about half the coconut cream. Put in the chicken, cover the pan, and simmer for 10 minutes. Uncover and pour in the reduced stock and the rest of the coconut cream. Bring back to a boil and leave to bubble gently for 15 minutes. Add the soy sauce and adjust the seasoning.

Take the chicken out of the pan and put it on a chopping board. Let it cool a little, while you continue to simmer the sauce. Then either cut the chicken into 4 equal portions, or carve it as you would carve a roast chicken, discarding the bones.

Arrange the chicken portions or slices on a heated serving plate and pour the sauce over them. Serve hot, with rice.

Serves 4–6

mild and
creamy

Adobong pusit Squid adobo

This is my adaptation of a recipe sent to me by my friend Pia Lim-Castillo in Manila. I like to serve this as a first course before a main course of, perhaps, a chicken curry or the Javanese lamb curry on p194. If you want to serve this *adobo* as a main course, offer a vegetable curry with it, and rice, bread, or a noodle salad.

INGREDIENTS

$1^1/_2$ lb (600 g) small squid, each 5–$6^1/_2$ in (12–16 cm) long, or 12–16 baby squid, cleaned and the tentacles and wings reserved for the stuffing

7 tbsp peanut oil

coarse sea salt

6 shallots, finely chopped

2 green chilies, seeded and thinly sliced diagonally

3 garlic cloves, chopped

2 kaffir lime leaves or bay leaves

6 ripe vine or plum tomatoes, peeled, partly seeded, and finely chopped

$3^1/_2$ oz (100 g) day-old bread, crust removed, soaked in water or milk and squeezed dry, or $^2/_3$ cup cooked rice

2 egg yolks, beaten

6 tbsp chopped flat-leaf parsley

$^1/_3$ cup rice vinegar or white wine vinegar

1 tsp sugar, if needed

METHOD

Dice the squid tentacles and wings into small cubes. Heat 2 tbsp of the oil in a wok or saucepan and stir-fry the chopped tentacles and wings for 2 minutes. Add a pinch of salt and remove from heat. Keep aside.

Heat 2 tbsp oil in another wok or saucepan and stir-fry the shallots, green chilies, and garlic for 2–3 minutes. Add the kaffir lime leaves and the chopped tomatoes. Simmer for 2 minutes. Season with a little salt, then remove from heat.

Using a slotted spoon, transfer half of this mixture to a bowl, leaving the cooking juices and leaves in the wok. Add the squid tentacles and wings to the bowl, being careful not to include the oil from the pan. Then add the bread or rice, egg yolks, and half the parsley. Mix well. Using a small spoon, fill the squid with this stuffing. Close the openings with wooden toothpicks or skewers.

Put the chili and tomato sauce back over low heat and add the vinegar. Simmer, without stirring, for 5 minutes. Add the rest of the parsley and a little water if the sauce looks too dry. Remove from heat. Taste the sauce and add the sugar, if necessary.

Heat the remaining 3 tbsp oil in a large flameproof dutch oven and carefully put in the stuffed squid. Cook until they are opaque all over, turning them once a minute. Pour in the vinegared sauce and turn the squid in this. Cover the pot and cook over medium heat for 10–12 minutes. Alternatively, you can cook in a preheated 300°F (150°C) oven for 30–60 minutes, depending on the size of the squid.

When cooked, remove the toothpicks from the squid. Serve whole or cut into thick slices, with the sauce spooned over the top.

Serves 4

sweet, sour, and savory

Karé-karé Braised oxtail with peanut sauce

We in Southeast Asia love variety meat, and oxtail is a favorite meat for soup. Sop Buntut (Indonesian oxtail soup) is a well-known and popular one-bowl meal served with rice or rice noodles. Karé-karé is a Philippines variation on the theme, using oxtail as the basis of a substantial main course. It is customary to serve it with two or three kinds of cooked vegetables, mixed with the peanut sauce. Filipinos also like to serve a chili-hot shrimp paste, which they call *guisadong bagoong alamang*, with this dish. My suggestion is to serve Karé-karé with the dried shrimp relish on p170.

INGREDIENTS

$^1/_4$ cup white vinegar

3–4$^1/_2$ lb (1.5–2 kg) oxtail, trimmed of excess fat and cut into segments 2$^1/_2$–3 in (6–8 cm) long

3 tbsp peanut oil

4 shallots, chopped

1 head of garlic, chopped (use less if preferred)

1 tsp shrimp paste

1 tsp coarse sea salt

1 tsp ground turmeric

1 tbsp black pepper

6–8 oz (175–225 g) yard-long beans, cut into 4-in (10-cm) pieces, or fine green beans

6–8 oz (175–225 g) white cabbage or Chinese cabbage, roughly sliced

6–8 oz (175–225 g) carrots, cut into thin rounds

1$^1/_4$ cups Sambal Kacang (p171)

METHOD

Add the vinegar to a bowl of water. Wash the oxtail pieces in this, then drain them in a colander and dry them with paper towels. Put the oxtail into a large saucepan and add enough cold water to cover. Bring to a boil and boil for 5 minutes. Drain the oxtail pieces.

In another saucepan, heat the oil over medium heat and fry the shallots, stirring often, until they start to color. Add the oxtail and stir the pieces around in the oil for a few minutes.

Crush the garlic, shrimp paste, and coarse salt together in a mortar, then add to the pan with the turmeric and pepper. Stir well, then add just enough cold water to cover the meat. Bring to a boil, then reduce the heat a little and cover the pan. Simmer for 2–2$^1/_2$ hours or until the meat is tender and the sauce quite thick. Skim every half hour or so during the simmering, and add a little hot water when the cooking liquid gets too low.

Remove the oxtail from the pan and transfer to an ovenproof serving dish; keep warm in a warm oven. Turn the heat under the saucepan to high and bring the cooking juices to a boil. Cook uncovered for 5–10 minutes or until reduced by half.

At the same time, cook the vegetables in boiling water for 3–4 minutes or until tender; drain. Arrange the cooked vegetables on top of the oxtail. Keep hot.

Stir the Sambal Kacang into the reduced cooking juices. Add $^1/_2$ cup hot water if the sauce is too thick. Heat until very hot, then pour all over the vegetables. Serve immediately, with rice.

Serves 4–6

nutty, garlicky, and rich

THAILAND

< A fish market, Bangkok

THAILAND

Thai food is one of the world's great cuisines. It has fine traditions and intricate culinary practices, great regional diversity and a vast array of ingredients. Together these combine to produce the most wonderful cooking. Thailand has a venerable past that stretches back to the arrival of the Thais on the plains of ancient Siam. During the ensuing thousand years, a remarkable cuisine evolved with a complex repertoire that reflects the ornate and sophisticated culture of the people.

Although Thailand is quite a small country, it has many distinct styles of cooking: royal and peasant food, street cooking and the diverse cuisines of the four major regions. The food of the court of Thailand is the most elegant, though sadly now almost extinct. It delights in unusual combinations with surprising textures and enticing perfumes, such as a red curry of shredded beef with orange blossoms accompanied by a dish of sweet and salty clams. Peasant food, on the other hand, is robustly flavored, firmly rooted in the land, and prepared with rudimentary techniques. A pungent curry of shrimp paste with shallots and chilies, with fish and local seasonal vegetables added, is perhaps the most common of peasant-style curries. But whatever the curry, rice is always served with it.

Rice is of fundamental importance to the Thais and their cooking. Its cultivation has transformed the countryside from impenetrable and uninhabited forests to verdant expanses of rice paddies feeding an increasing population. Its crucial role is reflected at the table. Rice is most often cooked with elemental simplicity, boiled or steamed, plain and unseasoned, although some cooks enhance its natural perfume by adding pandanus leaf. Normally, a selection of dishes arrives with the rice. While each and every dish shares the same importance as any other in the meal, they are merely accompaniments to rice.

Curries are perhaps the most familiar of Thai dishes, and many people will have eaten such standards as a red or green curry from the central plains. But the rich traditions make for a huge range of styles. From village to village, house to house and, of course, region to region, all have their own preferred type of curry. It can be made with coconut cream, a light stock, or even just with water, and the paste can be fried, grilled, steamed, or simply dissolved in simmering liquid. Almost all are seasoned with fish sauce, but some have the addition of palm sugar, tamarind, and, of course, chili to help lift it from the ordinary to the memorable. This is what makes Thai food so good: the interplay of textures and seasonings to create a deft balance of sweet, sour, salty, and hot tastes in each dish and every meal.

In every marketplace, there is always a section where prepared food is sold, and among these stands are those that specialize in curries. Some offer the curry paste already prepared—a boon that a Westerner can only dream of. Others, called *raan kao geng* in Thai, sell curries complete and ready to go. Up to 20 different varieties may be available. The national favorites are there, of course—sour orange, green, and red curries—as well as mussaman and aromatic curries and the more unusual local specialties.

There are four main regional styles of cooking, with a great many more variations in each area. The north of the country is mountainous and misty, and has a gentler style of cooking that seems to reflect the comparatively milder climate. Freshwater fish and pork are heavily used, as are uncultivated vegetables and wild mushrooms collected from nearby forests. Pork curry with shredded ginger, pickled garlic, and cardamom is a firm favorite.

The northeast is the poorest and most remote of the regions. The food here is extremely spicy and uses many fermented or preserved products, especially fermented fish in all its forms. A pork and mustard green curry is a typical dish. In both of the northern regions, the preference is for glutinous or sticky rice. Coconut cream is not much used, because at certain times of the year it becomes too cold for the coconut tree to grow well here.

The central plains are the heartland, dominating the country both politically and economically. Bangkok is at its center. The style of cooking here is the most familiar to non-Thais: a green curry of chicken, for instance, or red curries of many kinds. The south of the country winds sinuously around the Gulf of Thailand, so naturally this region's food is based on seafood. Shrimp, crabs, and fish are grilled or fried, and curries here are redolent of turmeric, coconut, and chilies.

Recipes have been honed, over generations, to ensure a harmonious balance. The recipes that follow are only a small selection from the huge repertoire of Thai curries, but they reflect the diversity, complexity, and elegance of this wonderful cuisine.

David Thompson

Frying the curry paste >
Simmer in cracked coconut cream until fragrant

The Taste of Thailand

1. Thai basil leaves
2. holy basil leaves
3. dried bay leaves
4. turmeric root
5. galangal
6. kaffir lime
7. kaffir lime leaves
8. wild ginger
9. cilantro stalks and root
10. lemongrass
11. garlic
12. fresh green bird chilies
13. dried red Thai chilies
14. dried large red chilies
15. cinnamon sticks
16. white cardamom
17. star anise
18. palm sugar
19. coriander seeds
20. cumin seeds
21. shrimp paste
22. tamarind
23. apple eggplant
24. heart of coconut
25. long green eggplant
26. pea eggplants
27. fresh green peppercorns

The raw materials

In the markets of Thailand, row after row of stands sell tempting produce along with inviting prepared curries of all kinds. Here is a brief description of the ingredients used in most curry pastes, in the order of addition if using a mortar and pestle, followed by the seasoning ingredients added to balance the hot, sweet, salty, and sour flavors, and vegetables, herbs, and other aromatics used as garnishes.

CURRY PASTE

Salt
This acts as an abrasive to help break down the other ingredients. It also seasons the curry paste and acts as a preservative to delay any fermentation that might develop during storage.

Chilies
Dried large, red chilies, which are fruity and hot, are most common in red curries; when fresh, large chilies (red or green) are only occasionally used in curry pastes. If large chilies are called for, it is best to remove the seeds and the surrounding membrane, which contains much of the heat. Then soak dried chilies in lightly salted water to remove yet more of the heat and to soften them. This means more chilies can be used without increasing the heat to lethal levels and gives a deeper, more substantial chili flavor to the paste. When small chilies are specified, either fresh or dried, the seeds and membranes are normally not removed. Those most often used are the very hot, fresh, green bird's-eye or bird chilies (what I like to call "scuds").

Galangal
Slightly older galangal is the best to use, because it has a stronger, more peppery taste than young galangal. It brings a sharp, almost medicinal quality to the paste, but use too much and the paste will be bitter. Peel the rhizome well and dice finely before pounding.

Lemongrass
This imparts a citrusy, floral perfume. The outer leaves, the top third, and the hard root need to be discarded before finely slicing the remainder. Prepare just before use, as its perfume dissipates quickly. Too much lemongrass makes a paste taste oily and bitter; too little and the paste has a metallic aftertaste.

< **Kaffir lime**

Wild ginger (grachai) >

Kaffir lime

Only the outer, green zest should be used—the white, fleshy pith is unrelentingly bitter—and it should be freshly grated, because the aroma—kaffir lime's essential role in a curry paste—dissipates quickly. A fresh kaffir lime is best, of course, but the frozen fruit can be used quite satisfactorily. Grate off the zest while the fruit is still frozen, because once thawed it becomes too soft. Too much lime zest in a curry paste will make it soapy and slightly bitter.

Although dried kaffir lime zest is available, the aromatic oils are so desiccated as to make it a worthless addition. If only dry is available, omit completely.

Cilantro root

The lingering herbaceous taste of cilantro root gives length to a curry's flavor. Before use, clean the root well, trim off the fuzzy strands at the bottom, and cut off most of the green stalk. Scrape or peel off the skin, then soak the root in water to dislodge any dirt that might still be lurking. Chop the root finely before pounding with the other ingredients.

Red turmeric

Fresh red turmeric is used mainly in curries from southern Thailand, although it also makes an appearance in a green curry paste to enliven the color. Although ground dried turmeric can be substituted, it must be used with caution—one-third of the quantity of fresh peeled root. Red turmeric has an agreeable mustiness that becomes bitter if too much is used.

Wild ginger

Also called Chinese keys, wild ginger (*grachai*) is a pencil-like rhizome. Its earthy heat is used to counteract the muddiness of freshwater fish and bloodiness of game. It is most used in jungle curries. Peel and trim before use.

Red shallots

Small red shallots are one of the most common ingredients used in Thai cooking, and they give a curry paste substance and sharp pungency. Although onions can be substituted, they are much stronger than shallots, so if using, reduce the amount slightly.

Garlic

Thai garlic has smaller cloves, and is sweeter and less pungent than Western garlic, although, of course, these larger cloves can be used instead. Garlic is an essential component in a curry paste, giving a rich sweetness to the flavor. It is good practice to remove the green germ, if any, which can give the curry a slightly bitter aftertaste.

Shrimp paste

Thai shrimp paste (*gapi*) is the soul of Thai food. It is made by fermenting small shrimp with salt—an unpromising start for a delicious result. The best quality varieties are rich and earthy. Sadly, the more common commercial versions are salty and can be acrid. Shrimp paste should be used carefully, as too much will smother the curry, making it murky and heavy, while too little will mean a curry without depth.

Spices

Most Thai curry pastes use very few dried spices—just enough to imbue the paste with aroma. The spices most employed are white peppercorns, Thai coriander seeds, and cumin seeds, with cassia bark, white cardamom, and star anise added occasionally. A large amount of spice usually indicates a Muslim origin for the dish. All dried spices should be roasted individually before being ground and then sifted (p322).

SEASONINGS

Sugar

Whether palm sugar or white sugar, this has always been a component of the Thai seasoning spectrum. White sugar imparts a simple, clear sweetness. It is most often used in boiled curries and in curries fried in oil. Palm sugar is richer and rounder in taste and gives body to a curry. It is most often used in curries where the paste is cooked in cracked coconut cream.

Tamarind

Tamarind water is the most common souring agent in Thai curries. It is best made fresh, using 1 part tamarind pulp to 2 parts water (p322). Take care after adding tamarind water to a curry as it can scorch quite easily.

Fish sauce

This salty seasoning is made by fermenting fish with salt in water. From such a dubious start comes one of the staples of Southeast Asia. Fish sauce (*nam pla*) should always be added last as it is the most pervasive seasoning and the most difficult to adjust if too much is used.

GARNISHES

Heart of coconut

This is the crunchy, nutty shoot of the coconut. It is ideal to use in curries where its texture poses a pleasing contrast. If cooked, this is done quite briefly. Before use, wash and then peel away any yellowing areas. The meat from a young green coconut is a possible alternative to heart of coconut.

Thai bay leaves

These dried leaves are only used in a mussaman curry, where their musty, spicy taste enhances the cardamom and peanuts. Bay leaves will make an almost undetectable alternative.

Thai basil

While Thai basil appears to be quite similar to European basil, it is very different: it has a pronounced anise taste. The leaves are usually added just before the curry is served so their aroma is at its best. Thai basil is used in many curries from the central plains, especially red and green curries.

Holy basil

The somewhat pointed, purple-tinged leaves of holy basil have a surprisingly clovelike intensity when very fresh. This volatile aroma dissipates quickly as the herb loses its freshness or is subjected to heat, so add just before serving. Once holy basil was used in many curries from the central plains, but now it is mainly reserved for jungle curries.

Eggplants

There are many kinds of eggplants used in Thai cooking, but perhaps the three most common are the pea, apple, and long green varieties. The little pea eggplant grows in clusters and should be picked from the stalk before being washed and added to a curry. It imparts a pleasing

bitterness. Apple eggplant has a less pronounced flavor and is mainly used for its texture. Top and slice just before adding to a curry, otherwise it will oxidize and the once-white flesh will develop an unsightly black-mottled tone. Some Thai cooks steep the sliced eggplant in salted water to delay this, but it can then take on too much salt. The long green eggplant needs to be cooked and tender to eat it at its best. Once sliced and simmered, it is rich and silken in both taste and texture.

Peppercorns

The peppercorn is indigenous to this region and was the main spicing component before the arrival of the chili in the 16th century. Thais use three types of peppercorns: green, white, and black. Green peppercorns are the fresh berries, simply washed and perhaps stemmed before use. White peppercorns are soaked in brine, then rubbed to remove the skin so that only the spicy kernel is dried. Black peppercorns retain the skin, which blackens as the berry dries.

Green peppercorns are mainly used as a finishing garnish in jungle curries but are rarely, if ever, used in a curry paste itself, whereas dried and processed pepper is an important spice in almost every curry paste. White pepper is used mostly in curries from the central plains, black pepper in curries from the south and those of Muslim origin.

Kaffir lime leaves

The verdant and aromatic leaves of the kaffir lime are normally added as a final garnish to a curry after it is cooked. Their perfume helps to cover any bitter or muddy flavors. When adding, crush the leaves slightly to help to release their fragrance. Frozen kaffir lime leaves have little of the characteristic smell, while dried leaves have none.

Deep-fried shallots

These are an important garnish in Thai cooking. Although they can be bought, it is much better to fry your own. Cut peeled shallots lengthwise into very thin, even slices, then deep-fry in hot oil, stirring constantly with tongs. As the shallots begin to color, they will lose their onionlike aroma and begin to smell enticingly nutty. When they become quite golden, remove from the oil and spread out on paper towels to drain. They will crisp as they cool. Deep-fried shallots will keep for 2 days in an airtight container.

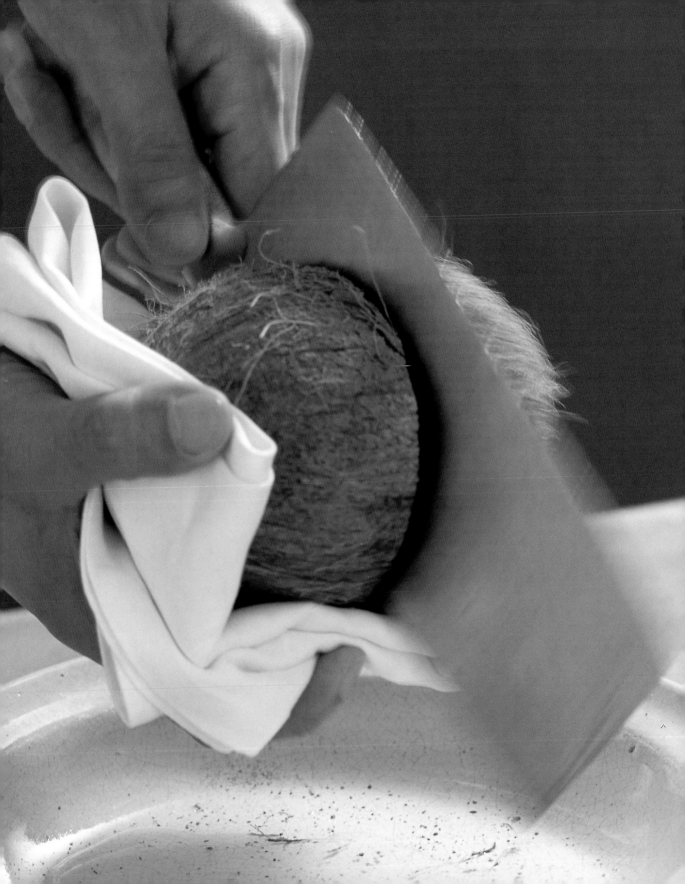

Coconut milk and cream

The taste of fresh coconut cream is incomparably luscious, with a complexity and depth of flavor that justifies the labor required to produce it. Both coconut milk and cream are best used within a few hours. They can be refrigerated for 1–2 days, but will harden and become difficult to use. One Thai trick worth trying is to add a bruised chili to retard the hardening.

Step 1
Use the back (blunt) side of a cleaver or a light hammer to split open the coconut, hitting it all the way around. Score the flesh or cut it into segments, to make it easier to pry from the shell. Peel away and discard the brown inner skin, then chop the flesh and blend in a food processor with an equal amount of hot water.

Step 2
*Pour the coconut mixture into a piece of muslin—or a very clean dish towel—draped over a glass, china, or plastic bowl (metal taints the cream). Gather up the cloth and squeeze the flesh to extract the liquid. If a recipe calls for **thick coconut milk**, use immediately, before separation occurs (see below).*

Step 2

Step 3
*For **coconut cream,** leave for at least 20 minutes. The cream is the thicker, opaque liquid that separates and floats on top of the thinner liquid, which is called **coconut milk** in the recipes in the book. No matter how much water is added when blending the coconut flesh, the yield of cream will always be the same. Normally one good coconut yields about 1 cup of coconut cream. Often the squeezing process is repeated, but this second pressing will yield more coconut milk than cream.*

"CRACKED" COCONUT CREAM
Curries that are fried in coconut cream often call for the cream to be "cracked," or separated. To do this, simmer the cream until most of the water evaporates. The cream then separates into thin oil and milk solids. Once cracked, coconut cream lasts for several weeks—longer if frozen. The separated oil can also be used for deep-frying, and the solids are sometimes used in desserts when a weighty sumptuousness is required.

Step 3

< Step 1

Cooking Thai curries

The Thai word for curry, *geng*, has a much looser meaning than its English equivalent. In its widest sense it means a liquid seasoned with a paste and can include soups and braised dishes, but when the paste is spicy it comes closer to our understanding of the word. At its most basic, then, a curry can be a simple paste of chilies, red shallots, and shrimp paste dissolved in simmering seasoned stock or water, quite similar to the sour orange curry on p222. This is the most common and probably most popular type of curry in the Kingdom. From this, curries become increasingly complex, reaching the harmonious intricacy of a mussaman curry, where up to 20 ingredients go into the paste, not to mention the subsequent seasoning, meat, and garnishes.

There are three main parts to making a Thai curry: preparing the paste, cooking and seasoning the paste, and adding garnishes, such as herbs, aromatics, and meat, fish, and so on.

Preparing the curry paste

While making a curry paste in a blender or food processor is undoubtedly more convenient, purists believe that the best paste is made by hand, using a mortar and pestle (p217). The larger the mortar, the more practical, since it allows for easier, quicker production of a fine paste.

However it is made, a good-quality paste is one where the original, often rough initial state is reduced to a fine purée. To ensure this, each ingredient should be pulverized completely before the next is added. The normal order is the hardest, most fibrous ingredients first, the softer ones last.

All the ingredients must be prepared in advance. This means that most ingredients need to be washed, peeled, and chopped prior to adding to the mortar. The more finely chopped, the less time required to reduce the ingredient to a pulp. Perhaps this is rather obvious, but it is certainly a welcome relief when actually pounding.

Cooking the paste

There are two methods for cooking the paste. The simplest and oldest is to dissolve it in simmering seasoned liquid, be it water, stock, or, in southern Thailand, coconut milk. After this, the "boiled curry" is seasoned, usually with fish sauce and tamarind water. Sometimes a pinch of white sugar is added to balance the tartness.

The alternative method is to fry the paste. Depending on the style of curry and the region, frying is done either in oil (some older recipes use rendered pork fat) or in cracked coconut cream (p213). With oil, the paste is fried over searingly high heat for just a minute or two, until it smells piercingly aromatic. Pastes cooked in oil are mostly seasoned with fish sauce, rarely with sugar, and are then moistened with stock. This forms the basis of "jungle" curries and many other curries from the north and northeast of the country, where coconuts are less common.

More familiar are curries based on coconut, where the paste is fried in coconut cream that has been simmered until the oil begins to separate out ("cracked"). The frying takes quite a long time—up to 5 minutes over moderate heat, stirring regularly. The aroma develops and deepens, conveying the changes in the paste as it cooks. The longer the cooking, the more mellow the flavor becomes as the disparate elements become unified.

Seasoning

Seasoning transforms the curry paste—it is this process that so distinguishes Thai food. Thai cooking is a deft balance of hot, sweet, salty, and sour. Most curries are salty, some are also sweet, many can be sour as well, and a few have all these elements. Wise cooks refrain from complete seasoning at this stage, since it removes the possibility of a final adjustment just before serving. After the seasoning process, the curry is moistened with either stock or coconut milk and then simmered gently for a few minutes to incorporate all the components.

Adding the garnishes

The third stage is where the garnishes are added. To the Western sensibility, this defines a curry, but to a Thai it is just one element in a complex dish. Garnishing is quite straightforward with a boiled curry, since it is usually only made with fish or seafood cut up into bite-sized pieces that cook quickly. Any vegetables, fresh herbs, and other aromatic garnishes are added in order of the time it takes to cook them.

With a fried curry, the meat is cut into very small pieces to allow for an easy and equal share for all, as well as to ensure that tough meat will become tender. Then the aromatic garnishes are added, usually including kaffir lime leaves, fresh chilies, and picked herbs such as holy, Thai, or lemon basil. Once garnishing is completed, the curry is left to rest for a minute or so, to allow the flavors to mingle and mellow. Then the seasoning is checked one more time so any final adjustments can be made before serving.

Making a Thai curry is a complex process in which the layers of taste are finely poised and the seasonings finely balanced: it is as sophisticated as Thai culture itself.

Kreaung geng geng gwio warn Green curry paste

Some of the paste recipes in the curries in this chapter make more paste than is needed for the individual dish. This is because when making a paste, either using a mortar and pestle or a blender, a certain volume is required before the ingredients will purée successfully. Leftover paste can be stored for up to 2 weeks in the refrigerator: put it in an airtight container, pressing plastic wrap against the surface of the paste before closing the top.

INGREDIENTS

1 heaped tbsp bird's-eye chilies
1–2 long green chilies, deseeded
pinch of salt
1 rounded tbsp chopped galangal
2^1/$_2$ tbsp chopped lemongrass
1 tsp chopped kaffir lime zest
2 tsp chopped cilantro root
2 tsp chopped red turmeric

1 rounded tbsp chopped wild ginger
2^1/$_2$ tbsp chopped red shallots
2^1/$_2$ tbsp chopped garlic
1 tsp Thai shrimp paste
1 tsp white peppercorns
1 tsp roasted coriander seeds
a few blades of mace, roasted (optional)

METHOD

Step 1
Pound the fresh ingredients with a mortar and pestle, adding them one at a time and starting with the hardest, driest, and most difficult (which is always the chilies), and working through to the softest and wettest. (In recipes where dried chilies are used, they are often soaked first; this means they are no longer the driest or hardest, but they are still pounded first.) Follow the order of ingredients as listed. Reduce each ingredient to a pulp before adding the next.

Step 2
Grind the peppercorns, coriander seeds, and mace, if using, then sift to be sure the powder is fine. Combine the spices with the rest of the ingredients in the mortar and pestle.

Step 2

USING A BLENDER

Put all the ingredients into the blender at once and blend to a paste, adding a little water to facilitate the blending. Stop the machine and scrape down the sides of the jar from time to time. Take care not to overwork the paste—3–4 minutes should be sufficient.

 Step 1

Kao suay Steamed jasmine rice

Most Asian cooks now use electric rice cookers, which make perfectly cooked rice simple and almost foolproof. However, you need to be careful not to overfill the cooker: one-third full is enough. Any more and the rice might cook unevenly. Below is the method for cooking rice in the traditional way.

INGREDIENTS

jasmine rice
water
pandanus leaf (optional)

METHOD

Wash the rice in cold water, carefully combing your hands through the rice grains in the water to remove any husks and excess starch and dust that aided in polishing the grains. With cupped hands, gently rub the grains together. Drain and repeat two or three times until the water is clear. This washing prevents gloopy rice.

Put the rice in a heavy pot—tall rather than wide for small amounts, but the converse for larger amounts—and cover with cold water. Traditionally, the water level should be about an index-finger joint above the rice. Surprisingly, this joint is almost always the same length! For the less traditional, the proportions of approximately $2^1/_2$ cups of rice to $3^1/_2$ cups of water will give you plenty of rice for 4 people. Significantly, the rice is not seasoned with salt—the accompanying dishes are sufficiently seasoned.

Cover the pot with a tightly fitting lid and bring quickly to a boil, then turn the heat down very low and cook for 10–15 minutes. Do not stir rice during cooking, because this breaks down the grains, releasing starch and making the rice gloopy.

Remove from heat and allow the rice to rest for 10 minutes or so—it will remain quite warm for 30 minutes, covered in the pot. A pandanus leaf is sometimes added after the rice is cooked, while it rests, to enhance its perfume.

If the rice on top is dry at the end of cooking, sprinkle with a little warm water and cover with a piece of banana leaf or parchment paper. Return to low heat for a few minutes, and the top rice should be cooked and moist.

Geng guwa pla dtaeng Coconut and turmeric curry of red snapper

Most southern curries are rich with coconut cream, and this curry should be hot, salty, and a little tart. It is important that the cream does not separate but forms a smooth emulsion with the paste. Naturally, almost any seafood can be used in place of the snapper. I find crab is an especially good alternative. Serve with slices of cucumber, sprigs of mint and cilantro, grilled shrimp, and rice.

INGREDIENTS

2 cups coconut milk (p213)
1 cup light chicken stock or water
2 stalks lemongrass, bruised
white sugar
$1/4$ cup tamarind water (p322)
$1/4$ cup fish sauce, or to taste
7-oz (200-g) red snapper fillet or 14-oz (400-g)
 whole red snapper, gutted and scaled
handful of torn betel leaves (optional)
$1/2$ cup coconut cream (p213)
5 kaffir lime leaves, finely shredded

Curry paste

6 dried long red chilies, soaked and chopped
3–4 dried small red chilies
pinch of salt
a few bird's-eye chilies
$1^3/4$ oz (50 g) chopped lemongrass
$1/4$ cup chopped red shallots
$2^1/2$ tbsp chopped garlic
1 rounded tbsp chopped red turmeric
1 rounded tbsp Thai shrimp paste

Serves 4

salty and
sour

METHOD

First, make the curry paste (p217).

Combine the coconut milk with the stock in a saucepan, add the lemongrass, and bring to a boil. Season with a little sugar, the tamarind water and fish sauce, and add 4 tbsp curry paste. Simmer for a minute before adding the fish and betel leaves. Continue to simmer until the fish is cooked.

Adjust the seasoning, then finish by stirring in the coconut cream. Serve sprinkled with the shredded kaffir lime leaves.

Geng som plaa ling maa Sour orange curry of brill and Asian greens

This is perhaps the most common of all Thai curries—certainly in the central plains. In every marketplace you will see pots of prepared boiled curries made with all manner of ingredients. It is extremely versatile: almost any seafood or freshwater fish can used and many alternative vegetables can be added, such as Siamese watercress, *cha-om*, or green onions. Traditionally, it is served with pickled ginger, salted beef, steamed eggs, and, of course, rice.

INGREDIENTS

2 cups light chicken stock or water
pinch of salt
9 oz (250 g) brill, turbot, sea bass, barramundi, or whiting fillets, cut into elegant lozenges (keep the trimmings)
1 bunch of *choy sum* or other Asian greens, trimmed into $1\frac{1}{4}$-in (3-cm) lengths
$2\frac{1}{2}$–4 tbsp tamarind water (p322), as needed and to taste
pinch of white sugar (optional)
$2\frac{1}{2}$ tbsp fish sauce, or more to taste
pinch of chili powder (optional)
a few deep-fried or roasted, dried small or long red chilies (optional)

Sour orange curry paste

3–4 dried long red chilies, soaked and chopped
2–3 dried small red chilies (optional)
1–2 bird's-eye chilies (optional)
pinch of salt
$\frac{1}{4}$ cup chopped red shallots
2 tsp chopped cilantro root
1 rounded tbsp Thai shrimp paste

METHOD

First, make the curry paste (p217).

Bring the chicken stock and salt to a boil over medium heat. Reduce the heat to low, add some of the fish trimmings, and poach for 5 minutes. Remove with a slotted spoon, draining well, and allow to cool, then pound to a fine paste with a mortar and pestle. Keep the poaching liquid.

Combine 1 heaped tbsp of the pounded fish paste with $2\frac{1}{2}$ tbsp of the curry paste.

Strain the stock and return to the saucepan. Bring back to a boil, then add the *choy sum*. Reduce the heat to low and simmer for a few minutes or until quite tender. Season with tamarind water, sugar, and fish sauce.

Stir in the curry paste mixture, increase the heat to high, and boil for a minute or so. Then add the fish to the boiling curry, turn down the heat, and poach for 5–6 minutes or until cooked.

Add the deep-fried chilies. Check the seasoning and adjust as required, then serve.

Serves 4

thin, salty, sour, and hot

Krua gling neua Southern curry of chopped beef

This is quite possibly the hottest curry of them all—certainly in Thailand. It comes from the southern area around the ancient city of Nakorn Siri Thammarat. Although pork or chicken could be used, the most popular version is made with beef. Having a little of the fat attached prevents the meat from becoming too dry when cooking. However, this curry is not oily—it is in fact very dry, and it looks deceptively mild. As with most pungent curries from the south, a plate of raw vegetables and herbs makes a welcome and cooling accompaniment. In Thailand, local herbs such as mango shoots and cashew nut sprouts are eaten with it, but cucumber, snake beans, and apple eggplants are perhaps more likely candidates to soothe the palate of Western cooks.

INGREDIENTS
10 oz (300 g) boned beef brisket and blade
   with some fat attached
2 cups light chicken stock
   or water
pinch of salt
$1/4$ cup vegetable oil
$1^1/_2$–$2^1/_2$ tbsp fish sauce
palm sugar, to taste
5 kaffir lime leaves, shredded

Curry paste
1 cup dried small red chilies
20 bird's-eye chilies
pinch of salt
$1/2$ cup sliced lemongrass
$2^1/_2$ tbsp chopped galangal
2 tsp chopped kaffir lime zest
$1/2$ cup peeled red shallots
$1/2$ cup peeled garlic cloves
1 tsp chopped red turmeric
1 rounded tbsp mixed white and black
   peppercorns, ground
1 rounded tbsp Thai shrimp paste

METHOD
First, make the curry paste (p217).

Trim the beef and cut into roughly $1/4$-in (5-mm) pieces. Add to the stock with the salt and bring to a boil, then simmer until cooked. Drain the beef, reserving the braising stock.

Heat the oil and fry the curry paste for 5 minutes or until fragrant. Add the beef and continue frying for 10–15 minutes or until it is quite dry. The curry can be moistened with a little of the braising stock during frying, but it must be simmered until dry again.

Season with fish sauce and a little palm sugar. Serve sprinkled with the kaffir lime leaves.

Serves 4

dry, very
hot, and
salty

Bpuu pat pong garee Crab stir-fried with curry powder

Although not technically a curry, this easy street dish is eaten throughout the country and I thought its inclusion was justified by the use of curry powder. Most Thai cooks would use a prepared curry powder and, I must confess, it is one of the few instances where store-bought is better than homemade. While crab is the most common version of this dish, on the streets and along the beaches, shrimp, squid, and sea bass are also used. Serve with rice and, perhaps, a grilled fish or some stir-fried Chinese broccoli with oyster sauce.

INGREDIENTS

1 crab, about $2^{1}/_{4}$ lb (1 kg)
1 egg, lightly beaten
2 garlic cloves, peeled
equivalent amount peeled fresh ginger root
pinch of salt
$1^{2}/_{3}$ cups cracked coconut cream (p213)
$^{1}/_{4}$ cup curry powder
4 tsp fish sauce

smallest pinch of white sugar
4 tsp rice vinegar
$^{1}/_{2}$ cup coconut cream (p213)
$^{1}/_{2}$ cup coconut milk (p213)
1 small bunch of Asian celery, cleaned and cut into $^{3}/_{4}$-in (2-cm) lengths, about 1 oz (30 g)
$^{1}/_{2}$ small white onion, sliced
handful of chopped coriander leaves

METHOD

Kill the crab humanely (drowning in fresh water is probably the best, least stressful way for the creature). Clean by lifting off its carapace, scraping out but retaining any mustard and roe, and removing its tail and the "dead man's fingers." Rinse, then segment the crab into about 8 pieces, cracking the claws. Mix the mustard and roe with the beaten egg.

Using a pestle and mortar, pound the garlic, ginger, and salt into a rather coarse paste. Heat a wok, add the cracked coconut cream, and, when sizzling, add the paste.

As the paste mixture is just beginning to color, add the crab and fry for a few moments over moderate heat. Sprinkle in the curry powder. Continue to fry for a few more moments, stirring constantly. When fragrant, season with the fish sauce, sugar, and vinegar.

Enrich with the fresh, uncracked coconut cream and moisten with the coconut milk, stirring well to mix. Cover the wok and simmer until the crab is cooked, tossing and stirring the pieces of crab regularly to ensure that they cook evenly.

Remove the lid and turn up the heat, then stir in the egg and roe mixture. Stir until the egg has thickened and begun to separate.

Adjust the seasoning. Mix in the celery and sliced onion, then sprinkle with cilantro and serve.

Serves 4

aromatic, rich, and salty

Geng lao ubon rachtani
Northeastern curry of pork ribs and mustard greens

This curry comes from the northeast of the country. The dominant tastes are of *pla raa* (fermented fish), peppery mustard greens, the sweetness of the pork, and dill. Dill is quite a common culinary herb in this region, where it is called *pak chii lao* (Laotian parsley). The curry can be either very hot or mild, according to the cook's preference. Normally, however, it is searingly hot. The northeast is a poor area, and most food is pungently seasoned, because a meal consists mainly of rice with just a little curry mixed into it. There are many alternatives to pork. Since this is such a pungent curry, the choices should also be pungent. A rich freshwater fish like carp is ideal, or an eel. Duck or chicken chopped on the bone with their variety meats is another option. Rather than making fermented fish sauce, ordinary fish sauce can be used. However, much of the character of this curry would be lost and it would become indistinguishable from its central plains equivalents.

Serves 4

hot, salty, and aromatic

INGREDIENTS
2$\frac{1}{2}$ tbsp pork fat or oil, less if using pork belly
6 oz (150 g) boned pork belly or ribs, sliced
2 cups light chicken or pork stock or water
5 tbsp Nahm Pla Raa (opposite)
$\frac{1}{2}$ cup picked pea eggplants
1 cup mustard greens, shredded
1 cup (20 g) dill, coarsely chopped

Northeastern curry paste
10–15 dried red chilies, soaked and chopped
a few small dried red chilies
$\frac{1}{2}$ tsp salt
1 rounded tbsp chopped galangal
1 rounded tbsp chopped lemongrass
1 rounded tbsp chopped red shallots
1 rounded tbsp chopped garlic

METHOD

First, make the curry paste (p217).

Heat the fat or oil in a heavy pan or wok. Add 2^{1}/$_{2}$ tbsp of the curry paste and cook until fragrant. Add the pork and continue to fry over medium heat for several minutes as the pork begins to cook and the paste deepens in color. Moisten, if necessary, with a little stock to prevent the paste from sticking and burning.

Season with the *nahm pla raa* and cover with the remaining stock. Simmer gently until the pork is tender. Replenish with more stock if the curry becomes too dry during the cooking.

When the meat has cooked sufficiently, add the eggplants and mustard greens and simmer for a further 10 minutes or so, or until the vegetables are cooked. Finish with the dill.

Check the seasoning and adjust as preferred, then serve.

Nahm pla raa Fermented fish sauce

INGREDIENTS

3 stalks lemongrass
5 red shallots
3 cilantro roots, or a handful of cilantro stalks
7 oz (200 g) fermented fish (*pla raa*)
1 whole kaffir lime, or several kaffir lime leaves
10 slices galangal

METHOD

Bruise the lemongrass, shallots, and cilantro. Combine all the ingredients in a pot and cover with 2 cups water. Bring to a boil, then simmer for at least 10 minutes or until the fish has completely dissolved.

Strain and let cool. Refrigerated, the sauce keeps indefinitely. Store in an airtight container.

**Makes about
2 cups**

Geng bpaa gai Jungle curry of chicken with vegetables and peppercorns

A jungle curry is a country curry that is simple and robust in flavor and technique. Coconut cream is never, used but either a green or a red curry paste can be its base. This version is perhaps the most common; however, there are many variations, using frogs, game, freshwater fish, and shrimp as well as a myriad of vegetables reflecting the bounty of the local market. It can be served with pickled red shallots and dried fish or shrimp.

INGREDIENTS

7 oz (200 g) boneless chicken thigh
   or breast, skinned if preferred
2 apple eggplants
1^1/$_2$ tbsp vegetable oil
2^1/$_2$ tbsp fish sauce
1–1^1/$_4$ cups light chicken stock
2 heaped tbsp picked pea eggplants
2 heaped tbsp snake beans cut into
   ^{3}/$_4$-in (2-cm) lengths
3 baby corn, cut into small pieces
a little sliced boiled bamboo (optional)
3 stalks wild ginger, julienned
1 long green chili, thinly sliced at an angle
2 kaffir lime leaves, torn
handful of holy basil leaves
3 sprigs of fresh green peppercorns

Red jungle curry paste

10 dried red chilies, seeded, soaked,
   and chopped
3–4 dried small red chilies, soaked and chopped
a few bird's-eye chilies (optional)
good pinch of salt
2 tsp chopped galangal
2^1/$_2$ tbsp chopped lemongrass
1 rounded tbsp chopped wild ginger
1 tsp chopped cilantro root
1 tsp chopped kaffir lime zest
2^1/$_2$ tbsp chopped red shallots
2^1/$_2$ tbsp chopped garlic cloves
1 tsp Thai shrimp paste

Garlic and chili paste

2 garlic cloves, peeled
pinch of salt
3 stalks wild ginger
3–5 bird's-eye chilies

METHOD

Slice the chicken into pieces about ^{3}/$_4$ in (2 cm) long and ^{1}/$_4$ in (5 mm) thick. Remove the stems from the apple eggplants, then cut each one into sixths; keep in salted water to prevent discoloration.

Next, make the curry paste (p217). To make the garlic and chili paste, grind all the ingredients with a mortar and pestle. Heat the oil in a wok or heavy saucepan and, when very hot, add the garlic and chili paste. Fry over high heat until golden and almost starting to burn. Quickly add 2^1/$_2$ tbsp of the curry paste and continue to fry, stirring to prevent scorching, until explosively fragrant.

Season with the fish sauce, then add the stock and bring to a boil. Add the chicken and all the eggplants. Simmer for a minute or so or until cooked.

Add the remaining ingredients. Simmer for a few more moments. Adjust seasoning, then serve.

Serves 4

hot and
salty

Geng taepo Red curry of oyster mushrooms and tofu

This is a tart, rustic curry from the central plains. Quite often a piece of freshwater fish or cut of pork is simmered in this curry, but it can be equally enjoyed as a vegetarian curry, as here. Siamese watercress is a vegetable common throughout all of Asia. Sometimes it is referred to invitingly as morning glory, less happily as swamp cress, or in Chinese as *ong choi*. But whatever its appellation, this soft green vegetable with its long crunchy stalks and spearlike leaves is a perennial favorite.

INGREDIENTS

$1/2$ cup cracked coconut cream (p213)
1 rounded tbsp palm sugar
pinch of salt
2 tsp light soy sauce
about $2^1/2$ tbsp tamarind water (p322)
2 cups coconut milk (p213)
7 oz (200 g) oyster mushrooms
1 small cake soft tofu,
    about 8 oz (225 g)
4 oz (100 g) Siamese watercress,
    cut into $1^1/4$-in (3-cm) lengths
7 kaffir lime leaves
2 small kaffir limes, cut in half and deseeded

Red curry paste

5–10 large dried chilies, deseeded, soaked,
    and chopped
pinch of salt
$1/4$ cup chopped lemongrass
6 slices galangal
$2^1/2$ tbsp chopped wild ginger
1 rounded tbsp chopped cilantro root
$2^1/2$ tbsp chopped red shallots
$2^1/2$ tbsp chopped garlic
1 tsp toasted coriander seeds

METHOD

First, make the curry paste (p217).

Simmer $2^1/2$ tbsp of the curry paste in the cracked coconut cream until fragrant. Season with the palm sugar, salt, soy sauce, and tamarind water. Add the coconut milk and, when it has come to the boil, add the mushrooms, tofu, watercress, and kaffir lime leaves.

Squeeze the kaffir limes and add them and their juice. Simmer until the mushrooms and watercress are cooked. Check the seasoning and adjust accordingly, then serve.

Serves 4

sour, salty, hot, and sweet

< A pandanus tree

Geng panaeng neua Red curry of beef with peanuts

A *panaeng* curry is rich and thick, redolent of peanuts, cumin, and nutmeg. A firm favorite in the Thai repertoire, its origins are in the Muslim community, probably from the south. Beef is the most common meat used in this style of curry, and with beef, nutmeg—and plenty of it—must also be used. However, chicken or shrimp are common alternatives, and long, green eggplants can be used for a vegetarian option. The curry paste must be cooked for at least 10 minutes to ensure that it is mellow and well balanced before seasoning it. Some regions prefer a decidedly sweeter version of this curry, which can be shocking to the Western palate. While this version uses some sugar and is sweet, it is not unsettlingly so. Add only half the amount of sugar called for, and taste; then add as much of the remaining sugar as preferred. Serve with steamed rice, naturally. Some pickled ginger or shallots would be nice too, and as an accompanying dish perhaps steamed fish or scallops.

INGREDIENTS

10 oz (300 g) boned beef shank, shin, or
   flank, trimmed
about 1 quart (liter) coconut milk
   (p213) or stock
1 pandanus leaf (optional)
2–3 Thai bay or cardamom leaves (optional)
Thai basil stalks (optional)
salt

Panaeng curry paste

6–12 dried long red chilies, seeded, soaked,
   and chopped
1 rounded tbsp chopped galangal
$2\frac{1}{2}$ tbsp chopped lemongrass
1 tsp chopped kaffir lime zest
1 tsp chopped cilantro root
$2\frac{1}{2}$ tbsp chopped red shallots
4 tbsp chopped garlic

1 tsp Thai shrimp paste
2 tsp coriander seeds, roasted
$1\frac{1}{2}$ tsp cumin seeds, roasted
good pinch of freshly ground white pepper
1 tsp freshly grated nutmeg
$2\frac{1}{2}$ tbsp roasted peanuts

Curry

$\frac{1}{2}$ cup cracked coconut cream (p213)
good pinch of freshly grated nutmeg
2–3 tbsp palm sugar, to taste
3–4 tbsp fish sauce, to taste
$\frac{2}{3}$ cup coconut milk (p213)
chili powder (optional)
2 kaffir lime leaves, torn
2 long red or green chilies, thinly sliced at an
   elegant angle and seeded
good handful of Thai basil leaves

Serves 4

rich, salty,
spicy, and a
little sweet

METHOD

For the braised beef, put the meat in a pan of cold salted water and bring to a boil, then drain and rinse. Put the coconut milk in a large pan and bring to a boil. Add the beef with the optional pandanus leaf, cardamom leaves, and basil stalks, and salt to taste. Braise over a low heat for

about 1 hour or the beef is until tender. Replenish with additional coconut milk, if necessary. While the beef is simmering, make the curry paste (p217).

Once sufficiently cooked, remove the beef from the liquid and allow to cool. Keep the braising liquid to moisten the curry paste. Trim off excess fat and sinew, then slice the beef into elegant pieces across the grain, about $^5/_8$ in (1.5 cm) wide and $^1/_4$ in (5 mm) thick.

To make the curry, heat the cracked coconut cream over moderate heat, then add $^1/_4$ cup of the curry paste and the grated nutmeg. Cook for at least 10 minutes, stirring often to prevent it from sticking. Season with the palm sugar and then, after a minute or so, the fish sauce.

Moisten with the coconut milk (some of the beef braising liquid can be used, too, but do not just use this, as it makes the curry very meaty). Add the coconut milk a bit at a time and allow it to evaporate while simmering for no less than 5 minutes; within reason, the longer the better, as this not only gives depth to the curry, ensuring that the paste is completely cooked and mellow, but encourages a good separation—a defining characteristic of this curry. It may be necessary to add a little chili powder and a pinch more grated nutmeg, to ensure that the curry is sufficiently spicy.

Add the beef. Continue to simmer for several minutes, then finish with the remaining ingredients.

Geng sapparrot hoi malaeng puu Pineapple curry of mussels

This curry comes from Phetchburi, a prosperous trading province to the southwest of Bangkok. The most traditional version uses the roe of the helmet crab, a sinister-looking beast with very firm, almost chalky eggs. Shrimp, clams, mussels, pork, or chicken can very easily be used as more readily available alternatives. Some cooks like to take the mussels out of the shell and cook them directly in the curry. It is served with steamed rice, as well as, perhaps, steamed salted duck eggs, salted beef, or pork. If the pineapple is either too green and tart or too sweet, wash it briefly in salted water to reduce its pungency.

INGREDIENTS

$1/2$ cup cracked coconut cream (p213)
$2-2^1/2$ tbsp palm sugar, to taste
$2^1/2$ tbsp fish sauce
$2-2^1/2$ tbsp tamarind water (p322)
2 cups coconut milk (p213)
$1^1/2$ cups finely chopped pineapple
10 oz (300 g) mussels, scrubbed and debearded
3 kaffir lime leaves, torn
1 long red or green chili, seeded if preferred and thinly sliced at an elegant angle

Curry paste

10 large dried red chilies, soaked and chopped
3 heaped tbsp red bird's-eye chilies
pinch of salt
$2^1/2$ tbsp chopped galangal
5 tbsp chopped lemongrass
2 tsp finely chopped kaffir lime zest
1 tsp chopped cilantro root
5 tbsp chopped garlic
$2^1/2$ tbsp chopped red shallots
1 rounded tbsp Thai shrimp paste

METHOD

First make the curry paste (p217).

Heat the cracked coconut cream over moderate heat, add $1/4$ cup of the curry paste, and fry until it is fragrant and redolent of the fish in the paste. This can take as long as 10 minutes, much longer than a normal red curry.

Season with the palm sugar and fish sauce (not too much, since the mussels will add their own salt) and then the tamarind water. Do not fry the paste for more than a minute or so after adding the tamarind water, otherwise it will develop a somewhat scorched taste.

Moisten with the coconut milk, then add the pineapple and the mussels. Simmer until the shells have opened, stirring regularly. (Discard any mussels that remain closed.)

Finish with the lime leaves and chili. Check the seasoning and adjust as needed, then serve.

Serves 4

salty, smoky, sweet, and sour

Ngob pla dtaa dtiaw Grilled halibut curry

This is a refined, restaurant version of a simple market-style curry. Cook the curry paste in plenty of cracked coconut cream to ensure that the fish does not dry out as it cooks. The addition of freshly grated coconut gives body and substance to the curry. Almost any fish can be used, as can any shellfish. To accompany it, this doesn't need much more than steamed rice, although it is nice with a soup, salad, and so on. Once the curry is cooked, seasoned, and wrapped, broil or grill it gently and slowly, charring the banana leaves. They impart a pleasing bitterness to the curry and help give it an inviting crust.

INGREDIENTS

1–2 large banana leaves
1 cup cracked coconut cream
  (p213)
$2^1/_2$ oz (70 g) Thai basil leaves
6–10 kaffir lime leaves, finely shredded
1 cup coconut cream (p213)
4 skinned halibut fillets, each weighing
  6 oz (180 g)

$^1/_4$ cup chopped lemongrass
1 rounded tbsp chopped galangal
1 tsp chopped kaffir lime zest
1 tsp chopped cilantro root
1 tsp Thai shrimp paste
good pinch of freshly ground white
  peppercorns
good pinch of freshly ground mace (optional)

Red curry paste

6–10 dried red chilies, soaked and chopped
a few bird's-eye chilies
pinch of salt
$^1/_4$ cup chopped garlic
5 tbsp chopped red shallots

Coconut mixture

$^1/_2$ cup cracked coconut cream (p213)
$2^1/_2$ tbsp palm sugar
$^1/_4$ cup fish sauce, or to taste
4 oz (100 g) freshly grated coconut
$^1/_2$ cup coconut cream (p213)

METHOD

First, make the curry paste (p217).

To make the coconut mixture, simmer 5 tbsp of the curry paste in the cracked coconut cream over medium heat until fragrant, then season with the palm sugar and fish sauce.

Add the grated coconut and continue to simmer, adding some fresh coconut cream and/or water to moisten as required. The water will ensure that the grated coconut is completely cooked and that the mixture is sufficiently oily.

Simmer until the additional water has evaporated and the mixture is indeed oily. (The coconut mixture can be made in advance; if refrigerated, it lasts for a few days. When reheating, add a little water and simmer until quite dry and oily once more.)

Trim the hard ribbed edge from the banana leaf and discard any yellowed parts. Cut the leaf into

Serves 4

**rich, nutty,
hot, and
salty**

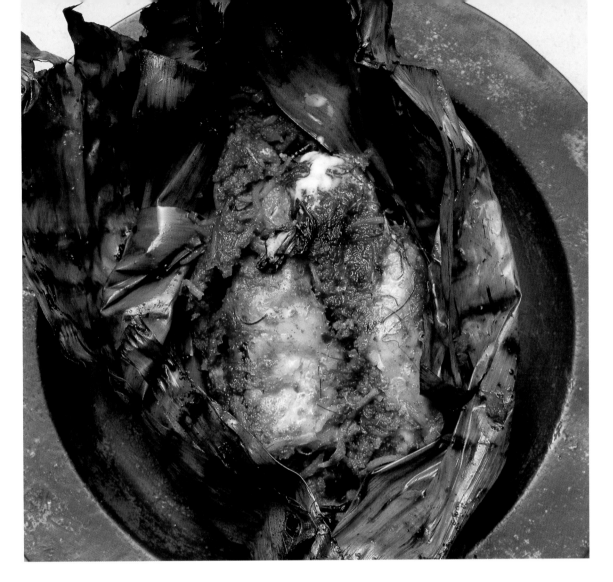

8 pieces, the first 4 about 6 in (14 cm) wide and the remaining 4 about 8 in (20 cm) wide. Wipe clean both sides of the cut pieces. Place each of the smaller pieces on top of a larger one, shiny sides facing outward.

Along half of each of the inner banana leaves, smear a little cracked coconut cream, then sprinkle on a few basil leaves. Spread with a layer of the coconut mixture before repeating alternate layers of small amounts of Thai basil, kaffir lime leaves, and fresh, uncracked coconut cream. Place the fish on top, then repeat the layering but in reverse.

Fold the inner banana leaf over to cover the filling, then wrap the outer banana leaf around this parcel quite tightly. Secure with wooden skewers or toothpicks, at least 3 per parcel.

Broil or grill the parcels, turning occasionally, for up to 30 minutes, depending on the degree of heat. The outer leaves should char; the inner leaves are used for serving.

Hor mok hoi shenn Steamed scallop curry

Mussels, clams, shrimp, and almost any fish, either saltwater or fresh, are happy alternatives to the scallops in this curry. Traditionally, the coconut cream is stirred in gradually, in one direction, to ensure that the cream does not separate during the cooking. I am not sure whether it is important to stir in one direction, but the cream should be added slowly. It is also imperative to have the cream at room temperature. If it is too cold, it will not bind with the fish. It must be coconut cream, too—if the thinner milk is used, it will introduce too much water and the mixture will be bound to separate and appear curdled. Some versions of this curry omit the fish purée and instead base it on a combination of fresh coconut cream, curry paste, and eggs. This makes a rich but very loose custard that requires gentle steaming. Once the mixture is made, it is normally steamed in a container fashioned from banana leaves. Sometimes a green coconut is used as the container. I've used scallop shells here. Serve with rice, as part of a meal.

Serves 4

rich, salty, and slightly hot

INGREDIENTS
2 oz (50 g) filleted white fish, such as
   turbot or sea bass
1/2 cup coconut cream (p213), cool
   but not too cold
1 1/2–3 tbsp fish sauce
pinch of white sugar (optional)
1 small egg
5 kaffir lime leaves, very finely shredded
4 medium to large scallops, without the coral,
   each cut into 3 slices
4 scallop shells, boiled in heavily salted water
   for several minutes to clean
handful of Thai basil leaves
1 *bai yor* leaf, very finely shredded (optional)
a few pieces of red chili julienne
a few cilantro leaves

Red curry paste
6–8 dried red chilies, soaked and chopped
pinch of salt
2 1/2 tbsp chopped garlic
1/4 cup chopped red shallots
1/4 cup chopped lemongrass
1 rounded tbsp chopped galangal
1 tsp chopped kaffir lime zest
1 tsp chopped cilantro root
2 tsp Thai shrimp paste
good pinch of freshly ground white
   peppercorns

Thickened coconut cream
good pinch of rice flour
5 tbsp coconut cream (p213)
pinch of salt (optional)

METHOD

First, make the curry paste (p217).

Purée the fish in a blender, then pass through a sieve. Combine $^1/_4$ cup of the curry paste with the fish purée. Work in the coconut cream, adding it gradually while stirring gently—and in the same direction—to ensure that the cream is thoroughly incorporated. Season the "mousse" with fish sauce and sugar. Finish with the egg. The mixture should have a rather sticky texture and silken sheen, and taste salty and slightly hot. Stir in most of the shredded kaffir lime leaves (reserve some for garnish) and the scallops.

Generously line the prepared scallop shells with the Thai basil and then the optional *bai yor*. Spoon in the scallop curry mixture. Steam in a Chinese steamer over low heat for about 15 minutes. When the "mousse" is slightly firm, it is cooked. Be careful not to overcook or it will split.

Meanwhile, make the thickened coconut cream. Mix the rice flour with 1 tbsp of the coconut cream to make a slurry. Bring the remainder of the coconut cream up to a boil, then stir in the rice flour mixture to thicken. Season with salt, if desired. Pass the thickened cream through a fine sieve to remove any lumps, if necessary.

Spoon the thickened coconut cream over the curry and garnish with the reserved kaffir lime leaves, the red chili, and the cilantro leaves.

Geng gwio warn yord maprao Green curry of heart of coconut

Green curries lend themselves to many variations. Given the Thai manner of eating, they usually include a meat, bird, or fish. But there is a strong tradition of vegetarianism in this Buddhist country, and at some time all Thais refrain from meat, whether it be to commemorate a solemn occasion, or more regularly, say, once a week or throughout a whole month. Heart of coconut is an ideal vegetable for a curry. Its toothsome crunch offers a wonderful textural contrast. However, this is not a common vegetable to be found, so baby corn, Asian eggplants of any type, or even pumpkin can make a happy alternative. Make sure that the curry itself includes plenty of Thai basil to round out the flavors and at the end of cooking has a little coconut oil dappling its surface.

INGREDIENTS

$^1/_4$ cup plus 1 tbsp cracked coconut cream (p213)
6 oz (150 g) elegantly cut heart of coconut
4–5 baby corns, each cut in half lengthwise
$2^1/_2$ tbsp fish sauce, or to taste
2 cups coconut milk (p213)
a few picked pea eggplants (optional)
3 kaffir lime leaves, torn
3 young green chilies, deseeded and thinly
  sliced at an elegant angle
handful of Thai basil leaves

Green curry paste

1 heaped tbsp bird's-eye chilies
1 long green chili, deseeded
pinch of salt
1 rounded tbsp chopped galangal
$2^1/_2$ tbsp chopped lemongrass
1 tsp chopped kaffir lime zest
1 tsp chopped cilantro root
1 tsp chopped red turmeric
$2^1/_2$ tbsp chopped red shallots
2 tbsp chopped garlic
1 tsp yellow beans
good pinch of finely ground white
  peppercorns

Serves 4

thin, hot,
and salty

METHOD

First, make the curry paste (p217).

Heat the cracked coconut cream, add $^1/_4$ cup of the curry paste, and fry over high heat for 5 minutes, stirring regularly. During this time, add the heart of coconut and the corn. Fry until the paste looks scrambled and smells cooked, then season with fish sauce.

Moisten with the coconut milk. Bring to a boil and add the remaining ingredients. Check the seasoning and adjust if necessary, then serve.

Geng gwio warn gung Green curry of shrimp with eggplant and basil

This is quite a thin curry, commonly served with spiced salted beef. Kaffir lime leaves, fresh long chilies, and Thai basil are essential garnishes, to give the dish its characteristic flavors. Various eggplants are common but not always used. Sometimes breadfruit, corn, or heart of coconut are included. Tradition dictates that the shrimp be added to the frying curry paste, but I feel that this can lead to such quick-cooking items being overcooked, as they then continue simmering after the coconut milk is added. I think it is better—and safer—to add the shrimp once the curry is made, when adding the vegetables. Almost any meat or fish can be used in place of the shrimp; if more resilient, the meat or fish can be fried with the paste.

INGREDIENTS

5 tbsp cracked coconut cream (p213)
2½ tbsp Kreaung Geng Geng Gwio Warn (p217)
1½–3 tbsp fish sauce, to taste
1 cup coconut milk (p213) and/or chicken or shrimp stock
3 apple eggplants, stem removed and each cut into sixths (if cut in advance, keep in salted water to prevent discoloration)

4 oz (100 g) picked pea eggplants
8–12 good-quality large, raw shrimp, cleaned and deveined
3–4 kaffir lime leaves, torn
3 young green chilies, seeded and thinly sliced at an elegant angle
handful of Thai basil leaves
1 rounded tbsp shredded wild ginger

METHOD

Serves 4

thin, salty, and hot

Heat the cracked coconut cream, add the *kreaung* (curry paste), and fry over high heat for about 5 minutes, stirring regularly, until fragrant. Make sure the paste is quite oily.

Season with fish sauce, then moisten with the coconut milk or stock, or a mixture of the two. Bring to a boil, then add the apple and pea eggplants. Simmer for a few minutes to cook before adding the shrimp. Continue to simmer until they too are cooked.

Finish with the remaining ingredients, then allow to rest for a minute or so before serving. The curry should have a dappling of separated coconut cream floating on top.

Geng gari fak tong Aromatic curry of pumpkin

The curry paste recipe here is from a very old cookbook written by Thanpuying Pliang Pasonagorn, a noble cook from the late 19th century. The light and delicate spicing makes it perfect for a vegetarian curry. While pumpkin is a good standard, almost any root vegetables, such as potatoes (sweet or regular), mooli, or taro, are good alternatives. Serve with the cucumber relish on the opposite page. This cuts through the coconut cream to reveal the various spices, and so the aromatic curry is immeasurably improved.

INGREDIENTS

1 quart (liter) coconut milk (p213)
pinch of salt
7 oz (200 g) peeled pumpkin flesh, cut into
  bite-size chunks
$1/2$ cup cracked coconut cream
  (p213)
1 rounded tbsp palm sugar
$1/4$ cup light soy sauce
4 red shallots, sliced and deep-fried
  (p211)
Ajad Dtaeng Gwa (opposite), to serve

Aromatic curry paste

4–5 dried long red chilies, seeded, soaked,
  and chopped
large pinch of salt
$2^1/2$ tbsp chopped lemongrass
1 rounded tbsp chopped galangal
1 rounded tbsp chopped red turmeric
2 tsp chopped cilantro root
$1/4$ cup chopped red shallots
$1/4$ cup chopped garlic
$2^1/2$ tbsp roasted, ground, and sifted
  Thai coriander seeds (p322)
1 rounded tbsp ground white pepper

METHOD

First, make the curry paste (p217).

Put the coconut milk in a medium-sized saucepan, add the salt, and bring to a boil. (I like to mix in a little water, which helps to prevent the coconut milk from separating as the pumpkin cooks.) Add the prepared pumpkin and simmer gently over medium heat for about 10 minutes or until tender. Drain, reserving the cooking liquid, and set aside.

Serves 4

Heat the cracked coconut cream in a small pan, add $1/4$ cup of the curry paste, and fry over medium heat for about 5 minutes or until it is quite fragrant. Stir regularly to prevent the paste from scorching. Season with the palm sugar and soy sauce.

**salty and
aromatic**

Moisten with 1 cup of the pumpkin stock, then add the pumpkin and reheat if necessary. Check the seasoning and adjust accordingly. Serve sprinkled with the deep-fried shallots and accompanied with the cucumber relish.

Aromatic curry of pumpkin

Ajad dtaeng gwa Cucumber relish

This subtle pickle is a popular accompaniment to many dishes, as its sweet and sour taste counterbalances any richness and oiliness that is so often a part of a Thai meal.

INGREDIENTS

5 tbsp white vinegar
1 rounded tbsp white sugar
1–2 cilantro roots
1 small head pickled garlic and 1 tbsp or so of its liquid (optional)
pinch of salt

$^{1}/_{2}$ small cucumber, quartered lengthwise and sliced crosswise
1 red shallot, finely sliced
1 rounded tbsp julienned fresh ginger root
a few thin rounds of small, long red chili
pinch of cilantro leaves

METHOD

Combine the vinegar, sugar, $6^{1}/_{2}$ tbsp water, the cilantro root, pickled garlic and its liquid, and salt in a small saucepan and bring to a boil. Remove from the heat when the sugar dissolves. Cool, then strain. The liquid should taste sour, sweet, and a little salty, but not be too concentrated.

Mix the remaining ingredients together in the serving bowl and add the vinegar mixture.

Serves 4

Geng gari gai Aromatic curry of chicken and potatoes

This gentle curry of Muslim origin is one of the most popular in the Thai repertoire, and its agreeable spiciness makes it a favorite with Westerners too. The distinguishing characteristic that defines a *gari* curry is the use of spices. Very often it is a ground spice mix purchased from the market or medicine shops, but this old recipe is more specific. Beef or chicken are normally used, with a starchy root vegetable. *Gari* curries are always served with a cucumber relish.

INGREDIENTS
2 chicken quarters, about 1 lb 2 oz (500 g) total
3 cups coconut milk (p213)
pinch of salt
3–4 waxy potatoes, peeled and quartered
1/2 cup cracked coconut cream (p213)
1 rounded tbsp palm sugar
2 1/2 tbsp fish sauce, or to taste
1 1/2-in (4-cm) piece cassia, roasted
pinch of ground white pepper
pinch of chili powder
1 generous tbsp coconut cream (p213)
4 red shallots, sliced and deep fried (p211)
Ajad Dtaeng Gwa (p245), to serve

Aromatic curry paste
3–4 dried red chilies, seeded, soaked, and
  chopped
pinch of salt
2 1/2 tbsp chopped grilled red shallots
2 1/2 tbsp chopped grilled garlic
1 rounded tbsp chopped galangal
2 tbsp chopped lemongrass
1 tsp chopped cilantro root
1 tsp chopped red turmeric
seeds from 3–4 roasted Thai cardamom pods
pinch of white peppercorns, roasted
1/2 tsp coriander seeds, roasted
1/2 tsp cumin seeds, roasted
good pinch of fennel seeds, roasted
4–5 cloves, roasted
2 blades mace, roasted

METHOD
First, make the curry paste (p217).

Segment the chicken legs into thighs and drumsticks or cut into thirds. Trim off excess fat. Heat the coconut milk with the salt. Add the chicken and poach for about 30 minutes or until cooked.

Rinse the potatoes in cold running water for a few minutes to remove any excess starch, then cook in boiling salted water, or some of the chicken poaching stock, until cooked but still firm. Drain.

Meanwhile, heat the cracked coconut cream, add 5 tbsp of the curry paste, and fry for at least 5 minutes or until fragrant with the spices. Season with the palm sugar and fish sauce. Moisten with the chicken poaching liquid, adding it ladle by ladle, until a medium-thick curry is achieved. Add the chicken and potatoes. Finish with the roasted cassia, ideally still smoking.

Check the seasoning: often a pinch each of white pepper and chili powder will improve the taste. Drizzle with the coconut cream, sprinkle with the deep-fried shallots, and serve, with the relish.

Serves 4

rich, salty, and a little spicy

Geng hang lae muu Chiang Mai pork curry

There are many variations of this northern curry, which comes originally from Myanmar. Some versions are quite salty with little spice and no sugar. However, this curry, from Chiang Mai, is rich and spicy and sweetened by the pickled garlic and its syrup. Although chicken or beef could be used, pork is the most common meat. Most traditional recipes use both a fatty and a lean cut of pork.

INGREDIENTS
7 oz (200 g) boned pork belly
7 oz (200 g) pork ribs
$^1/_4$ cup vegetable oil
16 red shallots, peeled
3 cups fresh ginger root, coarsely shredded
1 cup pickled garlic, peeled and
  heads cut in half
1 cup pickled garlic syrup
$^3/_4$ cup roasted peanuts (optional)
$1^1/_2$–3 tbsp palm sugar, to taste
5 tbsp fish sauce
5 tbsp tamarind water (p322)
stock or water

Chiang mai curry paste
10 dried long red chilies, deseeded, soaked,
  and chopped
large pinch of salt
1 rounded tbsp chopped galangal
$^1/_2$ cup chopped lemongrass
$2^1/_2$ tbsp chopped fresh ginger root
1 rounded tbsp chopped red turmeric
$^2/_3$ cup chopped red shallots
$^1/_2$ cup chopped garlic
1 rounded tbsp coriander seeds, roasted
2 tsp cumin seeds, roasted
3 star anise, roasted
$^3/_4$-in (2-cm) piece cassia bark, roasted
4 cloves, roasted
seeds from 4 roasted Thai cardamom pods
  (optional)

METHOD
First make the curry paste (p217).

Cut the pork belly and ribs into $^3/_4$-in (2-cm) cubes. I like to blanch the pork before cooking it in the curry paste: cover the meat with cold water and bring to a boil, then drain and rinse. This gives the curry a lighter, less porky taste.

Heat the oil in a large, deep-sided frying pan. Add $^1/_2$ cup of the curry paste and fry until fragrant. Add the pork and simmer for several minutes, stirring regularly to prevent burning.

Add the whole shallots, ginger, pickled garlic, garlic syrup, and peanuts (if using). Season the curry with palm sugar, fish sauce, and tamarind water. Cover with stock or water and bring to a boil, then reduce the heat and simmer for 1 hour or until the pork is tender.

The finished curry will be quite oily. That is how it is supposed to be. Check the seasoning: it should be just a little sweet and sour, and perfumed with ginger and the spices.

Serves 4

salty,
aromatic,
and fatty

Geng mussaman Muslim-style curry of duck with potatoes and onions

This a rich and generously flavored curry. It is most often made with beef or chicken, but I find duck is an appropriate and delicious variation. As with most Muslim curries, the pieces of meat are considerably larger than in curries of Buddhist origin. The duck, potatoes, and onions are deep-fried to enrich the curry as well as to prevent them from breaking up during the braising. I like to marinate the meat briefly in a little soy sauce, which gives the duck an inviting mahogany color. The curry is cooked in a large amount of cracked coconut cream—its oiliness helps to make the complex spicing more unified and mellow—and is finished with fruit juice, normally Asian citron, but you can use puréed and sieved fresh pineapple.

INGREDIENTS

2 large duck legs or 3–4 duck breasts,
    about 10 oz (300 g) in total
4 tsp dark soy sauce
4 potatoes, peeled and cut into elegant pieces
vegetable oil for deep frying
8 small pickling onions or red shallots, peeled
$^{1}/_{4}$ cup peanuts
2 cups coconut milk (p213)
good pinch of salt
1 piece cassia, $^{3}/_{4}$ x $1^{1}/_{4}$ in (2 x 3 cm), roasted
5 or so cardamom pods, roasted
4 Thai cardamom leaves, roasted
2 cups cracked coconut cream (p213)
9–11 oz (250–325 g) palm sugar, to taste
1 cup tamarind water (p322)
$^{1}/_{2}$ cup fish sauce, or to taste
1 cup Asian citron or pineapple juice

Mussaman curry paste

8–12 dried red chilies
5 tbsp coriander seeds
$2^{1}/_{2}$ tbsp cumin seeds
1 rounded tbsp cardamom pods
5 or so cloves
2 pieces cassia
2 star anise
6 oz (150 g) unpeeled shallots
6 oz (150 g) unpeeled garlic cloves
2 oz (60 g) chopped lemongrass
5 tbsp chopped galangal
salt

METHOD

Serves 4

salty, sweet,
and sour

First, make the curry paste. Roast the chilies and all the spices, individually, in a wok. Remove the seeds from the cardamom pods, then grind with the other spices. Sift. Combine all the remaining ingredients and roast them in the wok, with a little water to prevent them from scorching, until brown and fragrant. Allow to cool slightly, then peel the shallots and garlic. Grind the browned fresh aromatics in a mortar and pestle to make a purée, then work in the ground spices.

Trim the duck legs of excess fat and skin. Segment the legs. If using breasts, cut them into cubes. Briefly marinate the duck in the dark soy sauce.

Rinse the potatoes in cold running water to remove excess starch. Drain well and dry. Heat vegetable oil in a large wok, then deep-fry the potatoes until they are golden. Remove and drain. Deep-fry the onions; drain. Then deep-fry the duck until it too is golden. Remove and drain. Finally, deep-fry the peanuts; drain. Set all of the deep-fried items aside.

Season the coconut milk with the salt and bring to a boil in a saucepan. Add the pieces of duck, the cassia, cardamom pods and leaves, and deep-fried peanuts. (There should be enough coconut milk to cover the duck.) Simmer until the duck is almost cooked: 10 minutes for breast, 30 minutes for leg. Add the deep-fried potatoes and then, a few minutes later, add the onions. Simmer until everything is just cooked.

Meanwhile, in a medium pot, heat the cracked coconut cream and add 2 cups of the curry paste. Reduce the heat and simmer for no less than 10 minutes, stirring regularly to prevent the paste from sticking. Be careful, as it may splutter as it fries and it is painfully hot. Cook until it is redolent of the spices. If the paste is not oily enough, moisten with some of the fat skimmed off the duck poaching liquid. When the paste is oily, hot, and sizzling, season it with palm sugar. Continue to simmer as the sugar dissolves and begins to deepen the color of the curry.

Add the tamarind water and continue to cook, then add the fish sauce. Carefully add the coconut poaching liquid from the duck, followed by the spices, then the potatoes, onions, and duck. Simmer for several more minutes, then stir in the juice. Check the seasoning; the curry should be spicy, oily, and quite thick. Set aside for several minutes to allow the flavors to develop, then serve.

MAINLAND
SE ASIA

< **Carrying vegetables,
Hanoi, Vietnam**

Cambodia, Laos, and Vietnam have had the fortune—good and bad—to be a cultural and military crossroads for centuries. Armies and artisans, conquerors and cooks have traversed the area, making its history one of empire, artistic accomplishment, and extraordinary cuisines. Curiously, perhaps, while China's very significant influence in the area can be linked to military dominance, the equally significant Indian influences were never military. The South Asians, it seems, came, traded, and cooked, but never fought.

Curry is rooted in the spicy cooked-down foods that date back to ancient times, and were recorded in Sumerian and Mesopotamian texts. Scholars generally agree that the word curry has its roots in the Tamil word *kari*, referring to spices, sauces, and stews. "Curry" itself seems to be an English corruptive form of the Tamil word, first appearing in European references in the late 16th and early 17th centuries.

Curries do not have to be hot, and the spicy mixtures that underlie them can be powders or pastes, or a combination of the two. The powders you buy in stores are primarily turmeric, cumin, coriander, and pepper. In general Asian, South Asian, and Southeast Asian use, however, the palette is considerably broader, and may include chilies, mustard seed, cinnamon, and black and white peppers for hot notes; cloves, anise, fennel, nutmeg, and mace for sweetish notes; and fenugreek, bay leaves, poppy seeds, and allspice for expansive flavor notes. In Cambodia, Laos, and Vietnam, lemongrass, cilantro root, and galangal may also appear, lending uniquely Southeast Asian flavors to the dishes.

The spectrum of flavors and ingredients beyond the spicy basics is tremendous, ranging from pungent vegetables and fresh fish, to richly flavored fowl, and white and—less often—red meats. What distinguishes Cambodian, Laotian, and Vietnamese curries, however, is their relative lightness in comparison to their Indian cousins. They are also unique in other ways. For example, they can be custards, as in the Cambodian steamed curried snails (p268); they can be noodle soups, as in the Laotian Kao Soi (p278); and they can be stir-fries, skipping any rich coconut sauce altogether.

Unlike the rice-based meals of the rest of Asia, curries in this region often employ starches other than rice as the main staple. Baguette, for example, is a crisp, baked bread derived from the familiar French variety, a remnant of the French colonial era here. It is widely enjoyed with curry, and used to soak and scoop up rich sauces. Significantly, the

Southeast Asian baguette has been regionalized: half the length and perhaps a bit fuller than its French cousin, it is made with a combination of white wheat and rice flours, rendering a lighter-textured loaf.

Side dishes play an important role in Cambodian, Laotian, and Vietnamese curry-based meals. Lightly stir-fried leafy greens balance the comforting curry stews, providing contrasting colors and textures while broadening the range of vitamins and minerals in the meal. Pickled vegetables, too, play an important role. Lightly brined and mildly spiced, they help with the digestion of rich foods. Their crunchiness introduces variety of texture to the braised and tender morsels of curried meals, and their intense colors brighten the table, contrasting with the often earthy hues of the main dishes.

As refrigeration is close to nonexistent in broad areas of Cambodia, Laos, and Vietnam, fresh ingredients are essential, so going to the market several times a day is normal and expected. Asian households often have food sitting on a table at room temperature throughout the day, stored in shade, covered with insect netting, and available for snacking. The food is unlikely to be kept for the next day.

Indian and other South Asian meals often employ milk-based cheeses, yogurt, and yogurt drinks such as *lassi* to mediate the heat of their spicier curries. Such milk-based products are relatively rare in Cambodia, Laos, and Vietnam, so cooks here often use fatty coconut milks and creams in their main curry dishes, to the same effect.

In summary, the delightfully surprising thing about Southeast Asian curries is their diversity, their broad range of influences, and their significant degree of sophisticated cooking. Regional variations can be subtle, as in the variations found in Vietnam, or so different as to be separate categories of cooking, as in the nature of Laotian versus Cambodian dishes. Not just spicy—as might be assumed—and always interesting, these recipes cover dishes exploring the spectrum from mild to very hot, from simple to complex, and from bitter to sweet.

Corinne Trang

Making a savory base >
Stir-fry curry paste with palm sugar
and ground pork until golden

The Taste of Mainland SE Asia

1. dried large red chilies
2. red Thai chilies
3. palm sugar
4. Vietnamese cilantro
5. dill
6. cilantro leaves and stalks
7. cilantro root
8. pea eggplants
9. annatto seeds
10. tamarind pulp
11. shrimp paste
12. *prahoc*
13. peanuts
14. cumin seeds
15. coriander seeds
16. green cardamom pods
17. star anise
18. fresh ginger root
19. galangal
20. turmeric root
21. kaffir lime leaves
22. kaffir lime
23. wild ginger
24. lemongrass
25. Thai basil leaves

The raw materials

With the ever-increasing interest in cooking, the advent of the Internet and online shopping, and the wider range of ingredients available in local stores, foods that at one time were thought of as "exotic" are becoming more familiar. Where once only soy sauce was available, now you can find fish sauce, tamarind pulp, and fresh lemongrass, for example. The Western palate has also developed, and fusion dishes show up in restaurants everywhere. Southeast Asian flavors are a large part of this trend. These are the key flavoring ingredients that will enable you to create Cambodian, Laotian, and Vietnamese curries at home.

Chilies

Asia first gained knowledge of chilies after the 15th-century voyages of Christopher Columbus—Spain introduced chili-hot foods to South Asia, and from there the influence spread across greater Asia. Several kinds of chilies are used in this region's curries, and they range in heat from mildly hot and sweet large red chilies, similar to the New Mexico chili, to Thai chilies and the tiny, thin bird's-eye or bird chilies, both of which are extremely hot. Dried large red chilies are an important part of the Cambodian spice paste called Kroeung (p264).

Kaffir lime

Kaffir limes have little juice, and instead are prized for their zest (the green part of the peel) and leaves. The zest is widely used in Southeast Asian curry pastes for its bitter, citrus, and floral notes. There is no real substitute, but for a different, yet still citrusy, flavor,

you can use regular lime zest. Fragrant kaffir lime leaves have strong lime and floral notes. They are best if fresh, although frozen leaves are also good. If slicing or chopping, remove the woody central rib first.

Galangal

Also called galingale, this rhizome (underground rootlike stem) is used in herbal and spice pastes. Its flavor is unique: less spicy than ginger, to which it is related, yet citrusy. Galangal is pale yellow throughout, including its translucent skin, although when young it has a pinkish hue. There is no substitute for it. Fresh or frozen galangal is best—dried slices and ground galangal are less pungent.

Wild ginger

Variously known as Chinese keys, fingerroot, and lesser galangal in English, and *krachai* in Southeast Asia, this rhizome looks like a knob with long slender fingers or

tentacles. It is widely used in herbal and spice pastes and to flavor soups and stews. Similar in flavor to galangal, it is available fresh, frozen, in brine, or as dried powder, though the latter tends to be flavorless.

Lemongrass

Much used in Southeast Asian cooking, lemongrass is a tall, clumping grass, yellow to light green in color. Before use, remove the tough, outer layers, starting from the hard root end. About 8 in (20 cm) of the tender inner stalk can be used. When making a spice or herbal paste, lemongrass should go into the mortar first, since it takes great effort to break down the fibers.

Tamarind

Tamarind is used to "sour" foods, or make them tangy. The whole fruit, which resembles a large, brittle, brown bean pod, contains a pasty pulp, fibers, and seeds. Solid blocks of tamarind pulp,

Fresh dill >

with fibers and seeds, are most commonly available, and for use the pulp is soaked to yield tamarind water (p322), in the proportion of $1/4$ cup of pulp to 1 cup lukewarm water. While the tamarind tree is native to eastern Africa, it is now widely grown in many other parts of the world, including Asia.

Cilantro root

The root of the cilantro plant, rather than the green stalks and leaves, is used in curry pastes, in part because it is white—it keeps a yellow or red curry paste from turning green, for example. The root can be stored, in enough cold water to cover, for up to 1 week in the refrigerator; the water should be changed daily.

Cilantro leaves

Widely used fresh all over Asia, cilantro leaves have a floral and somewhat citrusy aroma that perfectly complements Asian foods, including spicy curries.

Thai basil

Dark green with purplish stalks and flowerbuds, Thai basil has a pungent licorice-like flavor. Added fresh to soups or stir-fries, it gives a sweet note. Italian basil is not a good substitute.

Vietnamese cilantro

Also called Vietnamese mint and *rau ram* in Vietnam, this herb has narrow, pointy, dark bluish-green leaves and a strong floral aroma. There is no substitute, but you can use fresh cilantro for a very different yet still Asian flavor.

Dill

Also known as Laotian coriander, dill is widely used in Laotian and Vietnamese cooking, and is especially enjoyed with seafood dishes. Believed to soothe the stomach, tender dill fronds are generally added fresh and in small quantities to cooked dishes. This pungent herb has an aroma reminiscent of sweet grass.

Turmeric

Also known as curcuma (from its botanical name), turmeric is a rhizome with brown skin and bright orange flesh. When fresh, it has a subtle earthy, spicy flavor. Turmeric is most widely available in dried ground form, and it is this that is used as a colorant, giving curries their distinctive yellowish-orange hue.

Annatto seeds

These tiny, rust-red, triangular seeds are used for coloring food, as well as to dye fabrics. Annatto seeds are available whole or ground or as an extract.

Cardamom

Also known as the "grain of paradise," this spice is used in its whole form (green pods), or the tiny, sticky black seeds are taken out of the pods and ground to a powder. Cardamom has a unique pungent aroma and slightly bitter yet sweet, warm flavor.

Coriander seeds

Available whole or ground, coriander seeds are round or oval, about the size of rice grains, with longitudinal ridges. Coriander has been widely used as a spice for thousands of years.

Cumin seed

This strongly flavored spice is one of the most important ingredients in most Asian curry powders and other spice mixes. Roast cumin seeds in a dry pan before grinding to a fine powder.

Star anise

Shaped like a star (hence its name), this spice has a strong licorice flavor that is warm and sweet. It is widely used in Southeast Asian cooking.

Fish sauce

An indispensable seasoning in Southeast Asian cooking, fish sauce (*nuoc mam*) is made from a specific type of anchovy. Once salted, the fish are layered in wooden barrels and then left to ferment for 3 months. The juices are extracted and poured back into large barrels or earthenware jars and fermented for another 12 months or longer. The first extraction is the most prized, because it is 100 percent pure fish sauce—this is generally used as a last-minute seasoning at the table. Second- and third-grade fish sauces are made using the same fish, with salt water added to further ferment them. These lesser-grade fish sauces, which are also delicious, are primarily used in cooking or for making dipping sauces.

Prahoc

This unique, chunky fish paste is the backbone of Cambodian cooking; similar versions are used in Laotian food as well. It is the strongest of all the fermented fish-based products of Southeast

< **Palm sugar**

Asia. *Prahoc* is made from gouramy, gray featherback, or mud fish fillets, which are soft and easily flaked, and is light to medium gray in color, from the fish's skin pigment. The preferred version is made using boneless fish fillets, with or without rice as a fermenting agent. This is labeled "Siem Reap Style."

Shrimp paste

Pungent, dark grayish-purple shrimp paste is strong and salty in flavor. Cambodian shrimp paste, which is only produced in the Cambodian coastal region of Kampot, is the preferred seasoning for making curries in this region, but it is not widely available elsewhere. However, excellent versions are produced in Malaysia, Indonesia, and Thailand, and make perfectly acceptable substitutes. Before storing shrimp paste in the refrigerator, it should be wrapped well in several layers of plastic wrap so that its pungent aroma is not transferred to other foods in the refrigerator.

Palm sugar

This is produced from the boiled sap of the coconut palm. It is also called coconut sugar.

Pea eggplant

Only a bit larger than green peas, pea eggplants grow in clusters like grapes. They are slightly bitter in flavor, and tender yet still firm when cooked. Pea eggplants are best used fresh—the longer they are kept, the more bitter they will become. Although most often associated with Thai food, they are used in cooking throughout maritime and mainland Southeast Asia.

Coconut

Coconut milk, cream, and oil are major ingredients in curries of this region, lending naturally sweet and rich flavors to tame spicy ingredients, especially chilies. You can make your own coconut milk and cream (p213).

Peanuts

Unsalted roasted peanuts are widely used in Asian cooking, lending a crunchy texture and earthy, nutty note, as well as a thickening quality.

Pork

Relatively inexpensive in Asia, pork is occasionally used to enhance and deepen the flavor of vegetarian and seafood dishes.

Step 1

Step 2

Preparing dried chilies

In general, large, smooth chilies are much less hot than small, wrinkly chilies. Both are used dried and fresh. When dried, chilies are normally rehydrated before adding to a recipe. They may be seeded, too, to make them less hot. When preparing chilies, you may want to wear plastic or rubber gloves, as there is an alkaloid in chilies, called capsaicin, that can irritate your skin. After preparing chilies, thoroughly wash your hands with soapy water.

METHOD

Step 1
Put the chilies in a bowl of lukewarm water and place a small plate on top to keep them submerged. Leave to soak until soft and fully rehydrated (this can take as long as 15–30 minutes, depending on the size of the chilies).

Step 2
Drain the chilies and pat dry with paper towels. Tear the chilies open and remove the stalks, veins, and seeds. (It is the seeds and veins in a chili that contain the heat.)

Step 3
Chop the chilies, then grind in a mortar for a curry paste or use according to the recipe instructions.

Step 3 >

GROUND ROASTED CHILIES
Roast dried chilies (mildly hot red chilies or very hot bird's-eye or bird chilies) in a wok or pan over moderate heat, stirring regularly to prevent scorching, until they change color and smell toasted. Allow to cool, then grind to a coarse or fine powder with a mortar and pestle, a clean coffee grinder, or a spice mill. The powder will keep well in an airtight container in a dark, cool place for up to 1 year.

CAMBODIA

Kroeung Cambodian herbal paste

This is an all-purpose Cambodian herbal paste. Similar in many ways to Indian and, especially, Thai curry pastes, it belies the idea that Cambodia does not have curry pastes, or curries in general for that matter. *Kroeungs* come in several versions that include yellow (using additional turmeric), green (using green lemongrass leaves) and red (using red chilies), just like Thai curry pastes. It is essentially (or arguably) the foundation to many Cambodian hybrid curries, and contains seven main ingredients: lemongrass, galangal, wild ginger (*krachai*), garlic, shallot, kaffir lime zest, and turmeric. Other more complex *kroeungs* may also include kaffir lime leaves, cilantro root, and chilies. For a basic curry base, stir-fry the paste with 1 tbsp Indian curry powder and 1 tbsp or more shrimp paste, until it becomes two shades darker. Add thick coconut milk and/or stock and proceed as you would with other types of curries, adding meat, poultry, or seafood, and vegetables.

INGREDIENTS

1 stalk lemongrass, outer leaves removed,
  then chopped
1 oz (30 g) galangal, chopped
1 oz (30 g) wild ginger
2 large garlic cloves, crushed
1 large shallot, chopped
grated zest of 1 kaffir lime
4 kaffir lime leaves (optional)
3 tbsp finely chopped cilantro root (optional)
1 oz (30 g) turmeric root, chopped, or
  1/2 tsp ground turmeric

Other ingredients

2 lemongrass leaves (if making a green
  kroeung), chopped
extra 1/2 oz (15 g) turmeric root or 1/4 tsp
  ground turmeric (if making a yellow *kroeung*)
2–4 dried large red chilies (if making a red
  kroeung), soaked until soft, seeded,
  and chopped

METHOD

Traditionally, this paste is made using a mortar and pestle, pounding the most fibrous ingredients first, as they will need more pulverizing than anything that is tender. However, it is easier, and quicker, to use a food processor or blender: blend the ingredients, adding water (1 tbsp at a time as necessary) to ease the process. The amount of water, if needed, all depends on how naturally juicy the ingredients are.

The paste is always best freshly made, but can be kept in an airtight container in the refrigerator for 2–3 days.

Cari k'hom Cambodian red curry paste

This red-colored curry paste is a variation on the basic *kroeung* (p264), and closer to the Indian (rather than the Thai) roots of much Cambodian cooking. In general, Cambodian curry pastes are lightly spiced, using mild to moderately hot chilies. Note that unlike a *kroeung*, this curry paste also includes dried spices similar to those used in Indian cooking.

INGREDIENTS

2 tbsp coconut oil
2 dried large red chilies, soaked, seeded and
    coarsely chopped, or 1 tbsp mild or hot paprika
3 in (7 cm) cinnamon stick, broken into pieces
1 tsp grated nutmeg
2 star anise
5 cardamom pods
$1/2$ stalk lemongrass, outer leaves removed,
    then sliced
2 kaffir lime leaves
2 tbsp coarsely chopped cilantro root
4 large garlic cloves, coarsely chopped
2 medium shallots, coarsely chopped
3-in (7-cm) piece galangal, chopped
1 tbsp shrimp paste
$1/2$ tsp ground turmeric

METHOD

Heat the oil in a frying pan over moderate heat. Stir-fry the chilies, cinnamon, nutmeg, star anise, cardamoms, lemongrass, kaffir lime leaves, cilantro root, garlic, shallots, and galangal for about 5 minutes or until fragrant and lightly toasted.

Transfer the ingredients to a blender. Add the shrimp paste and turmeric and blend until smooth, adding water (1 tbsp at a time as necessary) to ease the process. The paste can be kept in an airtight container in the refrigerator for up to 3 days.

Prahoc kroeung k'tih Curried fermented fish and pork dip

Seasoned with the fermented fish paste called *prahoc*, this is an example of the unique flavor combinations Cambodian cuisine has to offer. Serve the dip with plain rice and with crunchy raw vegetables, such as green beans, cabbage, cucumber, or eggplant, and fruit in season.

INGREDIENTS

2 tbsp *prahoc*
$\frac{1}{4}$ cup coconut oil
8 oz (225 g) coarsely ground pork
4–5 tbsp red Kroeung (p264)
4 tbsp palm sugar or granulated sugar
1–1$\frac{1}{2}$ cups thick coconut milk
   (p213)
$\frac{1}{2}$ cup tamarind water (p322)
4–6 kaffir lime leaves, bruised
3–6 oz (100–150 g) pea eggplants
salt

METHOD

Crush the *prahoc* with 5 tbsp hot water in a bowl, then leave to soak for 10 minutes. Pass through a sieve set over a bowl, pressing the *prahoc* solids against the sieve. Discard any remaining solids and reserve the extract.

Heat the coconut oil in a saucepan over moderately high heat and stir-fry the pork, breaking it up, for about 5 minutes or until lightly golden. Stir in the *kroeung* and sugar and cook for 1 minute or until fragrant. Add the coconut milk, tamarind water, *prahoc* extract, and kaffir lime leaves and bring to a boil. Reduce the heat to moderately low, add the pea eggplants, and season to taste with salt. Cook for a further 5 minutes.

Remove the kaffir lime leaves and transfer to a serving bowl. Serve at room temperature.

Serves 4

rich, mildly
sweet, and
spicy

Amok chouk Steamed snails in curry custard

Amok is a curried coconut custard that is generally steamed in a small container hand-formed from a section of banana leaf. A specialty of Malaysia, hybrid versions appear in both Thai and Cambodian cooking. While freshwater fish such as catfish is used in many *amok* recipes, this delicious and dramatic version uses snails, and the snails and custard are cooked in the shells. Serve this as an appetizer or light lunch or as part of a dinner with vegetables and rice on the side. Be sure to buy canned Burgundian snails, which are usually sold in a package with clean shells. The exact snail-to-custard ratio will depend on the relative size of the snail and shell; the custard should not overflow the shell.

INGREDIENTS

1/4 cup red Kroeung (p264)
2 cups thick coconut milk (p213)
1 tbsp shrimp paste
1 tbsp fish sauce
2 tsp palm sugar or superfine sugar (optional)
1 large egg, beaten
grated zest of 1/2 kaffir lime
salt

1 stalk lemongrass, leaves separated and cut
    into 24 pieces, each 4 in (10 cm) long
24–36 snail shells, well cleaned
24–36 cooked Burgundian snails (about 2 cans),
    rinsed and drained
6 kaffir lime leaves, very finely julienned
4 red Thai chilies, seeded and very thinly
    sliced into rounds

METHOD

In a mixing bowl, stir and mash together the *kroeung*, half of the coconut milk, the shrimp paste, fish sauce, and sugar to a smooth consistency. Add the remaining coconut milk, the egg, and kaffir lime zest and mix well. Season with salt, if necessary.

Fold a piece of lemongrass leaf and set it inside a snail shell so both ends of the leaf stick out. Half-fill the shell with the coconut mixture. Place a snail in the center and fill with more coconut mixture. Set the snail, open end up, on a bamboo steaming rack. Repeat with the remaining lemongrass pieces, shells, coconut mixture, and snails. As you fill the steaming rack, the snails will butt up against each other and find enough support to stand. (If using a 6- or 12-portion stainless steel or ceramic snail plate, simply set the snails directly on the plate, and the plate on the bamboo steaming rack.)

Half-fill a wok with water and set the covered bamboo steamer on top (the base of the steamer should not touch the water). Bring to a boil over high heat, then reduce to medium-low and steam the snails for about 15 minutes or until the custard is set but still moist.

Serve the snails hot, garnished with the kaffir lime leaves and chilies. To eat, simply pull out the lemongrass strands, dislodging the snail in the process.

Serves 4

aromatic,
mildly sweet,
and spicy

Kari trey Catfish curry with rice noodles

In Cambodia, fish accounts for 70 percent or more of the protein in the daily diet, and catfish, caught in the Tonle Sap (Great Lake) near Siem Reap and the Mekong River, has long been one of the most widely eaten fish. White-fleshed and mild in flavor, it absorbs all the spices and herbs a curry sauce has to offer. In this recipe, tender catfish morsels complement crunchy bamboo and water spinach. Thin, delicate rice noodles make a perfect canvas on which the exotic flavors and contrasting textures meet. If using fresh, round rice noodles (spaghetti-shaped), dip them in boiling water for a few seconds to heat them. If using dried rice sticks, (linguine-shaped), rehydrate them in water until pliable, then cook in boiling water for 1–2 minutes.

INGREDIENTS

3 tbsp coconut oil
4–5 tbsp yellow Kroeung (p264)
1 tbsp shrimp paste
1 1/2 tbsp palm sugar
6 oz (175 g) coarsely ground pork (optional)
1 quart (liter) thick coconut milk (p213)
2 lb (900 g) catfish fillets, cut into
  2-in (5-cm) pieces
1 stalk lemongrass, outer leaves discarded,
  then sliced

6 kaffir lime leaves, bruised
1 large bamboo shoot, parboiled and thinly
  sliced lengthwise
1 bunch of water spinach, halved crosswise
fish sauce to taste
1 lb (450 g) fresh thin, round rice noodles or
  rice sticks, cooked (see above)
red Thai chilies, seeded and thinly sliced
  into rounds

METHOD

Heat the coconut oil in a pan over medium-high heat and stir-fry the *kroeung* and shrimp paste, breaking up the paste with the back of a spoon, for about 2 minutes or until just golden and fragrant. Add the palm sugar and pork and stir-fry, breaking up the pork fully, for about 5 minutes or until cooked and lightly golden.

Reduce the heat to moderately low. Add the coconut milk, catfish, lemongrass, and kaffir lime leaves. Cook for 5 minutes. Add the bamboo shoots and water spinach, cover, and cook for a further 5 minutes. Adjust the seasoning with fish sauce.

Place a serving of rice noodles on each of 4 plates. Ladle the fish curry into 4 bowls. Serve with the chilies on the side. To eat, simply grab some noodles with chopsticks and dip them in the coconut curry, adding chilies to taste.

Serves 4

sweet,
savory, and
mild to spicy

Kari mouan Chicken curry with young jackfruit

This Cambodian chicken curry is a sensual delight. Jackfruit, which is widely grown and eaten throughout Southeast Asia, is sweet with floral notes when ripe. The unripened fruit, although not as complex in flavor, is used much in the same way a vegetable would be in savory dishes. In this curry, crunchy young jackfruit morsels complement the tender chicken, giving the dish a wonderful range of textures. If you cannot find fresh jackfruit, brined jackfruit in cans or jars, sometimes labeled 'young green jackfruit', makes a good substitute. Be sure to soak and rinse the brined jackfruit in several changes of water before use. Serve Kari Mouan with rice or baguette (p290) and stir-fried leafy greens.

INGREDIENTS

1 chicken, about $2^1/_2$ lb (1 kg)
3 tbsp coconut oil
4–5 tbsp red Kroeung (p264)
1 tbsp shrimp paste
1 tbsp Vietnamese Cari (p282) or
   store-bought Indian curry powder
$1^1/_2$ tbsp palm sugar

1 quart (liter) thick coconut milk (p213)
1 stalk lemongrass, outer leaves discarded,
   then sliced
6 kaffir lime leaves, bruised
8–12 oz (225–350 g) young jackfruit chunks
fish sauce to taste

METHOD

Remove the legs from the chicken and split them at the joint into thighs and drumsticks. Remove the wings and discard the tips. Split the chicken in half down the breastbone. Cut out the back and discard or reserve for making stock. Cut each breast crosswise into 2 equal pieces. You should have 10 pieces in total.

Heat the oil in a large pan over medium-high heat. Add the chicken pieces, skin side down, and brown for about 10 minutes, turning to color all sides. Remove the chicken from the pan.

Add the *kroeung* and shrimp paste and stir-fry, breaking up the paste with the back of a spoon, for about 2 minutes or until just golden and fragrant. Add the curry powder and palm sugar and stir for a further minute or until fragrant.

Reduce the heat to medium-low. Return the chicken to the pan and add the coconut milk, lemongrass, and kaffir lime leaves. Cover and cook for 20 minutes. Add the jackfruit, adjust seasoning with fish sauce, and cook for a further 10 minutes. Serve hot.

Serves 4

light and
aromatic

Saraman Cardamom and ginger beef curry with peanuts

Full of meat such as beef or duck and rich by Asian standards, Saraman is often served in restaurants or prepared for special occasions, when it is eaten in modest quantities. A classic Cambodian-style braised curry, it has dominant cardamom and ginger flavors, and the addition of peanuts helps to thicken the stew to a crème anglaise consistency. Serve over rice or with baguette (p290) for soaking up the "gravy," with pickled vegetables (p283) and stir-fried leafy greens as side dishes.

INGREDIENTS

3 oz (85 g) fresh ginger root, finely grated

1½ lb (675 g) boneless beef shin steak or thin flank, cut into 1½-in (4-cm) cubes

2 tbsp coconut oil

2 dried large red chilies, soaked, seeded and torn in half

1 tsp coarsely chopped galangal

4 large garlic cloves, crushed

1 large shallot, coarsely chopped

1 stalk lemongrass, outer leaves discarded then sliced

3 in (7 cm) cinnamon stick

2 star anise

7 green cardamom pods

1 tsp grated nutmeg

½ tsp ground mace

1½ tbsp finely chopped cilantro root

¼ tsp ground turmeric

3 tbsp vegetable oil

1 tbsp shrimp paste

1 quart (liter) thick coconut milk (p213)

¼ cup palm sugar or granulated sugar

¼ cup tamarind water (p322)

2 tbsp fish sauce

3 oz (75 g) unsalted roasted peanut halves

salt

2–4 red Thai chilies, seeded and thinly sliced (optional)

METHOD

Squeeze the grated ginger in your hand to extract the juice into a bowl. Discard the dry fibers. Add the beef to the bowl and toss to coat with the ginger juice, then leave to marinate for 30 minutes.

Meanwhile, heat the coconut oil in a saucepan over medium heat and stir-fry the chilies, galangal, garlic, shallot, and lemongrass until fragrant. Add the cinnamon, star anise, cardamoms, nutmeg, and mace and stir-fry for 5–7 minutes or until fragrant and lightly toasted. Transfer the ingredients to a blender. Add the cilantro root and turmeric and blend until smooth, adding water (1 tbsp at a time as necessary) to ease the process. Set this curry paste aside.

Heat the vegetable oil in a large pan over medium-high heat and stir-fry the shrimp paste, breaking it up with the back of a spoon, for 15–30 seconds or until a shade darker. Add half of the coconut milk and the curry paste. Stir well. Add the beef. Cook for 20 minutes, stirring occasionally.

Reduce the heat to low and add the remaining coconut milk, the sugar, tamarind water, fish sauce, and peanuts. Season with salt, if necessary. Simmer, covered, for 1½–2 hours or until the meat is fork-tender, adding more coconut milk if the stew thickens too much. Serve garnished with chilies.

Serves 4

rich, creamy, nutty, and mild to spicy

Kore Laotian all-purpose curry paste

Laotian curries are hybrids, taking their herbal base from Thai curries and their flavorful dry spice notes from Indian curries in making a basic paste. Accordingly, the fresh ingredients lemongrass, galangal, ginger, kaffir lime zest, shallots, garlic, chilies, and cilantro root, and the dry spices cumin, turmeric, and coriander seed make up the foundation of any good Laotian curry. Sometimes a Laotian curry paste will include a small amount of Indian curry powder to deepen and broaden the dry spice flavor.

INGREDIENTS

1½ tsp cumin seeds
1 tbsp coriander seeds
1 stalk lemongrass, outer leaves discarded then chopped
1 oz (30 g) galangal, chopped
grated zest of 1 kaffir lime
3 large garlic cloves, crushed
1 large shallot, chopped

3 tbsp finely chopped cilantro root
1 oz (30 g) turmeric root, chopped, or ½ tsp ground turmeric
1 oz (30 g) fresh ginger root, chopped, or ½ tsp ground ginger
4 or more green or red Thai chilies, seeded
2 tsp shrimp paste
1 tbsp Indian curry powder (optional)

METHOD

Heat a dry frying pan over moderate heat and roast the cumin and coriander seeds for about 2 minutes or until fragrant.

Put the lemongrass, galangal, kaffir lime zest, garlic, shallot, cilantro root, turmeric, ginger, chilies, and roasted cumin and coriander seeds in a blender. Blend the ingredients to a smooth consistency, adding water (1 tbsp at a time as necessary) to ease the process. Add the shrimp paste and curry powder, if using, and blend well.

The paste can be kept in an airtight container in the refrigerator for up to 3 days.

Kore pou gali Stir-fried yellow curried crabs

This seafood curry is a stir-fry rather than the more usual stewed dish. The fierce cooking heat elevates the aromas of the herbs and spices, caramelizing their natural sugars and intensifying the overall flavor of the dish. Kore Pou Gali is prepared using small, rice-paddy-raised freshwater crabs, but any small crabs will do as long as they are halved or quartered to allow the curry flavors to mingle with the natural juices of the crabmeat. The dish is a perfect appetizer or light lunch served with steamed sticky rice and pickled vegetables (p283). As with many Laotian foods, this can be served at room temperature and eaten with the hands. Some Lao cooks make this curried crab using only Indian curry powder; others use a fresh curry paste such as the one called for here; and still others combine the two. These approaches betray the cultural underpinnings of Laotian food. Equally delicious stir-fries can be made using cut-up lobster, clams, or mussels.

INGREDIENTS
1/4 cup vegetable oil
5 tbsp Laotian Kore (opposite) or store-bought
   Thai curry paste
1 tsp Indian curry powder (optional)
8 small crabs, about 8 oz (225 g) each,
   halved or quartered
2 green onions, thinly sliced diagonally

METHOD
Heat the oil in a wok over high heat and stir-fry the curry paste for about 5 minutes or until golden and fragrant. Add the curry powder, if using, and stir-fry to blend well.

Reduce the heat to moderate and add the pieces of crab, tossing them to coat each piece with the curry paste. Cover the wok and cook for 5 minutes. Toss the crabs again and cook, covered, for a further 5 minutes.

Transfer the crabs to a serving platter and garnish with the green onions.

Serves 4

light and
spicy-hot

Gang keo goung Green shrimp curry with fresh dill

Fresh dill, sometimes referred to as Laotian coriander, is widely used in Laos for fish or other seafood dishes. Never used dried or cooked, the dill fronds are added at the last minute as a garnish. Here they enliven a green shrimp curry, also helping to mellow the sometimes intense flavor of kaffir lime leaves. Eat this curry at room temperature with steamed sticky rice on the side: with your fingers, pinch and shape a small amount of rice into a ball and dip into the curry, eating shrimp along with dill in the same bite.

INGREDIENTS

3 tbsp vegetable oil
5 tbsp Laotian Kore (p274) or store-bought
  Thai curry paste
1 tbsp shrimp paste
1 tbsp palm sugar or granulated sugar
2 cups thick coconut milk (p213)
2 cups chicken or vegetable stock

4–6 kaffir lime leaves, bruised
fish sauce to taste
2 large waxy potatoes, peeled and cut into
  1-in (2.5-cm) pieces
1^1/$_2$ lb (675 g) raw tiger shrimp, peeled
  and deveined
1 bunch of dill

METHOD

Heat the oil in a pan over moderately high heat and stir-fry the curry paste for about 2 minutes or until just golden and fragrant. Add the shrimp paste (breaking it up) and palm sugar, and stir-fry for 1 minute or until fragrant. Reduce the heat and add the coconut milk, stock, kaffir lime leaves, and fish sauce. Add the potatoes, cover the pot, and cook for 20 minutes.

Add the shrimp and stir well, then cover again and cook for about 5 minutes or until they turn pink. Serve hot, garnished with dill fronds.

Serves 4

lemony
and
sweet

Kao soi Noodles with pork in red curry broth

This curry noodle soup is a specialty of the Laotian northern region of Luang Namtha and is similar to a dish of the same name from northern Thailand. It is widely believed, however, that Kao Soi originated in Myanmar. This version combines coconut milk with a light pork stock, creating a delicious, subtle broth. The steaming liquid is poured over raw vegetables, and it is completed with tender rice noodles and bits of sweet pork. If preparing the dish with Laotian Kore, omit the optional Indian curry powder in that recipe, as it is added here.

INGREDIENTS

1 lb (450 g) boned pork shoulder
2 oz (60 g) fresh ginger root
6 green onions, 4 of them crushed and 2 thinly sliced diagonally
2 tbsp fish sauce, or to taste
2 tbsp vegetable oil
5 tbsp Laotian Kore (p274) or store-bought Thai red curry paste
1 tbsp Indian curry powder
1 tsp shrimp paste
1 tbsp palm sugar
8 oz (225 g) coarsely ground pork

1 quart (liter) thick coconut milk (p213)
8 kaffir lime leaves, bruised
1 lb (450 g) fresh, thin, round rice noodles, or 8 oz (225 g) dried rice sticks, soaked in water until pliable
5–6 oz (150–175 g) Chinese leaf, cut into 1/8-in (3-mm) julienne
1 bunch of watercress, large stalks discarded
4 oz (100 g) beansprouts
2 tbsp torn mint leaves
2 tbsp torn cilantro leaves
1 lime, quartered

METHOD

Bring 1 1/2 quarts (1.5 liters) water to a boil and add the pork shoulder, ginger, crushed green onions, and 2 tbsp fish sauce. Reduce the heat and simmer, partly covered, for about 1 1/2 hours or until the liquid has reduced by half. Transfer the pork to a cutting board to cool, then slice thinly and cover with plastic wrap. Set the broth aside.

In another pan, heat the oil over moderately high heat and stir-fry the curry paste for 2 minutes or until just golden and fragrant. Add the curry powder, shrimp paste (breaking it up), and palm sugar, and stir-fry for about 1 minute or until fragrant. Add the ground pork and cook, stirring to break it up, for about 7 minutes or until just golden. Reduce the heat and add the coconut milk, pork broth, and kaffir lime leaves. Adjust seasoning with fish sauce. Cover and simmer for 30 minutes.

Bring a pot of water to a boil. If the fresh rice noodles are cold, heat in the boiling water for 5 seconds; if they are at room temperature, skip this step. If using rehydrated rice sticks, cook them for 3 minutes. Drain.

Divide the noodles among 4 large Asian-style soup bowls and top with Chinese leaf, watercress, beansprouts, and sliced pork shoulder. Bring the spicy coconut broth to a boil, then ladle into the bowls. Garnish with mint and cilantro, squeeze a lime wedge over each serving, and serve hot.

Serves 4

spicy, rich, and aromatic

Kang soh Bamboo shoot salad

This bamboo shoot salad is believed to have originated in the mountains of northern Laos, which are known for their particularly delicious wild bamboo shoots. While any bamboo shoot can be the basis for a tangy and savory salad, slender, young winter shoots are prized for their tenderness—shoots cultivated past the winter season, in spring or summer, tend to be more fibrous and less juicy. Always use a good-quality fish sauce that is golden amber in color to ensure a fresh and clean flavor (black indicates excessive aging). If using fresh bamboo shoots, peel and parboil for 15 minutes to get rid of any natural toxins, then drain. If using canned bamboo shoots, be sure to select whole shoots; drain and parboil them for 2 minutes to remove any canned flavor.

INGREDIENTS

1 small shallot, halved
1 large garlic clove, crushed
2 tbsp fish sauce
2 tbsp lime juice
1 red Thai chili, seeded and thinly sliced
1 lb (450 g) bamboo shoots, halved and thinly
    sliced lengthwise
1 green onion, thinly sliced diagonally
1/2 bunch of cilantro, stalks discarded
toasted sesame seeds

METHOD

Serves 4

refreshing,
crunchy,
and mild

Heat a dry frying pan and char the shallot and garlic over medium heat for about 2 minutes, turning to color all sides. Allow to cool, then finely chop the shallot and garlic.

Mix together the fish sauce, lime juice, shallot, garlic, and chili in a large bowl. Cover and set aside for 20 minutes.

Add the bamboo shoots, green onion, and most of the cilantro leaves to the bowl and toss to coat with the dressing. Transfer the salad to a serving platter and garnish with the remaining cilantro leaves and toasted sesame seeds.

Cari Vietnamese all-purpose curry powder

In contrast to other Southeast Asian cuisines, Vietnamese curries employ powders rather than pastes. This powder is based on traditional Indian curry powder, which can be used as a substitute if necessary. Freshly ground spices make for deep flavors and rich aromas. If you enjoy authentic flavors, making your own curry powder from scratch will be something you want to try. Freshly made versions differ from place to place and cook to cook, of course. This one includes star anise, a spice not generally included in Indian curry powders but enjoyed in Vietnam.

INGREDIENTS

8 curry leaves
2 star anise
1–2 dried red chilies, deseeded (optional)
$1/4$ cup coriander seeds
2 tsp cumin seeds
$1/2$ tsp mustard seeds
1 tsp fenugreek seeds
$1/2$ tsp whole cloves
1 tsp black peppercorns
1 tbsp ground turmeric
1 tsp ground ginger
1 tsp grated nutmeg
$1/2$ tsp ground cinnamon

METHOD

Heat a dry frying pan over medium heat. Add the curry leaves, star anise, red chilies (if using), coriander, cumin, mustard and fenugreek seeds, cloves, and peppercorns and roast, constantly shaking the pan to prevent the ingredients from burning, for about 1 minute or until a shade darker. Remove from the heat and leave to cool.

Transfer the spices to a spice mill or clean coffee grinder and process to a fine powder. Put into a jar and add the turmeric, ginger, nutmeg, and cinnamon. Close the jar and shake to blend. Store the curry powder in a dark, cool place, where it will keep for 3–6 months.

Rau chay chua Pickled vegetables

Pickled vegetables are an integral part of the Southeast Asian diet, considered essential accompaniments to meals. Believed to aid digestion of rich, fatty or oil-based dishes, pickled vegetables are appropriately served with curries, "cutting" the fat while "lifting" and cleansing the palate to allow a deeper enjoyment of the food.

INGREDIENTS

1 lb (450 g) ridge cucumbers, peeled (optional) and deseeded
1 lb (450 g) daikon radish, peeled
1 lb (450 g) carrots, peeled

3 tbsp sea salt
$1/2$ cup sugar
$1^1/2$ cups white rice vinegar

METHOD

Cut the cucumbers and mooli into sticks $1/4$ in (5 mm) thick and $1^1/2$ in (4 cm) long. Cut the carrots into sticks of the same length but $1/8$ in (3 mm) thick.

Put the vegetables in 3 separate colanders set over mixing bowls. Sprinkle each vegetable with 1 tbsp salt and toss, then leave to drain for 1 hour.

Gently squeeze any remaining juice out of the vegetables, then transfer them to a large, resealable plastic bag.

In a bowl, whisk together the sugar and rice vinegar until the sugar is completely dissolved. Add this pickling liquid to the vegetables. Close the bag, squeezing out any air. Leave to marinate for 3 hours before serving. You can keep the pickles in the refrigerator for a week or two; the longer they are kept, the softer they will be and the more pronounced the pickle flavor.

Serves 4–8

crunchy,
sweet and
sour

SALTED LEMONADE

Believed to aid digestion, this unsweetened lemonade (called da chanh muoi*) made with salt-preserved lemons (sometimes limes) is enjoyed at the end of a meal, either served at room temperature or chilled with ice cubes. It is also drunk during the day as a thirst quencher and restorative, particularly in warm weather. The ratio of lemon to water given here can be adjusted to taste. For 1 serving, rinse $1/3$ preserved salt-brined lemon and put in a bowl. Crush the lemon with a fork. Place $1–1^1/2$ tbsp of the crushed lemon in a large glass. Add ice cubes to taste, if using, and top off with 1 cup still or sparkling mineral water. Stir a few times, then drink. While best made fresh, large quantities (full pitchers) can be prepared a few hours ahead of time and kept in a cool place or chilled.*

Cari ga Chicken curry with sweet potatoes and carrots

Vietnamese curries are a specialty of the south of the country, where the Indian culinary influences are pronounced. While herbal pastes are generally employed in Cambodian or Laotian curies, they are absent from Vietnamese versions, and fresh herbs such as lemongrass and kaffir lime leaves are used whole as flavor enhancements. Another difference is that for a chicken curry such as this one, the Vietnamese cook will marinate the chicken in a sweetened curry powder before cooking. Potatoes are an integral part of Vietnamese curries, with the preferred type being sweet white yams. Serve this with rice or baguette (p290).

INGREDIENTS

1 chicken, about 2^1/$_2$ lb (1 kg)
2 tbsp Vietnamese Cari (p282) or
   store-bought Indian curry powder
1 tsp sugar
1 tsp salt
^{1}/$_4$ cup vegetable oil
2–3 white yams or sweet potatoes, peeled
   and cut into 1-in (2.5-cm) cubes
3 large garlic cloves, crushed
2 shallots, cut into wedges

1 quart (liter) thick coconut milk (p213)
2 tsp annatto seed extract (optional)
2 stalks lemongrass, outer leaves removed,
   then bruised
2 kaffir lime leaves
2 tbsp fish sauce
3 large carrots, peeled and cut into
   1^1/$_2$–2-in- (4–5-cm-) long pieces
salt

METHOD

Remove the legs from the chicken and split them at the joint into thighs and drumsticks. Remove the wings and discard the tips. Split the chicken in half down the breastbone. Cut out the back and discard (or reserve for making stock). Cut each breast crosswise into 2 equal pieces. You should have 10 pieces in total.

Mix together 1 tbsp of the curry powder, the sugar, and the salt in a large bowl. Add the chicken and toss well to coat. Marinate for 1 hour.

Heat the oil in a large pan over medium-high heat and brown the yams all over for about 5 minutes. (The yams should be browned only, not cooked through.) With a slotted spoon, transfer the yams to paper towels to drain.

Add the chicken, skin side down, to the pan and cook for about 10 minutes, turning to brown all sides. With a slotted spoon, transfer the chicken to paper towels to drain.

Add the garlic and shallots to the pan and stir-fry for about 5 minutes or until lightly golden. Add the remaining curry powder, the coconut milk, annatto seed extract, lemongrass, kaffir lime leaves, fish sauce, and carrots, then return the chicken and yams to the pan. Bring to a boil. Reduce the heat to a gentle boil, cover, and cook for 20 minutes or until the chicken and yams are tender.

Serves 4

rich, slightly
spicy, and
fragrant

Cari chay Vegetable and tofu curry

Tofu, which originated in China millennia ago, came into Vietnamese cuisine during China's thousand-year rule of Vietnam, from approximately 100 BCE to 1000 CE. Today, with the high cost of meat (usually reserved for special occasions and holidays) and the religious preferences of vegetarian Buddhism, tofu still plays an important role in the country's cooking. Cari Chay combines tofu, bamboo, and Asian eggplant in a relatively light dish suitable for any season. It is subtle with a light coconut milk broth spiced with curry powder. The last-minute addition of Vietnamese cilantro lends a floral finish. Serve with rice or baguette (p290).

INGREDIENTS

3 tbsp vegetable oil
2 large garlic cloves, crushed
1 large shallot, thinly sliced
1–1¹/₂ tbsp Vietnamese Cari (p282) or store-bought Indian curry powder
1 tbsp palm sugar
1 quart (liter) thick coconut milk (p213)
juice of 1 lime
2 tbsp fish sauce (optional)
2 tsp annatto seed extract (optional)

2 stalks lemongrass, outer leaves discarded, then bruised
2 kaffir lime leaves, bruised
salt
2 lb (900 g) firm tofu, cut into 1-in (2.5-cm) cubes
1 large boiled bamboo shoot, thinly sliced
2 Asian eggplants, halved lengthwise and cut into 1-in (2.5-cm) pieces
24 Vietnamese cilantro leaves or Thai basil leaves

Serves 4

light,
sweet, and
lemony

METHOD

Heat the oil in a pan over high heat and stir-fry the garlic and shallot for about 5 minutes or until they are golden. Add the curry powder and palm sugar and continue to stir-fry for 1 minute or until fragrant. Add the coconut milk, lime juice, fish sauce, annatto seed extract, lemongrass, and kaffir lime leaves. Bring to a boil, then reduce the heat to low. Adjust the seasoning with salt and add the tofu, bamboo shoot, and Asian eggplants. Simmer, covered, for 10–15 minutes or until the eggplants are tender.

Serve garnished with Vietnamese cilantro or Thai basil.

Rau muong xao Stir-fried water spinach

Also known as water convolvulus, swamp cabbage, or swamp morning glory in English, and *rau muong* (Vietnamese), *bongz* (Laotian), and *trakuon* (Cambodian), this leafy green vegetable is abundant in Southeast Asia. Prized for being versatile, flavorful, nutritious, and well-textured, it has tender, narrow, and pointy leaves with crunchy, hollow stalks. Water spinach can be added whole to soups or to stir-fries such as this one, where it is seasoned with fish sauce, garlic, and a pinch of sugar. Thought of as a wonderful embodiment of the ancient Chinese philosophy of yin and yang (balanced opposites), it combines tender and crunchy textures in each bite.

INGREDIENTS

2 tbsp vegetable oil
2 large garlic cloves, chopped
1 lb (450 g) water spinach
1 tbsp fish sauce, or 1 tbsp (1–2 cubes)
    fermented bean curd
pinch of sugar
pepper to taste

METHOD

Heat the oil in a frying pan or wok over high heat and stir-fry the garlic for about 2 minutes or until fragrant and lightly golden. Add the water spinach, fish sauce, sugar, and pepper and cover the pan. Cook for 5 minutes.

Remove the lid, toss a few more times, and serve hot.

Serves 4

savory,
crunchy,
and tender

< **Floating market,
Mekong Delta**

Banh mi Saigon baguette

Originating from the French colonial era of the mid-1800s to mid-1900s, Banh Mi is made from a mixture of rice and wheat flours. Shorter (about half the length) and lighter than their French cousins, and sometimes almond-shaped rather than long and slender, these breads have become an integral part of the everyday Vietnamese and Cambodian diet. In lieu of the more traditional rice or noodles, baguette is often eaten with coconut curries, where it is used as a scoop. Smeared with butter, it is also enjoyed for breakfast; when sliced lengthwise and filled with pork, vegetables, and chili paste it is a popular lunchtime sandwich.

INGREDIENTS

$^1/_2$ oz (15 g) fresh yeast
$1^1/_2$ cups lukewarm water
1 cup rice flour

$2^3/_4$ cups white bread flour, plus
   extra for kneading
2 tsp salt

METHOD

Put the yeast in a small bowl and add the lukewarm water. Stir until dissolved.

Sift the flours and salt into a large mixing bowl. Make a well in the center and add the yeast liquid. With a wooden spoon, incorporate the wet and dry ingredients until fully combined. The dough should be soft, not wet, and definitely not stiff.

Turn the soft dough onto a floured work surface and knead for about 5 minutes or until smooth and elastic. Shape into a ball. Grease a large mixing bowl and place the dough ball in it. Cover with plastic wrap and leave to rise at warm room temperature for 3 hours or until doubled in size.

Punch down the dough, bringing the sides toward the center. Turn the dough out onto a floured work surface and knead for 2 minutes, then shape into a ball once again. Divide the dough into 4 equal pieces. Make sure they are separated by 2 in (5 cm) or so, then cover them with plastic wrap and leave to rise at warm room temperature for 2 hours or until doubled in size.

Punch down each piece of dough, rolling and pulling it (against the work surface) back into a ball. Stretch each ball roughly into a $^1/_2$-in- (1-cm-) thick rectangle, then roll into a slender, almond-shaped loaf with tapered ends. Cover the dough with oiled plastic wrap and leave to rise at warm room temperature for 1 hour or until almost doubled in size.

Remove all but one rack from your oven. Place the rack at the bottom and set a pizza stone on it. Preheat the oven to 450°F (230°C).

Sprinkle a peel or baking tray with flour and place 1 or 2 shaped breads on it. Score each bread 3 times on the diagonal using a clean razor blade or sharp knife. Slide the breads onto the hot stone and bake for 20–25 minutes or until golden. Transfer the loaves to a wire rack and leave to cool for 1–2 hours before eating.

Makes 4

OUTPOSTS

< Brixton Market, London

Comforting, celebratory, and diverse, South Asian cooking styles have traveled well across thousands of miles, amassing worldwide acclaim from curry aficionados and connoisseurs alike. There are few classic cuisines that have evolved and been embraced by host countries in the same way as Indian food. Encapsulated in the blending of favorite spices is a cosmopolitan appreciation of global cooking styles. From South African *masalas*, Caribbean stews, colonial British curries, and Japanese-inspired spice formulas, the variety and versatility of curry in all its guises have impressive credentials.

Over centuries, the sustained and successive movement of slaves, followed by indentured labor, economic emigrés, and businesspeople, laid the foundation for the changing flavors of displaced Indian kitchens. Familiar food and preparations—the aroma of toasted cumin seeds, the rhythmic pounding of *masalas*, and a pot of bubbling rice on the stove— were the only culinary links to a country left far behind. Adept home cooks soon learned to adapt meals to suit the produce of their newly adopted country. And in doing so, they won over the local populace and enriched national cuisines. Even in Japan, where Indian-style dishes arrived via the tenuous route of the Western palate, curries are malleable enough to be included on restaurant menus and for quick, accessible home cooking.

One of the tenets of Asian hospitality is sharing home-cooked food with family and friends, making sure that there's enough to go around. Even in homes with meager resources, there's usually an extra portion prepared "for the pot" or as a token offering to the gods. For unexpected guests, a handful of chopped vegetables added to chicken curry, or a fistful of peas tossed into rice as it simmers, is a life-saver. Whether in Durban, Glasgow, or Trinidad, cooks will all give a nod to their cultural heritage in the same way. Recipes are accommodating and rarely regimented—making an Indian curry is pretty much a laid-back affair, so nobody holds back from putting in their own add-ons.

At the same time, top chefs have fashioned a new approach, elevating curries to fine dining status, and these interpretations are an acknowledgment of the curry's versatility. Local produce—Jamaican chilies, Japanese noodles, or succulent Scottish salmon—are as likely to be found on modern menus as are the traditional stalwarts such as fresh cilantro, green chilies, and garam masala. The global reach of Indian cooking and the curry has long since crossed national boundaries, and is a tribute to, and an endorsement of, entrepreneurial flair, acculturation, and experimentation.

From hearty African staples to Cape Malay curries, fiery Indian *masalas*, and European mainstays, modern South African kitchens are a melting pot of world cuisines. Despite apartheid and its attempts at racial segregation, for centuries culinary curiosity for other cooking styles has tempted taste buds into trying new and adventurous dishes. Indian and Cape Malay dishes have stood the test of time, seasoning South Africa's meals with sweetly spiced offerings, succulent kebabs, and an array of pickles and *sambals*.

To appreciate South Africa's richly diverse food history, it's worth tracing the journey of immigrants, settlers, and slaves who made the arduous journey across the seas hundreds of years ago. Their arrival transformed the culinary scene, as they brought with them an appreciation for kitchen specialties traced to what is now Indonesia and India. Cape Malays, the descendants of the original slave population, are skillful cooks, and evoke a love of flavorsome Southeast Asian cooking, often combining sweet fruity flavors with tart-tasting tamarind and aromatic spices. Their culinary heritage is celebrated in the kitchen with exotic sun-kissed produce, including lemon leaves, fennel seeds, cinnamon, and cardamoms.

In the 19th century, Indian laborers were brought to Natal to work in the sugar-cane fields. Because time for cooking was limited, curries were adapted to suit the needs of the day, with many dishes taking on a fiery stewlike character that included an assortment of lentils, beans, and herbs. Spotting a new market, Indian entrepreneurs, particularly from the Gujarati community, established trade links, plying spices, foodstuffs, and textiles. Many settled in eastern and southern Africa, adapting their curries to take in local ingredients, such as cornmeal and African legumes. In Kenya, this acculturation process went even further, with Indian "curries" adopting Swahili titles for local consumption. In South Africa, decades of a shared immigrant experience and a common identity forged around surviving apartheid have tended to ease traditional caste differences and regional and linguistic variance. For the most part, culinary and cultural diversity has been swapped for an all-embracing approach to pan-Indian cooking, notable for its distinctive South African character.

From Bobotie, Cape Malay's tasty take on shepherds' pie, to Bunny Chow, a seriously spicy, curry-filled bread loaf, it is family food cooked for everyday meals that really showcases the best flavors. Indian-inspired South African cooking can never be fussy or fanciful. The crackle of curry leaves, the nutty aroma of popped mustard seeds, and the sweet whiff of toasted fennel seeds is always within sniffing distance. Indian cooking, in all its guises, is as steeped in South African culinary culture as biltong, *boerewors* (farmers' sausages), and the ultimate in barbecues, the *braai*.

Roopa Gulati

Frying spices >
Toast curry leaves, cinnamon, and mustard seeds in hot oil

Butter bean curry

Durban ground spice *masalas* are sold by weight from market stalls, and there's a different spice blend for almost every style of curry. One favorite is "mother-in-law's tongue" *masala*—and what a lashing of chilies it unleashes. In this recipe, which is also called sugar bean curry, I've recreated my own mother-in-law's special spice blend. It's milder than many *masalas* and has an almost nutty character, spiked with the bite of refreshingly sharp chilies. The creamy blandness of butter beans works especially well with the pungency of Indian spices.

INGREDIENTS

3 tbsp vegetable oil
1 tsp mustard seeds
2 sprigs of curry leaves (about 2 tbsp leaves)
3–4 fenugreek seeds
2 onions, diced
1$^{1}/_{4}$-in (3-cm) piece fresh ginger root, finely chopped
3 garlic cloves, finely chopped
2 green chilies, seeded and chopped
4 plum tomatoes, peeled and chopped
1 carrot, scrubbed and cut into 1$^{1}/_{4}$-in (3-cm) chunks
$^{3}/_{4}$ tsp ground coriander

$^{1}/_{4}$ tsp ground turmeric
$^{1}/_{2}$ tsp red chili powder
$^{3}/_{4}$ tsp ground cumin
$^{1}/_{2}$ tsp ground garam masala
1 red pepper, seeded and cut into 1$^{1}/_{4}$-in (3-cm) chunks
3 oz (75 g) green beans, cut into 1$^{1}/_{4}$-in (3-cm) lengths
14 oz (400 g) canned butter beans, drained
2 tbsp chopped cilantro leaves

METHOD

Heat the vegetable oil in a *karahi* or wok. When hot, toss in the mustard seeds, followed by the curry leaves and fenugreek seeds. After about 30 seconds, the spices will give off a nutty aroma.

Add the onions and soften over low heat for about 10 minutes. Stir in the ginger, garlic, and green chilies and continue frying until the onions are flecked golden.

Turn the heat up slightly, add the chopped tomatoes to the pan, and cook until thickened and darkened in color. Add the carrot and sprinkle with the ground coriander, turmeric, chili powder, cumin, and garam masala. Fry briskly for 1 minute before adding $^{2}/_{3}$ cup hot water. Cover the pan and simmer for 10–15 minutes or until the carrots are just tender.

Stir in the red pepper and green beans and continue cooking, uncovered, for 10 minutes or until the vegetables are softened.

Add the butter beans and pour in another $^{2}/_{3}$ cup hot water. Half cover the pan and simmer for a further 10 minutes. You might need to add more water as the beans cook.

Garnish with chopped cilantro and serve with boiled rice.

Serves 4

warmly
spiced and
aromatic

Mtuzi wa samaki Kenyan fish curry

Fiery, brothlike curries, sharpened with tamarind and enriched with coconut milk, are typical of the Gujarati-inspired dishes from East Africa. Most Gujaratis are vegetarian, and although this curry is made with fish, the recipe also works well with vegetables—green beans, baby eggplants, and chunks of carrot make a tasty combination. The best accompaniment to this dish would be generous helpings of rice, enough to soak up the delectably soupy *masala*.

INGREDIENTS
juice of 1 lime
1 tsp cracked black peppercorns
1$\frac{1}{4}$ lb (600 g) haddock fillet, skinned
  and cut into 2-in (5-cm) pieces
6 tbsp vegetable oil

Spice mixture
2 dried red chilies
$\frac{3}{4}$ tsp coriander seeds
$\frac{3}{4}$ tsp cumin seeds
1 tsp mustard seeds
$\frac{1}{4}$ tsp ground turmeric

Masala
1 red onion, finely chopped
1 red pepper, seeded and shredded
1 red chili, finely shredded
4 garlic cloves, finely chopped
9 oz (250 g) plum tomatoes, peeled
  and finely chopped
$\frac{3}{4}$ cup thick coconut milk (p213)
$\frac{1}{2}$ cup tamarind water (p322),
  or to taste

METHOD
To make the spice mixture, roast the chilies and seeds, then grind to a powder (p322). Combine with the turmeric. Set aside.

Combine the lime juice with the cracked peppercorns and pour over the fish. Heat the oil in a deep-sided frying pan. Pat the fish dry with paper towels, then fry for about 1 minute on each side until lightly colored but not quite cooked through. Using a slotted spoon, transfer the fish to a plate, cover with foil, and set aside while you make the *masala*.

Add the red onion to the pan you used for frying the fish. Cover and cook for about 5 minutes or until softened. If the onion looks like it is sticking to the bottom of the pan, add a dash of water. Add the red pepper, chili, and garlic, and continue frying, uncovered, for 10 minutes or until the onions are on the verge of turning color. Stir in the spice mixture and fry briskly for 1 minute.

Stir in the chopped tomatoes and bring to a boil, then pour in $\frac{3}{4}$ cup water. Simmer the curry for about 15 minutes or until thickened.

Pour in the coconut milk and add enough tamarind water to lend a pleasant tang. The curry shouldn't be too thick—aim for something almost brothlike in consistency.

Return the fish to the pan and simmer for 5–10 minutes or until cooked through. Serve hot.

Serves 4

soup-like and tangy

Crab and mango curry

Brimming with sunshine ingredients, this delectable curry from the Maldives marries tropical fruit with sizzling spices and fresh seafood. As with many Asian-inspired dishes, once you get a feel for the ingredients, feel free to experiment—try adding a few cloves, green chilies, or white peppercorns, for example. Other fruits that work well with seafood curries include star fruit, papaya, and pineapple.

INGREDIENTS

juice of 1 lime
$1/4$ tsp ground turmeric
$3/4$ tsp cracked black peppercorns
8 uncooked crab claws
1 firm, slightly underripe mango,
  cut into $3/4$-in (2-cm) cubes
1 tbsp palm sugar or muscovado sugar

Masala
$1/4$ cup vegetable oil
$3/4$ tsp mustard seeds
2 sprigs of curry leaves (about 2 tbsp leaves)

$1^{1}/2$ in (4 cm) cinnamon stick
1 large onion, sliced
2 red chilies, seeded and chopped
3 garlic cloves, finely chopped
$3/4$-in (2-cm) piece fresh ginger root,
  finely chopped
$1/2$ tsp ground cumin
$1/2$ tsp chili powder
1 tsp fennel seeds, roasted and ground (p322)
4 large plum tomatoes, peeled and
  finely chopped

METHOD

Combine the lime juice with the turmeric and cracked peppercorns. Coat the crab claws in the spiced juice and set aside.

Heat the oil in a wok or *karahi* and add the mustard seeds—they should start popping almost right away. Toss in the curry leaves and cinnamon stick. After about 30 seconds, once all the spluttering has settled down, add the sliced onion. Turn down the heat, cover the pan, and soften the onions for about 5 minutes.

Stir in the chilies, garlic, and ginger and cook for a further minute before adding the ground cumin, chili powder, and ground fennel. Stir to mix everything together, then add the tomatoes. Fry this *masala* until the tomatoes have cooked down and most of the liquid has evaporated.

Add the crab claws to the pan along with any spiced lime juice from the bowl. After a few seconds, add the mango cubes and sprinkle with the sugar. Turn the heat up high and continue frying for about 10 minutes or until the crab claws turn color and the meat is tender. If the *masala* looks like it is sticking to the bottom of the pan, add a dash of water now and again.

You'll need a small hammer or a pair of crackers to break open the crab shells for eating—it's quite a messy affair, but great fun. Serve with flatbreads or rice.

Serves 4

tangy and
slightly
sweet

Crab fishing >

Plantain curry

Kwazulu Natal has a large Indian population, and as a result there are plenty of South Indian–inspired dishes to season its diverse cooking styles. Affordable and plentiful, plantains are a staple food for many locals, and make a versatile curry that can be served as a side dish or snack. This recipe, inspired by my mother-in-law, Ambi Pillay, is lighter than most, because she steams the plantains before frying them with peppery curry leaves and popped mustard seeds. Deliciously tart, it's particularly good served with spiced and pickled chilies and relishes.

INGREDIENTS

4 plantains
3 tbsp vegetable oil
$^3/_4$ tsp mustard seeds
$^1/_2$ tsp cumin seeds
1 sprig of curry leaves (about 1 tbsp leaves)
1 onion, finely chopped

$1^1/_4$-in (3-cm) piece fresh ginger root, finely chopped
2 green chilies, seeded and chopped
pinch of ground turmeric
2 tbsp chopped cilantro leaves
lemon juice, to sharpen

METHOD

Put the unpeeled plantains in a steamer basket set over a pan of simmering water. Steam for about 10 minutes—they should still be quite firm to the touch.

While the plantains are cooking, make the *masala*. Heat the oil in a *karahi* or wok and toss in the mustard seeds followed by the cumin seeds and curry leaves. As soon as the seeds pop and sizzle, add the onion, ginger, and green chilies. Turn the heat down low, cover the pan, and cook for about 10 minutes or until the onion is softened.

When the plantains are cool enough to handle, strip off the peel with a sharp knife and grate along their length so you have long, coarse shreds. It's best to do this just before you add them to the onion mixture because they discolor really quickly.

Add the turmeric to the *masala* while still on the heat, and stir well to combine. Add the grated plantains and fry for a further 5–7 minutes, keeping an eye on them—you want them to keep some texture and bite. If it looks like it is sticking, add a dash of water.

Sprinkle with the chopped cilantro, sharpen with a squeeze of lemon, and serve with boiled rice.

Serves 4

mildly spiced and light

Bunny chow Curried beans in a loaf

The last word in South African street food, Bunny Chow began life as an affordable and filling meal for workers in the city. No one is quite sure when it originated, but most people believe it's named after a *baniya*, an Indian term for a trader, who coined the idea of stuffing bean curry into a hollowed-out bread loaf. The word *baniya* has been shortened to "bunny," and "chow" translates to "food." Besides beans, there's a choice of vegetable, chicken, and lamb bunny chows—they're all incredibly spicy and best enjoyed late at night with plenty of cold beer.

INGREDIENTS

1 large loaf white sandwich bread, unsliced
4–6 tbsp vegetable oil
3 sprigs of curry leaves (about 3 tbsp leaves)
2 onions, diced
2-in (5-cm) piece fresh ginger root, shredded
2 tsp crushed dried chilies
1 potato, about 6 oz (150 g), peeled and diced

14 oz (400 g) canned chopped tomatoes
1 tsp ground garam masala
6 oz (150 g) green beans, roughly chopped
2 cans (14 oz/400 g each) kidney beans
juice of 1 small lemon
large handful of cilantro leaves, chopped

METHOD

Lay the loaf flat and slice a 1¼-in (3-cm) layer horizontally off the top. Reserve the top. Pull out most of inside of the loaf, leaving ½-in- (1-cm-) thick sides on the bread case. Set aside.

Heat the oil in a large saucepan and toss in the curry leaves. After about 10 seconds, turn the heat down low and stir in the onions, ginger, and chilies. Cover the pan and cook for 10–15 minutes or until the onions are really soft. Uncover and continue frying the onions until they are tinged golden.

Add the diced potatoes, cover the pan again, and cook for about 10 minutes or until they're almost tender. Lift the lid every few minutes and give the potatoes a good stir to prevent them from sticking to the bottom of the pan.

Add the tomatoes and garam masala and fry briskly until the tomatoes darken in color and the *masala* thickens. Stir in the green beans and cook for 1 minute. Add the kidney beans along with the liquid from the cans. Stir well, then bring to a boil and simmer for about 10 minutes or until the curry thickens.

Preheat the oven to 350°F (180°C).

Sharpen the curried beans with the lemon juice and stir in the chopped cilantro. Ladle the hot curry into the hollowed-out loaf, being careful not to fill it all the way up to the top. Replace the lid, pushing down well, so that the bread has a chance to soak in the *masala*. Wrap the loaf in foil and bake for 15 minutes.

Bring the filled loaf, still wrapped in foil, to the table. Place on a big board and unwrap. Break open the four corners and dig in—no cutlery needed!

Serves 4

full-
flavored
and fiery

Bobotie Spiced ground lamb with savory custard

Brought to South Africa by Southeast Asian slaves in the 17th century, Bobotie is a tribute to Cape Malay cooking styles and Islamic culinary influences. Boer settlers used to bake their interpretation of Bobotie inside a hollowed-out pumpkin. Today, it's usually baked in a round pot, with most cooks adding their own special twist—perhaps a handful of raisins or dried apricots, or more chilies for added strength.

INGREDIENTS

2 slices white bread, crusts removed
1/2 cup milk
2 tbsp vegetable oil
3 tbsp butter
2 onions, roughly chopped
2 red chilies, seeded and chopped
4 large garlic cloves, finely chopped
1 1/2 lb (600 g) ground lamb
2 1/2 tsp mild curry powder
3/4 tsp ground cinnamon
3/4 tsp cracked black peppercorns
grated zest and juice of 1 lemon

1 tbsp Mrs. Ball's Extra Hot Chutney, or
    other hot mango chutney, chopped
1 tsp demerara sugar
1 tbsp blanched almonds, halved
6 lemon leaves or fresh bay leaves

Savory topping

2 large eggs
1/2 cup heavy cream
1/2 cup milk
1/4 tsp crushed black peppercorns
pinch of grated nutmeg

METHOD

Tear the bread into rough pieces, place in a small bowl, and add the milk. Set aside for about 10 minutes.

Meanwhile, heat the oil in a flameproof dutch oven and, when hot, add the butter. Put in the onions and chilies and cook until golden. Add the garlic and ground lamb and continue frying, stirring frequently, until the meat browns. Sprinkle with the curry powder, ground cinnamon, peppercorns, and lemon zest. Stir and fry over medium heat for a further 5 minutes to cook the spices.

Squeeze excess milk from the soaked bread, then add the bread to the meat. Stir well to break up any lumps. Add the lemon juice, chutney, sugar, and almonds. Remove from the heat and leave to cool before turning the meat mixture into a 1-quart (1-liter) pie dish. Roll the lemon or bay leaves into cigar shapes and stand them upright in the spiced meat. They should peep through the lamb.

Preheat the oven to 350°F (180°C).

Serves 4

Whisk together the eggs, cream, and milk and stir in the peppercorns. Pour this savory custard over the meat and sprinkle with grated nutmeg. Set the pie dish in a roasting pan half filled with hot water. Bake for about 25 minutes or until the topping is golden and set.

**mild and
slightly
sweet**

Serve with boiled rice or baked sweet potatoes. Bobotie also works well with a crisp salad and some tangy chutney.

The laborers of the 1800s who were shipped over from the Indian subcontinent and China to work the plantations of the Caribbean left their mark in the best possible place—the bellies of the Caribbean people. From Arrival Day in 1845 to the present, the colors, flavors, and textures of Indian cooking pervade meals from breakfast through dinner and are enjoyed on holidays and high days as well as at the many Indian festivals and religious days celebrated throughout the islands. Just as those of African and Indian descent have mixed and married and blurred their ethnic descent, so the foods of these countries have jumped into the cooking pot and mixed themselves together to produce a vibrant cuisine.

Indian immigration to Trinidad spanned the period 1845–1917, and during this time over 140,000 Indians were transported to Trinidad and Tobago alone. These indentured laborers arrived to replace the black African workers who had been released from slavery in 1833. The Indians were a displaced population over 12,000 miles from home; the continuation of their culinary traditions offered comfort as they adapted to their new country. Today, Indo-Caribbeans form a large part of the population in Guyana, Surinam, and Trinidad and Tobago. Smaller groups live elsewhere in the Caribbean, especially in Barbados, Jamaica, Grenada, Martinique, and Guadeloupe.

In Trinidad and Tobago, 42 percent of the population is of Indian descent, and it is here that you find the largest variety of Indo-Caribbean dishes in the islands. The vast majority of street food is Indian-based: a typical early morning scene in Port of Spain, Trinidad, sees laborers and lawyers in the same line waiting for their day to start with a delicious snack called "doubles" (p316), which is generally eaten by the roadside, accompanied by ice-cold coconut water drunk from the cracked-open nut.

One of the most popular Indo-Caribbean street snacks is the *roti*. In India this is the name for a flatbread, but in the islands a *roti* is the bread with its curried filling. The bread by itself is called a *roti* "flap" or "skin," and it can be filled with just about any curry: goat, shrimp, chicken, beef, or chickpeas and vegetables. Bread is the most popular partner for curry in the Caribbean, although it is also served with rice. In fact, it was the Indian and Chinese laborers who introduced rice to the area.

The influence of curry even permeates the music of the region. "Chutney" is not only a condiment to accompany curry but also the name given to the Indian version of soca and soul. Drawing inspiration from the rhythms of pan and rap as well as Indian folk and Bollywood film music, chutney songs have become immensely popular.

Judy Bastyra

Caribbean chilies >
These give a hot and fruity
flavor to island curries

The raw materials

Green onions

Known as scallions or "cives" in the islands, these are an integral part of any fresh seasoning mix. Combined with celery, chives, parsley, *chandon beni*, and garlic, they make "green seasoning," which is used in Trinidad to season meat, poultry, and fish.

Chilies

It is hot chilies (or hot peppers, as they are called) that give Caribbean cooking its distinctive flavor. There are many varieties used, including Scotch bonnets, tiny bird or bird's-eye chilies and "seasoning peppers," but it is the Scotch bonnet that is the most popular. It is extremely hot, with a distinctive aroma and fruity flavor. It is so named because it resembles a little bonnet. Seasoning peppers also have a strong flavor, but they don't have the heat of the other chilies. If you are unable to find hot Caribbean chilies, a Caribbean hot pepper sauce will give a more authentic flavor than using other fresh chilies.

Thyme

This aromatic herb is used throughout the Caribbean, but especially in Trinidad and Tobago as an integral part of the "seasoning mix."

Chandon beni

Also called culantro (*Eryngium foetidum*), the leaves of this pungent wild herb are used as a flavoring in Trinidad and Tobago as well as on many of the Spanish islands. It is known by many other names: shadow bennie, shado beni, shadon bene, and chandon beni, among them. All seem to be descended from a French vernacular name, *chardon beni*, meaning "blessed thistle," because the plant has thistlelike leaves. In Jamaica it is known as "fit weed," because it is thought to cure seizures. Fresh cilantro leaves are a good substitute.

Curry powder

Unlike most other countries where curry is cooked, in the Caribbean curries are seasoned with locally manufactured curry powders. Each mix is a little bit different, with the spices and the proportions used varying according to local tastes. None of the curry powders is very hot. "Colombo" is a special mixture of Indian spices used in Guadeloupe when making a curry.

Allspice

Allspice is the dried berry of a tropical tree that is cultivated in Jamaica. The flavor is like a mixture of cloves, black pepper, cinnamon, and nutmeg, which is why it is called allspice. Its other names are pimento and Jamaica pepper. It is one of the core ingredients in many Jamaican dishes, such as jerk, as well as curries. Allspice is used much in the same way as cloves, either whole or ground to a powder.

< Allspice berries

Dhalpurie roti Ground split pea flatbread

There are two types of *roti* "skins" or "flaps" in Trinidad. One is plain and the other is stuffed with split peas. The latter is known as Dhalpurie Roti, or just Dhalpurie. *Roti* may be folded around a curry and eaten with the hands like a sandwich, or served to accompany a curry, with the torn pieces of *roti* being used as a utensil to scoop up the curry. Once made, *roti* can be frozen, then reheated in the microwave.

INGREDIENTS
2 heaped tbsp sugar
2 eggs
$1^2/_3$ cups whole milk
6 cups all-purpose flour
1 tbsp salt
$^1/_2$ tsp baking powder
$^1/_4$ cup vegetable oil
$^1/_4$ cup vegetable oil or melted margarine,
   or a mixture, for cooking

Split pea filling
8 oz (225 g) split peas
$^1/_2$ tsp ground turmeric
2 tsp salt
3 garlic cloves, chopped
1 tbsp vegetable oil
1 tbsp ground cumin

METHOD
To make the filling, put the split peas into a pan with the turmeric, half the salt, and the garlic. Cover with water, bring to a boil, and boil for 15–20 minutes or until cooked but still firm. Drain well and allow to cool.

Grind the split peas to a powdery paste in a food processor or coffee grinder. Heat the oil in a frying pan and fry the split pea paste over medium heat for 1 minute, stirring constantly to prevent it from sticking to the pan or burning. Add the cumin and remaining salt to taste. Set aside while you make the dough.

Mix the sugar and eggs with the milk in a small mixing bowl, stirring until the sugar has dissolved. Sift the flour into a large mixing bowl and stir in the salt and baking powder. Gradually add the egg and milk mixture and knead lightly to make a soft dough. Be careful not to work the dough too much or it will become stretchy. Cover with a damp cloth and leave to rest for 15 minutes.

Add the oil and mix lightly. Divide the dough into 12 pieces and shape each into a ball. Open each one and place 2–3 tbsp of the split pea mixture inside. Pull the sides over to enclose the filling and re-form into balls. Dredge lightly in flour, then carefully roll out the filled balls very thinly, using enough flour on the work surface to prevent sticking.

Heat an oiled griddle or *tawa* over high heat and place a rolled-out *roti* on top. Cook for 1 minute, then turn over and brush with oil or melted margarine. Cook for $^1/_2$ minute, then turn over again and brush with oil or margarine. Remove and set aside while you cook the remaining *roti* in this way. Serve hot.

Makes 12

mild and
filling

Trinidadian roti Curried shrimp in split-pea flatbread

One of the most popular street foods in Trinidad is *roti*, which can best be described as curry parcels—flatbreads wrapped around various curries and then eaten like a hot sandwich. *Roti* vendors are found throughout Trinidad and Tobago, but one of the best places is in St. James, down Port of Spain. On Friday nights the place is buzzing. The bars are full and people spill out on to the street. The action continues into the early hours, with fresh *rotis* being made throughout the night. The secret to this simple shrimp filling is the "green seasoning" (p310).

INGREDIENTS
2 lb (900 g) raw medium-sized shrimp, peeled
1 tsp finely chopped garlic
1 large onion, finely chopped
3 tbsp curry powder, preferably Trinidadian
2 tbsp vegetable oil
2 medium potatoes, about ¹/₂ lb (225 g) in total, cut into cubes, boiled for 5 minutes, and drained
1 tsp salt
1 Scotch bonnet chili, seeded and finely sliced
1 tbsp finely chopped *chandon beni*, or 2 tbsp finely chopped cilantro leaves
6 Dhalpurie Roti (p311)

Green seasoning
1 bunch of green onions, coarsely chopped
2 tbsp coarsely chopped chives
2 tbsp coarsely chopped parsley
3 tbsp chopped *chandon beni* or cilantro leaves
4 garlic cloves, peeled

METHOD
First, make the green seasoning. Put all the ingredients in a food processor or blender with ¹/₄ cup water and process until very finely chopped, almost puréed. (This makes more seasoning than is needed for the recipe, but the remainder can be kept in the refrigerator for up to 1 week. For keeping longer, substitute 1 tbsp cane or white vinegar for all the water.)

Season the shrimp with the garlic, half the onion, and ¹/₄ cup of the green seasoning, tossing well. Set aside for 30 minutes.

Mix the curry powder with ¹/₄ cup of water to make a paste. Heat the oil in a frying pan, add the remaining onion, and cook for 6 minutes to soften. Add the curry paste and cook for 1 minute. Stir in the potatoes and cook over a low heat for 5 minutes.

Add the shrimp with the salt and chili and stir for 1–2 minutes to coat the shrimp with the curry mixture. Pour in ¹/₂ cup water and cook over high heat for 3–5 minutes or until the shrimp have turned pink and are cooked through. Do not overcook, or the shrimp will become tough. Stir in the *chandon beni* or cilantro and serve hot, wrapped in the *roti*.

Serves 6

warmly spiced

Jamaican goat curry

No Jamaican party would be complete without a pot of goat curry. Goat is a very popular meat throughout the Caribbean, but it is a real Jamaican specialty—another Jamaican dish called "Mannish Water," which is a soupy stew made from all parts of the goat, is supposed to have aphrodisiac properties. You can use either the leg or the rib cut of the goat. Traditionally, it is cooked on the bone, which the butcher cuts for you into manageable pieces, and sucking the bones is part of the enjoyment (Jamaicans believe that the meat is always sweeter next to the bone). This recipe uses boned leg of goat, but with the bone cut up and added to the pot during cooking, to give extra body to the sauce. If you are unable to find goat, lamb tastes just as good. In Jamaica this is served with rice and peas, and fried plantain.

INGREDIENTS

4$\frac{1}{2}$-lb (2-kg) leg of goat, boned (bones reserved), washed, dried and cut into 1-in (2.5-cm) cubes
2 tbsp finely chopped chives
2 Scotch bonnet chilies, 1 seeded and chopped, the other left whole
4 garlic cloves, finely chopped
1 tsp ground allspice
1 small bunch of thyme, leaves chopped

4 tbsp Caribbean curry powder
2 tbsp vegetable oil
2 onions, finely chopped
1 tbsp grated fresh ginger root
1 tsp salt
1$\frac{2}{3}$ cups coconut milk (p213)

METHOD

Ask the butcher to cut up the bones for you. Season the cubes of meat with the chives, chopped chili, half the garlic, the allspice, half the thyme, and 2 tbsp of the curry powder. Cover and marinate for at least 4 hours, preferably overnight.

Heat the oil in a large flameproof dutch oven or "dutchie" (p317), and add the remaining garlic and thyme, onions, and ginger. Cook for about 5 minutes or until the onions start to turn golden.

Mix the remaining curry powder with 4 tbsp of water. Add to the pot and cook, stirring, until all the liquid has evaporated. Add the cubes of goat meat and cook over low heat for 5 minutes or until the meat is seared all over, stirring constantly to prevent it from sticking to the pot.

Add the bones, salt, and whole chili, then stir in the coconut milk and 1 cup water. Bring up to a boil. Reduce the heat to low, cover, and simmer for 2 hours.

Remove the lid and continue cooking for about 30 minutes or until the meat is soft and tender and the sauce is thick and glossy. Serve hot.

Serves 4–6

mild,
creamy,
and meaty

Doubles Bara and curried chickpeas

Doubles consists of two delicate pancake-type breads called *bara* filled with lightly curried chickpeas (*channa*), served with hot pepper sauce and mango chutney. My favorite Doubles vendor is George, who is located just outside the Brooklyn Bar in Port of Spain. Confusingly, just a few yards away there's another vendor selling Doubles, with a huge sign saying "George X." This is George's ex-wife.

INGREDIENTS

9 oz (250 g) dried chickpeas, soaked overnight
2 tbsp vegetable oil
1 large onion, finely chopped
4 garlic cloves, finely chopped
2 tbsp mild curry powder
1 tsp ground cumin
1 tsp salt
1/4 tsp chopped Scotch bonnet chili or
   hot pepper sauce (optional)
chopped *chandon beni* or cilantro leaves

Bara

3 cups all-purpose flour
1 1/2 tsp instant yeast
1/2 tsp sugar
1/2 tsp salt
1 tsp ground turmeric
1/2 tsp ground cumin
2 tablespoons melted margarine
1 cup vegetable oil for deep-frying

METHOD

Drain the chickpeas, then put them in a pan of fresh salted water. Bring to a boil and boil for 15–20 minutes or until they are tender. Drain well.

Heat the oil in a large frying pan, add the onion and garlic, and cook for a few minutes until golden. Stir in the curry powder and add 4 tbsp water. Cook for another few minutes. Stir in the chickpeas and cook for a further 5 minutes. Pour in 1 cup of water and season with the cumin, salt, and chili. Bring to a boil, then reduce the heat to low, cover, and cook for 15 minutes or until the chickpeas are soft and juicy, adding more water if necessary. Keep warm while you make the *bara* (or reheat for serving).

Mix the flour, yeast, sugar, salt, turmeric, cumin, and margarine together in a bowl. Add about 1 cup warm water to make a soft dough. Knead for a few minutes, then return to the bowl. Cover and set aside for 15 minutes.

Form the dough into 24 balls. On an oiled work surface, using your fingertips, pat each ball flat into a thin pancake about 3 in (8 cm) in diameter.

Heat the oil for deep-frying in a deep-sided frying pan. When the oil is hot, fry the *bara* one at a time: add to the oil and fry for just 5–7 seconds or until the dough starts to bubble, then turn over and fry for another 5–7 seconds. Remove with a slotted spoon and drain on paper towels. Keep warm in a warm oven while you fry the remaining *bara*.

Serve by making a sandwich: place 2 tbsp of curried chickpeas between a pair of *bara*, adding some *chandon beni* plus hot pepper sauce and/or mango chutney to taste.

Serves 8–12

mild and
appetizing

"River lime" curried duck

As you drive through the countryside in Trinidad, you will often see groups of Indo-Caribbean people gathered on a river bank, relaxing, enjoying each other's company, drinking icy-cold Carib beer and generally having a good time. This is what is known as a "river lime," and curried duck is one of the dishes often cooked in a "dutchie" over an open fire by the river. "Dutchie" is a local term for a "Dutch pot," which arrived in the Caribbean islands in the mid-1600s from the Netherlands, brought by the early explorers who used these cooking vessels on their expeditions into the interior. Made from aluminum scraps and river sand, the dutchie (also called a "coal pot") is still used all over the Caribbean.

INGREDIENTS

1 duck, about 5 lb (2.25 kg), skinned,
   trimmed of excess fat, and
   cut into serving pieces
1 bunch of thyme, stalks removed
1 tbsp finely chopped fresh ginger root
2 garlic cloves, pounded to a paste
1 red onion, cut into small dice
5 "seasoning peppers," finely chopped,
   or 1 Scotch bonnet chili, deseeded and
   finely chopped

1 bunch of *chandon beni* or cilantro
   leaves, chopped
5 tbsp Trinidadian curry powder
1 tbsp ground turmeric
1 tbsp roasted cumin seeds
4 tbsp vegetable oil
4–5 cups coconut
   milk (p213)
1 Scotch bonnet chili
salt and pepper

METHOD

Season the duck with the thyme leaves, ginger, garlic, onion, seasoning peppers, *chandon beni*, and 1 tbsp curry powder. Allow to marinate overnight, if possible.

Mix the remaining curry powder, the turmeric, and the cumin with 4 tbsp water. Heat the oil in a heavy frying pan, add the spice mixture, and fry for 12 minutes or until browned. Add the duck and stir well to coat with the spices. Cook for 15 minutes to brown the duck on all sides.

Add the coconut milk and bring to a boil. Lower the heat to a simmer and add the whole Scotch bonnet chili. Cover and cook for about 1$\frac{1}{4}$ hours or until the duck is tender.

Remove the lid and simmer for a further 10 minutes or until the liquid has reduced a little. Season with salt and pepper. Serve immediately, garnished with a few extra chopped *chandon beni* or cilantro leaves. Serve with rice.

Serves 4–6

strong and
full-flavored

Leila's Guyanese chicken curry

A Guyanese friend of mine gave me this delicious recipe, which I have used time and time again. What makes it slightly different from other Caribbean curry recipes is that you make your own spice mix and then combine it with some ready-made curry paste. The spice powder can be kept in an airtight container for several weeks. Although the recipe is for chicken, both lamb and beef would taste equally delicious. I have skinned the chicken, making the dish less fatty. Also, without the skin, the spices can soak deeper into the chicken meat.

INGREDIENTS

1 tsp ground turmeric
1 tbsp Madras curry paste
2 tbsp vegetable oil
1 large onion, finely chopped
5 garlic cloves, finely chopped
1 tsp grated fresh ginger root
2 red chilies, chopped
1 chicken, about 3½ lb (1.5 kg), skinned and
    cut into 8–10 pieces
4 medium tomatoes, peeled and chopped
6 curry leaves
2 medium potatoes, peeled and quartered

Curry powder

2 tbsp coriander seeds
1 tbsp cumin seeds
1 tbsp cardamom pods
1 tsp black peppercorns
1 tsp cloves
1 cinnamon stick
2 tsp black mustard seeds

METHOD

To make the curry powder, roast and grind all the spices (p322). Mix 2 tbsp of the curry powder with the turmeric and curry paste. Add 2 tbsp water and mix well.

Heat the oil in a large heavy-based saucepan and fry the chopped onion, garlic, ginger, and chilies until golden brown. Add the curry mixture and fry for 3–5 minutes, stirring constantly to ensure that the mixture does not burn. Add the chicken pieces to the saucepan and turn them so that they are thoroughly coated with the spice mixture.

Add the tomatoes and curry leaves and cook for 1 minute, then add the potatoes and ½ cup water. Cover the saucepan and simmer for 20 minutes or until the chicken is cooked. Stir the curry occasionally during the cooking, to make sure that it does not stick to the pan. Serve immediately with rice or *roti*.

Serves 4–6

warmly
spiced and
aromatic

Indian cuisine is omnipresent in Britain—so much so that Chicken Tikka Masala has been voted Britain's favorite national dish. Two centuries of colonial presence in the Indian subcontinent fostered a much-flaunted love affair with the Indian kitchen, and Britain, reinventing a centuries-old culinary heritage, has made "going out for a curry" and "having a takeaway" celebrated symbols of multiculturalism.

The British *memsahib* adapted Indian *masalas* to suit Western palates, and in so doing, threw "authenticity" out the window. Colonial-style curries were made up of meat, fried with a curry paste before being stewed in water. Anglicized curries, made popular by returning expatriates, were often embellished with chopped bananas, shredded coconut, and raisins, a style of cooking virtually unknown in South Asia.

Of course, new flavor combinations and cooking styles have been making the rounds for centuries. The fact is that no cuisine remains static: India didn't have chilies until the Portuguese brought them from the New World. And spices are not new to Britain—in addition to being a valuable trade commodity, aromatic spice blends have long played a key seasoning role in British cooking styles.

South Asian immigrants arrived in Britain's big cities from India, Bangladesh, Pakistan, Sri Lanka, and East Africa during the sixties and seventies, and many entered the restaurant and catering industry. Adept at adapting menus to suit local tastes and expectations, the South Asian restaurant sector was the success story of the second half of the last century.

Most Indians prefer lamb or chicken curry made with meat cooked on the bone, the advantage being that while the meat simmers, it makes its own flavorsome sauce. In Britain, however, meat cooked this way can be tricky to negotiate on the plate, especially with cutlery, which might explain why boneless meat is preferred.

While menus at many British curry houses have remained largely unchanged over the past two decades, the emergence of newer styles of cooking at fine restaurants has elevated modern Indian cooking to a privileged position. More recently, supermarkets have developed new product ranges championing regional gems, including Keralan fish curry and biryani from Hyderabad.

But it's the tried-and-tested stalwarts of Indo-British cooking that continue to hold their own, such as Madras Curry (p326), creamy kormas, and Chicken Tikka Masala (p330). The difference today is that there's a culinary curiosity to lift the lid off the Indian spice box and cook authentic recipes at home.

Roopa Gulati

**Curry houses,
Brick Lane, London >**

Step 1

Roasting and grinding spices

Dry-roasting whole spices makes them more aromatic and brings out their flavor. It also dries them and makes them easier to grind to a powder.

Step 1
Heat a small, heavy-based frying pan or griddle over moderate heat. Add the whole spices and roast for about 1 minute, stirring constantly or shaking the pan to prevent the spices from scorching.

Step 2
As soon as they start to darken and you catch the spicy aroma, remove from the heat and pour the spices onto a plate. Cool.

Step 3
Transfer the spices to a mortar and grind to a fine powder using the pestle. Alternatively, use a spice mill or clean electric coffee grinder.

Step 4
For a very fine result, pass the powder through a sieve to remove any remaining bits of husks and seed.

Step 3 >

Step 2

Tamarind water

As a general guide, use a walnut-sized piece or about 1 oz (30 g) of pulp and ½ cup water. To make thick tamarind water, use twice as much pulp.

Step 1
Break a piece of tamarind pulp from the block, put it in a bowl, and cover with hot water. Leave to soak for 10–15 minutes or until the pulp has softened, then squeeze and mash the pulp with your fingers to loosen and separate the fibers and seeds.

Step 2
Strain the thick brown water through a sieve into a bowl; discard the solids. Tamarind water can be stored in the refrigerator for 2 weeks.

Dhansak Lamb with lentils and tamarind

In its purest form, Dhansak is a labor of love to prepare and far removed from often formulaic British interpretations. This lamb curry, with its blend of spiced lentil and vegetable purée with refreshingly tart tamarind, marries modern cooking styles with the rich culinary heritage of the Parsees. In India, Dhansak is always made with lamb, but variations with chicken are just as popular in Britain.

INGREDIENTS

6 garlic cloves, roughly chopped
1¼-in (3-cm) piece fresh ginger root, roughly chopped
¼ cup vegetable oil
1 star anise
2 onions, very finely chopped
1½ lb (600 g) boned shoulder or leg of lamb, cut into 1¼-in (3-cm) cubes
¾ tsp ground coriander
½ tsp each cracked black peppercorns, ground cinnamon, crushed cardamom seeds, chili powder, and ground cumin

Lentils

1 oz (25 g) split gram lentils (*chana dal*)
1 oz (25 g) split red lentils (*masoor dal*)
1 small eggplant, diced
handful of fresh fenugreek leaves or mustard greens
3 oz (75 g) pumpkin flesh, diced

To finish

½ cup tamarind water (p322), or to taste
1 rounded tsp palm sugar
2 tbsp shredded mint leaves

METHOD

Wash the gram lentils and put in a pan with enough water to cover. Bring to a boil and simmer for about 15 minutes or until half-cooked. Add the red lentils, diced eggplant, fenugreek leaves, and pumpkin. Simmer until the lentils and vegetables are very soft. Remove the pan from the heat and leave the lentil mixture to cool slightly before blending to a smooth purée. Transfer it to a bowl and set aside.

Put the garlic and ginger in the rinsed-out blender and pour in ½ cup water. Process to make a thin paste, then transfer to a small bowl.

Preheat the oven to 325°F (170°C).

Heat the oil in an flameproof dutch oven over medium heat. Add the star anise and leave to sizzle for a couple of seconds, then stir in the onions and fry until just beginning to turn golden.

Add the meat to the pan and cook, stirring frequently, until browned. Gradually stir in the garlic and ginger paste. Sprinkle in all the spices and fry for 1 minute, stirring all the time. Add enough hot water to reach three-quarters of the way up the meat. Bring the curry to boiling point, then cover the pan and transfer to the oven. Cook for about 40 minutes or until the meat is tender.

Stir the puréed lentil mixture into the curry and continue cooking for 10 minutes. To finish, add enough tamarind water to sharpen the flavor, and stir in sugar to sweeten. You should aim for a sweet-sour taste. Serve garnished with the mint and accompanied by rice.

Serves 4

sweet and tart

Madras curry Fiery lamb curry

You're likely to draw a blank if you go to Chennai and ask for a Madras Curry—it's almost as British as Yorkshire Pudding. Take a culinary journey around numerous curry houses, and you'll find as wide a variety of Madras curries as there are restaurants. What they do all have in common is fiery chili heat. Simple to make at home, Madras Curry tastes far better than takeaway meals, and you remain in charge of how many chilies go into the pot.

INGREDIENTS
3 tbsp vegetable oil
2 onions, very finely chopped
9 oz (250 g) plum tomatoes, peeled and finely chopped
2 tsp tomato paste
1½ lb (600 g) boned shoulder or leg of lamb, cut into 1¼-in (3-cm) chunks
⅔ cup thick coconut milk (p213)

Dry spice blend
1 tsp coriander seeds
1 tsp cumin seeds
½ tsp mustard seeds
3–4 dried red chilies
½ tsp black peppercorns

Coconut paste
¼ tsp ground turmeric
½ tsp ground cinnamon
4 garlic cloves, roughly chopped
¾-in (2-cm) piece fresh ginger root, roughly chopped
3 tbsp freshly grated coconut
3 tbsp white wine vinegar

METHOD

To make the spice blend, roast and grind the spices (p322). Set aside.

For the coconut paste, combine all the ingredients in a food processor and process until smooth. You might need to add a dash of water.

Heat the oil in a large flameproof dutch oven and fry the onions until golden. Stir in the tomatoes, tomato paste, and dry spice mixture. Cook briskly, stirring frequently, for about 10 minutes or until the sauce has thickened.

Add the meat to the pan and fry over high heat until it starts to color. While the meat is cooking, gradually add the spiced coconut paste. Turn the heat down low and pour in enough hot water to reach three-quarters of the way up the meat. Cover the pan and simmer for about 30 minutes or until the lamb is tender.

Just before serving, add the coconut milk and gently reheat the curry, stirring frequently. Serve with rice or Indian breads.

Serves 4

chili-hot
and
robust

Rogan josh Lamb curry with aromatic spices

More upmarket than earthy baltis, Rogan Josh evolved from Kashmiri roots and was one of the earliest curries to achieve mainstream popularity with British diners. It isn't a chili-laden curry, but it does have an appealingly intense flavor. Kashmiri chilies, noted for their mildness and bright color, are traditional but not that easy to get hold of; paprika makes a super substitute. If you can, make this curry a day ahead, to give the *masala* a chance to mature and mellow.

INGREDIENTS

1 large onion, roughly chopped
4–5 garlic cloves, roughly chopped
4 tbsp vegetable oil
1 brown cardamom pod, split (optional)
8 green cardamom pods, split
2 cinnamon sticks, 1¼ in (3 cm) each
1 dried bay leaf
5 cloves
¾ tsp black peppercorns
1 blade mace
4½ cups (600 g) boned shoulder or leg of lamb,
  cut into 1¼-in (3-cm) cubes
5 OZ (125 g) plain yogurt

Spice mix

2 tsp fennel seeds, roasted and
  ground (p322)
¾ tsp ground coriander
¾ tsp ground cumin
2 tsp mild paprika
½ tsp chili powder
½ tsp ground ginger
¼ tsp ground turmeric

METHOD

To make the spice mix, combine all the ingredients. Set aside.

Put the onion in a food processor, add a dash of water, and blend to a smooth paste. Put the onion paste into a small bowl. Alternatively, you can grate the onion. Blend the garlic in the food processor with 1 tbsp water, then transfer to another bowl.

Heat the oil in a wok or *karahi* over medium heat and add the brown and green cardamoms, cinnamon sticks, bay leaf, cloves, peppercorns, and mace. Swirl everything around in the hot oil for about 30 seconds or so, until the spices give off a nutty scent. Add the onion paste to the pan, turn down the heat, and fry until golden. Stir in the garlic paste and continue cooking for 1 minute.

Put the lamb into the pan, turn the heat up, and fry for about 10 minutes or until browned. If it looks like it is sticking to the bottom of the pan, add a couple of tablespoons of water. Stir in the spice mixture. Gradually add the yogurt to the pan, stirring well between additions. Pour in enough hot water to barely cover the lamb, then cover the pan and simmer, stirring occasionally, for about 40 minutes or until the lamb is tender and the sauce thickened.

Serves 4

mild and
fragrant

If, at the end of cooking, the masala is a little thin, take the lamb out of the pan and boil the liquid until thickened. Return the meat to the curry and serve piping hot.

Chicken korma Creamy chicken curry with nuts

Served at Indian banquets and main-street curry houses all over Britain, *kormas* come in many guises. The mild, creamy sauce is best suited to timid palates, so *korma* is often suggested as a first taster of Indian cooking. South Asian *kormas* are steeped in regal tradition, and even today remain the ultimate party dish. What makes the evolution of British-style *kormas* so intriguing is that they're a global celebration of curry rather than being solely derived from a single regional cuisine. You could use lamb instead of chicken. Just remember to give it a longer cooking time, adding more water as it simmers.

INGREDIENTS

$^1/_4$ tsp saffron threads
3 tbsp vegetable oil
1 tbsp ghee or clarified butter
1 blade mace
5 cloves
6 cardamom pods, split
$1^1/_2$ in (4 cm) cinnamon stick
1 onion, very finely chopped
$1^1/_4$-in (3-cm) piece fresh ginger root, roughly chopped
6 garlic cloves, roughly chopped
4 boned chicken thighs, about $1^1/_2$ lb (600 g) in total
$^1/_2$ tsp mild chili powder or paprika
1 tsp ground coriander
$^1/_2$ tsp ground garam masala

Browned onion paste

1 onion, thinly sliced
salt
vegetable oil for deep-frying

Nut paste

1 tbsp cashew nuts
1 tbsp blanched almonds

To finish

$^1/_3$ cup thick coconut milk (p213)
$^1/_3$ cup heavy cream
1 tbsp chopped cilantro leaves

METHOD

For the browned onion paste, sprinkle the sliced onion with salt and set aside for 20 minutes. Pat the onion dry with paper towels. Heat vegetable oil in a deep-fryer or wok and fry the onion slices until golden. Drain on paper towels. Transfer the warm fried onion to a food processor. Add 2 tbsp hot water and process until smooth. Set aside.

For the nut paste, soak the cashew nuts and almonds in boiling water, covered, for 30 minutes. Drain the nuts, reserving 2–3 tbsp of the liquid. Grind the nuts to a paste in a food processor, adding a dash of the soaking liquid.

Put the saffron threads in a small bowl and cover with 2 tbsp hot water. Leave to soak for at least 10 minutes. Meanwhile, heat the oil in a *karahi* or wok and add the ghee. Once melted, stir in the mace, cloves, cardamom pods, and cinnamon stick. Swirl the spices around for about 30 seconds.

Serves 4

mild and aromatic

Curry stand, Camden Market, London

When you smell a warm, nutty aroma, add the chopped onion. Turn the heat down low and cook for about 5 minutes or until the onion is soft but not colored.

While the onion is cooking, put the ginger and garlic in a food processor and add 2 tbsp water. Blend to a smooth paste. Add this paste to the onions and fry, stirring well, for a further 1 minute. Stir in the nut paste and continue cooking, stirring all the time, for 2–3 minutes or until most of the liquid has evaporated.

Add the chicken pieces to the pan along with the chili powder, ground coriander, and garam masala. Combine everything and fry for 5 minutes to cook the spices. Add about 1/2 cup water and turn the heat down low. Cover the pan and simmer for 10 minutes or until the chicken is cooked, stirring occasionally. If the curry looks like it is sticking to the bottom of the pan, add a dash more water.

Add the browned onion paste and stir to combine. Pour the coconut milk and cream over the curry. Bring to a simmer, then add the saffron and its soaking liquid. Sprinkle with the chopped cilantro and serve piping hot with naans.

Chicken tikka masala

The popularity of Chicken Tikka Masala is a testament to Britain's centuries-old love affair with Indian food. Don't be shy with the garlic and ginger—this dish is big on bold flavors. Simple to make, this curry also embraces other ingredients. For a vegetarian version, cut a block of *paneer* or tofu into large cubes and add the pieces, without marinating, to the tomato sauce at the end of cooking.

INGREDIENTS

6 boned chicken thighs, about $1^1/_2$ lb (675 g) in total, skinned
juice of 2 limes
1 tsp paprika
$1^1/_2$ tsp cumin seeds
$^1/_2$ tsp coriander seeds
2 shallots, roughly chopped
4 large garlic cloves, roughly chopped
$1^1/_2$-in (4-cm) piece fresh ginger root, roughly chopped
2 green chilies, seeded and roughly chopped
$4^1/_2$ oz (125 g) plain Greek-style yogurt

$^1/_2$ tsp ground garam masala
1 tbsp vegetable oil

Sauce

14 oz (400 g) canned chopped tomatoes
1 rounded tsp tomato paste
handful of coriander leaves, roughly chopped
$1^1/_4$-in (3-cm) piece fresh ginger root, grated
1 tsp lime juice
$^1/_2$ tsp sugar
3 tbsp unsalted butter
$^1/_2$ cup heavy cream

METHOD

Cut the chicken thighs into $1^1/_4$-in (3-cm) chunks. Combine the lime juice and paprika and mix with the chicken. Set aside while you roast and grind the cumin and coriander seeds (p322).

Put the shallots, garlic, ginger, and chilies into a food processor. Drain the lime juice and paprika mixture from the chicken and add to the onion mixture. Process until smooth. Pour into a mixing bowl and stir in the yogurt, garam masala, and add half the coriander and cumin powder.

Pour the spiced yogurt mixture over the chicken, turning every piece so that it's evenly coated. Cover with plastic wrap and marinate overnight in the refrigerator. If you can, flip the chicken over once or twice while it's marinating.

Preheat the broiler, with the broiler pan in place, to its hottest setting.

Take the chicken out of the yogurt marinade and arrange on the hot broiler pan. Drizzle with the oil and broil for about 5 minutes on each side or until beginning to char around the edges. Pour any cooking juices into a bowl and skim off any fat. Keep the chicken warm while you make the sauce.

Combine the tomatoes, tomato paste, coriander leaves, ginger, lime juice, sugar, and remaining cumin and coriander powder in a blender or food processor and process until smooth. Heat the butter in a saucepan and, when melted, add the spiced tomato mixture and cream. Bring to simmering point, then strain in the reserved cooking juices and add the cooked chicken pieces. Reheat and serve piping hot, with Indian breads.

Serves 4

rich and
full-
flavored

Shrimp balti

Having more in common with Birmingham than Pakistan, *baltis* are a star attraction for curry aficionados. Putting together a *balti* is a theatrical affair, best appreciated when ingredients are showered into a cavernous *karahi* and flash-fried over fierce heat. Expect robust garlicky notes, plenty of onions, and a sprinkling of tingling chilies—perfect for mopping up with an obliging naan. No one's really sure how they came into being—*balti* means "bucket" in Punjabi—hardly a prosaic description. However, chances are that *batti*, which means food, could well have been the inspiration behind naming Birmingham's most-loved curry.

INGREDIENTS

1¼ lb (500 g) raw jumbo shrimp, peeled
    but last tail section left on
juice of 1 lime
1½ tsp paprika

Masala

3 tbsp vegetable oil
1 red onion, diced
1½-in (4-cm) piece fresh ginger root,
    finely shredded
2 garlic cloves, finely chopped

2 green chilies, shredded
1 red pepper, seeded and shredded
14 oz (400 g) canned chopped tomatoes
¼ tsp ground turmeric
¼–½ tsp red chili powder
¼ tsp ground cinnamon
½ tsp ground garam masala
½ tsp ground coriander
½ tsp sugar
2 tbsp coarsely chopped cilantro leaves,
    to garnish

METHOD

Put the shrimp in a bowl, squeeze the lime juice over them, and stir in the paprika. Stir well, then set aside while you make the *masala*.

Heat the oil in a *karahi* or wok set over medium heat and fry the onion for about 5 minutes or until softened and just beginning to turn golden. Add three-quarters of the ginger, followed by the garlic, chilies, and shredded red pepper. Continue frying for 1 minute.

Turn the heat up and add the tomatoes, turmeric, chili powder, cinnamon, garam masala, ground coriander, and sugar. Cook briskly until the tomatoes have thickened and darkened in appearance. Pour in about ²/₃ cup hot water, stir well, and turn the heat down low.

Add the shrimp, along with any lime juice from the bowl, and simmer for 3–4 minutes or until they turn pink and are tender.

Garnish with chopped cilantro and the remaining shredded ginger before serving.

Serves 4

warmly
spiced

Curry was first introduced into Japan around the middle of the 19th century, by chefs who came with the British traders. The first published Japanese curry recipe in 1872 was "curried veal or fowl served with white rice." In fact, it was not an authentic Indian curry but a curried meat stew, which Westerners adapted from the original. Having traveled to the West, curry was brought back to the East, but this time bypassing India and starting a new life.

This was when Japan, a closed country for the preceding 200 years, opened up its borders to the outside world and also stopped being a vegetarian nation. Many people found eating meat quite intriguing but very challenging. Curry helped to overcome this by disguising the smell of meat with spices and a thick sauce. Also, stewed meat was more tender and easier to chew than grilled.

Over time, "Curry Rice," or, as it is sometimes called, "Rice Curry," successfully settled into the Japanese diet. Other meat dishes, such as beef steak, pork cutlet, and hashed beef, were introduced at around the same time. They are still called *Yo-Shoku*, which means "Western food." Eating these exotic foods was seen to be a sophisticated thing to do by open-minded Japanese people.

Today, numerous "curry houses" can be found all over Japan, and curry is the most popular dish made at home. Ever since the introduction of ready-to-use curry roux (p336) in shops and supermarkets in the sixties, Curry Rice has been a regular dish in the repertoire of Japanese home cooks. Seasonal vegetables can be added to the standard combination of potatoes, carrots, and onions, and seafood such as shrimp, clams, squid, or canned tuna can be used instead of meat.

In Japan there are those who like Japanese and European curries, those who prefer Indian curries, and those who want to eat other Asian curry varieties. One thing all have in common is that they eat them with sticky, white, short-grain Japanese rice, not basmati rice. This preference is a good example of the "Japan-ization" of foreign food. Another example is the way curry is combined with traditional Japanese dishes, such as curry and noodles or curry pancake.

At home, curry is eaten with just a spoon. However, at a restaurant the same curry may be served with a European table setting. The Japanese pickles that accompany the curry are presented in a special silver dish and the waiter bows to you politely before pouring curry sauce from a silver saucepot on to your plate of rice. As with so many other aspects of Japanese life, the serving of curry can be quite a formal affair.

Yasuko Fukuoka

< **Making noodles, Hyogo**

Seven-vegetable pickles (left) and pickled Japanese shallots

The raw materials

Curry roux mix

Solid blocks of "curry roux mix," which look like bars of chocolate, are sold in shops and supermarkets in Japan alongside other special flavorings such as "fond de veau" or "bouquet garni extract"—as if curry roux were also part of French cuisine. Using instant curry roux cuts the preparation time enormously. Consequently, not many Japanese venture to make their own roux at home anymore.

Seven-vegetable pickles

Often colored a bright red, these sweet pickles (which are called *fuku-jin-duke* in Japanese) were devised to be served with Japanese curry dishes as a substitute for Indian chutney. They contain mooli, shiso perilla leaves, white sesame seeds, small eggplants, sword bean pods, cucumber, and lotus root, all of which are finely shredded and pickled in a shoyu-based liquid.

The Japanese never make these pickles at home—the ingredients are not widely available, even in Japan, and the pickling method has remained a closely guarded secret since it was first created by a small specialty shop about 150 years ago. *Fuku-jin-duke* can easily be found in Japanese or Chinese food shops.

Pickled Japanese shallots

The Japanese shallot is smaller and sweeter than the European type, and the pickling liquid used to make *rakkyo* is sweeter than a Western pickle. You can make a nice substitute by mixing 1 tsp honey into a cup of pickled pearl onions along with their pickling liquid and leaving overnight.

Karashi-duke Radishes pickled with mustard

This is easy to make, and gives you an idea of the kinds of pickles served with a curry in Japan. It goes well with the recipes on the following pages.

INGREDIENTS
2^1/$_4$ lb (1 kg) red radishes, trimmed
1 garlic clove, crushed
2^1/$_2$ tbsp fine sea salt
^{1}/$_2$ cup sugar
1 tbsp Japanese or English mustard powder
^{3}/$_4$-x-2-in (2-x-5-cm) strip *dashi-konbu* (optional)

METHOD
Put the radishes, garlic, and salt in a large resealable plastic bag. Close and seal the bag, then "massage" the bag with your hands for 2–3 minutes, to rub the salt into the radishes and garlic. Some radishes will be cracked or broken up.

Add the sugar, mustard powder, and *konbu* (if using). Shake the bag to mix all the ingredients together well. Refrigerate overnight. The pickles will be ready to eat the following day, and will keep for a week in the refrigerator.

Makes 2^1/$_4$ lb
(1 kg)

Dashi Soup stock

Below is the traditional method for preparing Dashi, using seaweed and dried bonito flakes. For instant stock, simply dissolve a 5-g packet (about 1 heaped tsp) *dashi-no-moto* granules in 6 cups warm water.

INGREDIENTS
4-x-2-in (10 x-5-cm) piece of *dashi-konbu*
1^1/$_4$ oz (35 g) *katsuo-bushi* or *kezuri-bushi*

METHOD
Put the konbu in a large pan and pour in 6 cups water. Bring to a boil. When the water boils, reduce the heat and remove and discard the *konbu*.

Add the *katsuo-bushi* and boil over low heat for 2 minutes. Strain the stock through a sieve into a bowl. Discard the contents of the sieve.

Makes 6 cups

Curry nanban soba Curry noodle with chicken

A relatively recent innovation, Curry Noodle is a fusion of two favorite dishes that the Japanese love with a passion: noodles in hot soup and a light curry sauce. Three types of noodles can be used: soba (buckwheat noodles), udon (thick white wheat noodles), or ramen (Chinese-style yellow wheat noodles). Soba are used here. If the curry roux and soup are all made at home from scratch, it is a quite laborious dish to cook. However, to save time, Japanese cooks often make the stock with *dashi-no-moto* granules, available from Japanese food shops, and curry roux mix (p336). Then you only need to cook the chicken and noodles.

INGREDIENTS
6 cups dashi (p337)
9 oz (250 g) chicken thighs, skinned and cut into bite-sized pieces
1 onion, cut into 8 segments lengthwise
$^2/_3$ cup shoyu
$^2/_3$ cup mirin
14 oz (400 g) dried soba
1 green onion, cut into thin rings
8 snow pea pods, blanched for 1 minute, then cut diagonally into thin slivers

Curry roux
3 tbsp vegetable oil
1 onion, thinly sliced lengthwise
2 garlic cloves, finely chopped
$^3/_4$-in (2-cm) piece fresh ginger root, finely chopped or grated with a Japanese grater
3 tbsp all-purpose flour
$2^1/_2$ tbsp mild Japanese or Indian curry powder
1 tbsp tomato ketchup
1 tbsp mango chutney

METHOD

First make the curry roux. Heat the oil in a saucepan and fry the onion, garlic, and ginger over low heat for 20–30 minutes or until golden. Add the flour and curry powder and stir until the oil in the pan has been absorbed. Add the ketchup and chutney, mixing thoroughly. Remove from the heat and set aside.

To make the soup, pour the dashi stock into a large pan and bring to a boil. Add the chicken and onion and simmer for 5 minutes, skimming off any scum from the surface. Reduce the heat to low.

Scoop out about 2 cups of stock and mix little by little into the curry roux to make a smooth, thick paste. Pour the roux mixture into the rest of the stock in the large pan, then add the shoyu and mirin. Mix thoroughly. Bring to a boil, then reduce the heat and leave to simmer gently while you cook the soba.

Bring a large pan of water to a boil. Add the soba and cook for about 5 minutes or as instructed on the package. As with Italian pasta, soba should be cooked al dente and eaten as swiftly as possible. Drain the soba, then put it into the soup. Mix well.

Ladle the soup into 4 deep soup bowls. Sprinkle with the green onion and garnish with the snow peas. Serve immediately.

Serves 4

savory
and
warming

Curry rice

This dish is popular with Japanese of all ages. If using a store-bought curry roux mix (p336), break the roux bar into chunks and add them to the pan after the potatoes and carrots and bringing the stock to a boil.

INGREDIENTS

1 lb (450 g) Japanese rice
2 tbsp vegetable oil
3 tbsp butter
9 oz (250 g) stewing beef, cubed
1 onion, cut into 8 chunks lengthwise
2 potatoes, peeled and each cut into
  4–6 pieces
1 carrot, peeled and cut into
  $^3/_4$-in (2-cm) pieces
1 bay leaf
3 cups beef or vegetable stock

Curry roux

1 onion, thinly sliced lengthwise
2 garlic cloves, finely chopped
$^3/_4$-in (2-cm) piece fresh ginger root, finely
  chopped or grated with a Japanese grater
2 tbsp mild Japanese or Indian curry powder
4 tbsp all-purpose flour
1 tbsp mango chutney
2 tbsp tomato ketchup
2 tsp shoyu
salt and white pepper

METHOD

Put the rice in a bowl and wash under cold running water for 2 minutes. Drain in a sieve. Pour $2^1/_2$ cups water into a large pan with a tight-fitting lid, add the rice, and set aside to soak.

Heat the oil and half of the butter in a frying pan until the butter melts, then fry the beef over medium-high heat until browned all over. Remove with a slotted spoon and place on a plate.

To make the curry roux, add the sliced onion to the frying pan and reduce the heat to low. Fry for 30–40 minutes or until the onion is soft and well browned. Stir in the garlic, ginger, and curry powder and fry for 2 minutes. Add the flour and stir to absorb the oil. Add the chutney, ketchup, and shoyu and mix well. The roux should look like a thick brown paste. Remove from the heat.

Now start cooking the rice. Place the lid tightly on the pan and bring to a boil. As soon as you hear a bubbling noise, turn the heat down low and simmer for 10 minutes or until the bubbling noise disappears and a faint crackling noise starts. Remove the pan from the heat, without lifting the lid, and leave aside for at least 10 minutes before checking the rice.

While the rice is cooking, melt the remaining butter in another deep pan and add the onion chunks and then the browned beef. Fry for 3 minutes. Add the potatoes, carrots, and bay leaf and pour in the stock. Bring to a boil. Reduce the heat and simmer for 20 minutes or until the potatoes and carrots are tender. Skim off any scum from the surface.

Scoop out about 2 cups of the hot stock and add it to the curry roux in the frying pan. Mix well into a smooth and runny mixture. Add this to the rest of the stock in the deep pan and stir in thoroughly. Add salt and pepper to taste. Bring back to a boil and cook for a further 2 minutes.

Serve the curry on a bed of warm rice, with some pickles if you like (pp336–337).

Serves 4

thick and
slightly
sweet

Katsu curry Curry rice with pork steaks

The word *katsu* is derived from "cutlet" and generally means a piece of deep-fried boneless meat. Pork is widely used for this dish, although chicken breast is also popular. The pork rests on a bed of rice and the sauce is spooned over it. Serve with Japanese *ton-katsu* sauce or Worcestershire sauce and pickles (pp336–337).

INGREDIENTS

4 pork loin steaks, about 6 oz (150 g) each
2 tbsp all-purpose flour
1 egg, beaten
scant 1oz (25 g) fine, dry white breadcrumbs
vegetable oil for deep-frying
1 lb (450 g) Japanese rice, freshly cooked
   (see Curry Rice, p339)

Curry roux

2 tbsp vegetable oil
2 tbsp butter
1 onion, thinly sliced lengthwise
2 garlic cloves, finely chopped
$^3/_4$-in (2 cm) piece fresh ginger root, finely
   chopped or grated with a Japanese grater
2 tbsp mild Japanese or Indian curry powder

4 tbsp all-purpose flour
1 tbsp mango chutney
2 tbsp tomato ketchup
2 tsp shoyu

Curry sauce

1 tbsp vegetable oil
1 onion, thinly sliced lengthwise
14 oz (400 g) button mushrooms, halved or
   quartered if large
$^1/_2$ cooking apple, grated with skin
1 small carrot, peeled and grated
1 stick celery, finely chopped
$2^1/_2$ cups vegetable stock
salt and ground white pepper

METHOD

To make the curry roux, heat the oil and butter in a frying pan, add the onion, and reduce the heat to low. Fry for 30–40 minutes or until the onion is soft and brown. Stir in the garlic, ginger, and curry powder and fry for 2 minutes. Add the flour and stir to absorb the oil. Add the chutney, ketchup, and shoyu and mix well. Remove from the heat and set aside.

Next, make the curry sauce. Heat the oil in another frying pan and fry the onion for 3 minutes. Add the mushrooms and fry until soft. Add the apple, carrot, and celery and fry for 5 minutes over medium-low heat. Pour in the stock and bring to a boil. Stir in the curry roux little by little and add salt and pepper to taste. Cover and leave to simmer gently, stirring occasionally.

With a sharp knife, make shallow cuts around the edge of the pork steaks to prevent them from curling up when fried. Season the steaks. Dust lightly with flour, then dip in beaten egg and coat with breadcrumbs, patting them on well.

Heat oil for deep-frying to 325°F (160°C). Fry the pork steaks for about 3 minutes per side or until the breadcrumbs are golden brown and the meat is thoroughly cooked. Drain on paper towels, then cut the meat into strips about $^3/_4$ in (2 cm) wide. Make a bed of rice on each plate and arrange the pork on top. Spoon the hot curry sauce over the top and serve immediately.

Serves 4

mild, rich, and meaty

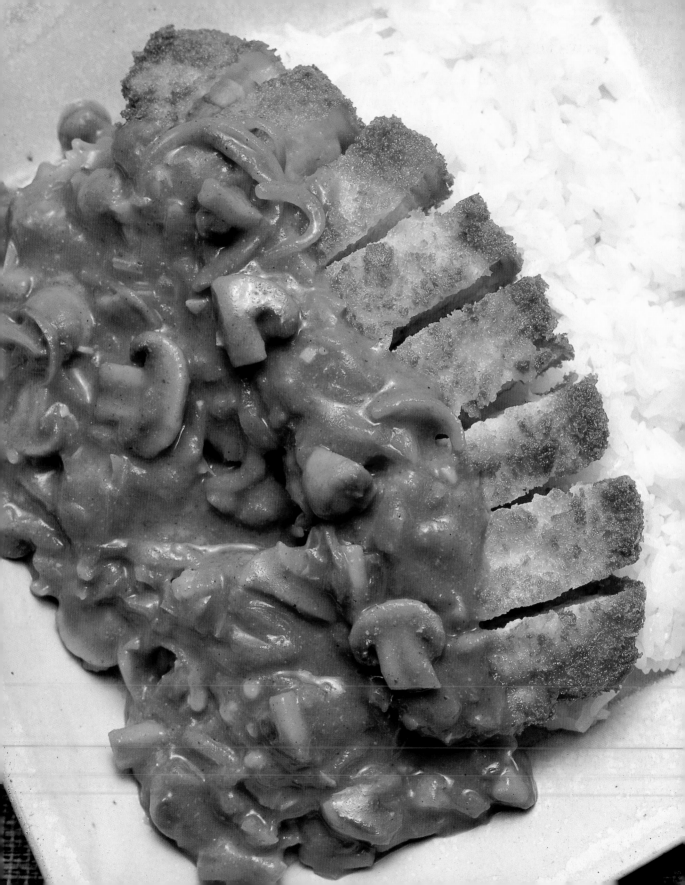

GLOSSARY

Asian celery
Also known as wild celery, this has a very strong, bitter flavor. Similar in appearance to flat-leaf parsley, it is often used as a flavoring in stir-fries and soups.

Bai yor leaf
Otherwise known as Indian mulberry leaf, this is a tobacco-like plant with a bitter, earthy flavor. In Thailand and the Philippines, young *bai yor* leaves may be shredded and added to curries. It is not readily available in the West.

Betel leaf
These are used in Thailand, predominantly as an edible wrapping for certain hors d'oeuvres. They can be replaced with spinach leaves.

Biryani
The original Persian spelling is *biriani*, meaning "fried," and refers to a spicy dish of meat and basmati rice flavored with saffron. The Moghul version was often elaborately garnished with gold leaf.

Cha-om
Not widely available in the West, this green herb is in fact the leaves of the Thai acacia tree. It has a bitter, nutty flavor and is commonly used in Laos and Thailand in soups, curries, omelets, and stir-fries.

Choy sum or Choi sum
Also known as Chinese flowering cabbage, this is a very popular vegetable in Cantonese cuisine, as well as being widely used throughout Asia and the West. It is sold as bunches of leaves, and can be used raw in salads or lightly boiled or steamed to add to meat dishes.

Dal
This can refer to either split lentils (or other legumes) as an ingredient, or, more generically, to a dish containing beans, peas, or lentils.

Halwa or Halva
Derived from the Arabic word for sweet, *hulw*, in India *halwa* refers to a semolina and sugar-based confectionery. The ingredients and flavorings vary widely, with the simplest recipe involving semolina being fried in ghee with syrup and raisins. In Pakistan, meanwhile, *halva* can be similar in texture and appearance to Turkish delight.

Jackfruit
A large fruit native to Southern India, but grown all over India and Sri Lanka. When unripe, it is treated more as a vegetable and added to savory dishes. As it ripens, it becomes much sweeter and is mainly used in desserts.

Kadhai or Karahi
Kadhai, or karahi, refers to an Indian wok, and also the dish it produces, namely a stir-fry. This rapid method of cooking is popular with youngsters and amateur chefs who do not want to spend hours in the kitchen.

Korma
A cooking term that, in India and Pakistan, originally referred to a slow-cooked dish with a sauce. Nuts, yogurt, and butter are the ingredients most commonly used to enrich an Indian korma.

Masala or Massalla
Meaning "spice mixture," *masala* can refer to any combination of spices, ground or whole, hot or mild, as a powder or paste. These mixes form the basis for most Indian dishes, and vary widely from region to region. *Garam masala* (p28) is the best-known example, though again, the blend will differ according to regional preferences. In terms of preparations, powders are generally preferred in North India, while pastes are favored in the south.

Mirin
Similar in appearance to rice wine, *mirin* is a liquid sweetener used in Japanese cuisine. It is only used in very small quantities, often in the place of sugar and soy sauce. It has a low alcohol

content, and in the 17th and 18th centuries was even drunk as an alternative to sake.

Pandanus leaf
An important ingredient throughout Southeast Asia, predominantly as a flavoring in Thai, Malaysian, and Indonesian cooking. They are added directly to rice dishes and desserts, allowing their delicate fragrance to infuse the food. The leaves should be bought fresh where possible, though they can be found frozen or dried.

Popadum or Papadum
These are thin, round wafers made from dough and fried in oil until crisp. Chickpea flour and lentil flour are both commonly used, and various spices may also be added. In North India they tend to be spicier, whereas in the south a milder recipe is preferred, to balance the hotter local cuisine.

Raita
This is a cooling, yogurt-based condiment, popular as an accompaniment to fiery curries. The yogurt is seasoned with herbs and spices, including mustard, cumin, mint and cilantro. In addition, various chopped vegetables may be added; cucumber is popular in western versions, though eggplant, potato, and spinach

are just as popular in authentic Indian *raita*.

Rice vinegar
Most Asian vinegars are brewed from rice; they have a lower acid content than malt vinegars and are relatively mild. Japanese brown rice vinegar is the best quality but is not easy to find.

Shoyu
An essential ingredient in Japanese cuisine, *shoyu* is a soy sauce that strongly differs in flavor from its Chinese counterpart. This is due to the presence of wheat, which gives the Japanese sauce a sweeter, more alcoholic taste.

Siamese watercress
More commonly known in the West as water spinach and in Thailand as *pak bung*, this leafy vegetable has excellent nutritional qualities. Full of protein and minerals, it is an inexpensive addition for curries and stir-fries.

Snake beans
Also known as yard-long beans, these are excellent eaten raw when very fresh and firm. They can be used as a garnish, or lightly cooked in stir-fries.

Sugar cane vinegar
Popular in the Philippines, this vinegar is mild in flavor, not dissimilar to rice vinegar. It is dark yellow or brown in color, and, unusually, is not at all sweet.

Tandoor
Essential to the way of life in North India and Pakistan, the *tandoor* is a clay oven used to bake breads and other dishes. It is the focal point of many homes, and some villages may even have a communal *tandoor* where gossip is as important as cooking. The fires are fueled by charcoal and are often kept lit all day.

Tawa or Tava
A flat, circular pan, often made from cast iron, used in Indian cooking to make *chapattis* and *parathas*.

India

Foods of India
www.food-india.com

Bombay Bazar
85 First Ave.
New York,
NY 10003
Tel: (212) 529 1815

548 Valencia St
San Francisco,
CA 94110
Tel: (415) 621 1717

Cham Gourmet
2943 Broadway
New York,
NY 10025
Tel: (212) 666 4190

Penzeys Spices
Tel: (800) 741 7787
www.penzeys.com

Thokalath
www.thokalath.com

Indian Grocery Stores
www.thingsindian.com/grocery

Indian Foods Company
www.indianfoodsco.com
www.ethnicfoodsco.com

GaramChai
www.garamchai.com/bazaar

Spice House, Inc.
99 First Avenue
New York,
NY 10003
Tel: (212) 387 7812

Pakistan

Natco
www.natcofoods.com

Desimart
www.desimart.com

Myanmar & Maritime SE Asia

Asian Foods
www.asianfoods.com

Yummy Taste
www.yummytaste.com

Foodie Site
www.foodiesite.com

99 Ranch Market
www.99ranch.com

Thailand

Bangkok Center Grocery
104 Mosco Street
(between Mott
and Mulberry Street)
New York,
NY 10013
Tel: (212) 732 8916
www.thai-grocery.com

Temple of Thai
www.templeofthai.com

Import Food
www.importfood.com

Thai-Food
www.thaifood.com

Thai Indochine Trading Inc.
www.thaiindochine.com

Mainland SE Asia

Ai Hoa Supermarket
860 North Hill Street
Los Angeles,
CA 90012
Tel: (213) 629 8121

Golden Country Oriental Food
www.goldencountry.com

Viet World Kitchen
www.vietworldkitchen.com

Africa

African Chop
www.africanchop.com

Afro Drive
www.afrodrive.com/
AfricanStores

African & Caribbean Supermarket
www.africanandcaribbean
supermarket.com

Enyi African Supermarket
414 South Bascam Avenue
San Jose,
CA 95128
Tel: (213) 947 7735

Caribbean

Walkerswood
www.walkerswood.com

Grace
www.gracefoods.com

eCaroh Caribbean Emporium
www.sweetsoca.com/caribbean_
foods

Japan

Maruwa
www.maruwa.com

Ethnic Grocer
www.ethnicgrocer.com

KoaMart
www.koamart.com

Food Service Direct
www.foodservicedirect.com

NYC Japan
www.nycjapan.com

General

Dean and Deluca
560 Broadway
New York,
NY 10012
Tel: (212) 226 6800

Kalustyans
123 Lexington Ave
New York,
NY 10016
Tel: (212) 685 3451
www.kalustyans.com

Seasoned Pioneers
www.seasonedpioneers.co.uk
Tel: 0800 068 2348

World Spice
www.worldspice.com

The Spice House
Tel: Evanston, IL: (847) 328 3711
Chicago: (312) 274 0378
Milwaukee, WI: (414) 272 0977
www.thespicehouse.com

The Spice of Life
www.thespiceoflife.co.uk

**The Great American
Spice Company**
www.americanspice.com

ACKNOWLEDGMENTS

DORLING KINDERSLEY WOULD LIKE TO THANK THE FOLLOWING:

Editorial
All of the contributors for being so efficient and accommodating throughout. Jeni Wright and Norma Macmillan for their tireless hard work and professionalism.

Food stylists
Bridget Sargeson and Alice Hart

Prop stylist
Victoria Allen

Index
Hilary Bird

DTP
Adam Walker and Emma Hansen-Knarhoi

On behalf of David Thompson
Tanongsak Yordwai, who prepared and styled David's food for photography.

Picture Credits
The publisher would like to thank the following for their kind permission to reproduce their photographs:

10–13 Susan Downing (Vivek Singh); Manoj Siva (Das Sreedharan); Oliver Wright (Mahmood Akbar); Susan Downing (Sri Owen); Martin Brigdale (David Thompson); Christopher Hirsheimer (Corinne Trang); Sharron Gibson (Roopa Gulati); Mike Dennis (Judy Bastyra); Paul David Ellis (Yasuko Fukuoka). 14–16 Alamy Images: Simon Reddy. 33 Alamy Images: Robert Harding Picture Library. 76–78 Corbis: Macduff Everton. 120–122 Rex Features: Ilyas J Dean. 141 Corbis: Mike Zens. 154–156 Corbis: Frank Lukasseck/Zefa. 191 Corbis: Tony Arruza. 200–202 Lonely Planet Images: Kraig Lieb. 231 Lonely Planet Images: Richard I'Anson. 250–252 Getty Images: David Noton. 288 Lonely Planet Images: John Banagan. 292–294 Rex Features: Ilpo Musto. 301 Corbis: Vince Streano. 321 Alamy Images: Andrew Hamilton. 334 Alamy Images: Pacific Press Service

All other images © Dorling Kindersley. For further information, see **www.dkimages.com**